MY MOTHER'S JOURNAL

A Young Lady's Diary

OF FIVE YEARS SPENT IN MANILA, MACAO, AND THE CAPE OF GOOD HOPE

FROM 1829–1834

EDITED BY

KATHARINE HILLARD

" Her children arise up, and call her blessed "

BOSTON

GEORGE H. ELLIS, 272 CONGRESS STREET

1900

GEORGE H. ELLIS, PRINTER, 272 CONGRESS ST., BOSTON.

CONTENTS.

BOOK VII.

BOOK VIII.

INTRODUCTION.

THE chief interest of this diary to those who had no personal acquaintance with the writer lies, of course, in the glimpses it gives of the conditions of life and travel in the third decade of this century, when steam navigation was in its infancy, and the luxuries that are now a matter of course to those that go down to the sea in ships were quite unknown. It is hard to realize that it then took four or five months, at best, to reach China, and that nearly a year must elapse before an answer could be received to a letter sent from there. In those days a ship of seventeen hundred tons was considered a marine marvel, and its accommodations were spoken of as "magnificent." There were no such things then as canned meats, fruits, and vegetables, or condensed milk; and we can readily imagine that provisions for the table, on so long a voyage, must have been somewhat monotonous. And, as there was no possibility of having anything washed on board ship, an enormous amount of linen had to be carried, a lady was obliged to provide herself with at least six dozen of every kind of under-clothing, not to mention the variety of other garments that were needed for a voyage that took the traveller from the temperate to the torrid zone and back again to the temperate.

Imagine, then, a lively young girl, just past her twentieth

birthday (who had been brought up in the midst of a family of twelve children, only one older than herself), suddenly transported from the dull and extremely provincial town of Salem, Mass., to live in China under the auspices of the East India Company, and in all the luxury and formality of the English society of that time. It must have been a bewildering change at first from the quiet and rather Puritanical régime of home, where Sunday was kept with the utmost strictness, and Saturday night was almost as rigidly observed, to the ceaseless round of dinners, balls, and Sunday visiting in Macao, from being one of the many superfluous females of Massachusetts to occupying the dazzling and somewhat hazardous position of the only " spinster " where men were so numerous and for much of the time so unoccupied.

But the society of an indifferent crowd soon palls upon an affectionate nature; and this girl of twenty, taken away from the companionship of her beloved elder sister and all the duties and pleasures of home, found many occasions to regret all she had left behind. There was much, too, to shock her prejudices in the manners and customs of society in Macao; and it took her some time to acquire that sweet tolerance and charity for which she was in later life so noted. It is interesting to a student of human nature to watch the development of her mind and character amid the pleasures and the trials of her residence in China; and it is to be regretted that so many of the more intimate details of that life were reserved for home letters (mostly lost) instead of being recorded in this Journal, kept for the benefit of her elder sister.

As there must necessarily be much repetition in a journal covering so long a space of time, a great deal has been cut out; but, with the exception of a few slips of the pen, nothing has been corrected or altered.

One book of the Journal is missing, that containing the most exciting incident of Miss Low's life in China, the trip to Canton when that port was closed to foreign women; but a few letters and fragments of letters have been found that give some idea of that rather perilous journey.

KATHARINE HILLARD.

DECEMBER, 1899.

THE JOURNAL.

BOOK I. PART I.

ON BOARD THE "SUMATRA," MAY 24 TO SEPT. 9, 1829.

Sunday, May 24, 1829.— Embarked on board the "Sumatra," bound to Manila, and thence to Macao, where I shall probably take up my residence for the next four years; and for you, my dear sister, shall this journal be kept. I left home at five o'clock (in the morning) with feelings not to be described nor *imagined* but by those who have been placed in a similar situation. We were escorted out as far as Baker's Island * by a few friends from Salem, which made it rather pleasanter for me, though I cannot say that I enjoyed anything that took place that day. The morning was as delightful as it could be, with a fresh breeze that soon wafted us beyond the sight of our native land. About nine our party left us. However, I behaved like the heroine I had resolved to be! At ten began to be sea-sick; and, though I suffered nothing in comparison to some people, it was enough to make me feel a state of *utter hopelessness*, and prostration of *strength* and *spirits* such as I never

* Just outside Salem Harbor.— *Ed.*

before knew nor desire to feel again. I remained on deck most of the day, but cared neither how nor where I was going. This journal was commenced a week after we sailed,— it seemed like a month.

May 27.—Becalmed to-day ; low in spirits, think a sailor's life the worst of all others ; tolerably well, though I have not yet felt bright, and cannot relish coffee or tea without milk. I lead a listless sort of life, not having the energy to do or say anything.

... You must excuse me, my dear sister, if you find many things in this book uninteresting ; but I give you free permission to omit reading any or the whole of it. I write as much for my own amusement as anything else. So few are the incidents at sea that I am obliged to put in more about myself than I otherwise should. A less partial eye than yours, however, must never see it.

May 29. — After dinner to-day I was called on deck to see a dolphin, which was playing round the vessel, a beautiful-looking fish in the water. Every day I take a lesson in the rigging of the ship. I now know the head from the stern, and likewise that it is a difficult matter for a ship to cut the water with her taffrail, which is more than I once knew. That is not the extent of my knowledge, but I shall keep the rest to myself. I think I am rather an apt scholar !

Sunday, May 31. — Rose this morning with a determination to spend the day as it should be. At half-past nine we assembled in the cabin, and Mr. A. read us a very good sermon : we then employed ourselves as we thought best till dinner-time, and at three Mr. A. read two more of Mr. Thatcher's sermons. We then walked the decks; and I stood at the stern, thinking of home and all associated with that sweet place, till I wished that I was there, and not condemned in foreign climes to rove. But for a moment, however. I drive all such thoughts away, and I have never repented of my resolution. Uncle and Aunt L. are as kind as they can possibly be. The weather has been much pleasanter than I had any idea it would be, and the days begin to seem shorter than they did. But you can have no idea how tedious this first week was!

June 2. — Head wind for the last few days. You cannot conceive what a wretched thing it is to have a head wind! It is worse than the toothache; it gives us all the blues. My motto is : —

> " To be resigned when ills betide,
>   Patient when favors are denied,
>   And pleased with favors given. "

But how far I act up to it, it remains for you to guess. O Molly, you would hardly recognize your once industrious sister Harriet if you were to see her now! I shall lose all my good habits on board this ship, but I as confidently hope I shall resume them when I quit this floating habitation. There is some excuse for me, which arises from my not feeling perfectly well; all my energy seems to have left me.

June 3. — Head wind again. Mr. A. prophesied something new for to-day, but nothing new have we seen; the same round of faces, which are not very fascinating in their appearance, I assure you. However, all are orderly in deportment, and there is no swearing, fighting, or anything of the kind among the crew; the greatest harmony prevails throughout. The captain first chop, the officers excellent, the sailors all good, the cook good, and so sanctified in his appearance that it seems as though he thought it a sin to smile, and the steward active and attentive. Uncle kind, Aunt L. ditto, Mr. A. agreeable, myself the same fascinating, engaging, enchanting, sweet-tempered, obliging, passive creature that I ever was. And, with all this, to still have a head wind!

June 5.— Soon after dinner the captain called me, saying there was a sail in sight. I immediately ran to the deck; and, though with some slight fear [of pirates], I was delighted to see it. I ran down again to the cabin, and wrote a letter, fervently in hopes that she was bound towards our dear native land; but, when she came near enough, she hoisted a *detestable Spanish flag*. We spoke her, but she was bound for Spain. Such a miserable-looking set as she had on board as I never saw. It was a great disappointment, I wish so that you might hear from us; but I hope we shall see another soon. Played whist this evening. It is almost impossible to read in the evening, the light flares so. You are obliged to have the wick long, or it will go out; and, if you get near enough to see, it smokes in your face, which is not peculiarly pleasant. So there is precious little comfort in reading in the evening at sea.

June 10.— Wind tolerably fair, a beautiful day. Another sail to-day. I begin to see them with less delight, as they do not do us any good. We have agreed to-day to choose a committee to wait upon Mr. A. and request him to deliver an oration upon the 4th of July. Uncle W. is to write an ode for the occasion, I am to read the Declaration of Independence; to conclude with a good dinner. After tea, walked as usual,— a most splendid evening. All I want is some of my nearest, dearest friends about me!

June 11.— Another beautiful day, fair wind, though but little of it; studding-sails all set, which looks cheerful. We have an awning spread all over the quarter-deck, and I generally take my book and go up there as soon as breakfast is over, saunter about a while, see all there is to be seen, hear the news of the day, find out how she heads, take a look at the fowls and the pigs, and then to my book. By the bye, the pigs are a great amusement to us, they quarrel so. Any little thing amuses us. Oh! I would not be a sailor all my days for the wealth of the Indies! I would sooner live on potato skins and eggshells, provided I had one friend in the world.

June 16.— Fine wind, feel as bright as a lark. We live as comfortably on board ship as I could wish. All that is wanting is one near friend who can partake of all your feelings; the heart will at times feel alone. Though you may live comfortably, peaceably, and happily, still there is a feeling of loneliness within, an indescribable something that will not be satisfied.

You will perhaps say, "Silly creature, to put such an idea in a journal!" but this is not what can be called a regular journal, I think, and I did not mean it should be; for, I am sure, to sit down and write you an account of the weather and of what happens daily on board would be drier than this is, which is needless. If that is what you wish, you can send to the captain and get his log-book; but, remember, this is written for you and me, so that, when I feel like it, I can sit down and open my heart.

June 18.— About five o'clock we saw a sail. They tried to make me think it was a pirate, did not succeed, however. They felt a little suspicious themselves, I believe, as she hoisted both her topsails at once, which is not very common except with a man-of-war, they say now, though they did not tell me at the time. She cut some queer pranks, but kept her distance, and did us no injury. I do not wish to see any more sails at present, as there is no chance of our sending home by them.

June 27, *Lat.* 1.57.— Old Neptune will soon visit us, we are almost on top of the world. A beautiful day again, another week has passed rapidly away. Time flies swifter at sea than on shore. You will say it must go pleasantly, then. True, but I account for it in this way; the time is passed in so monotonous a style that, when the week closes, we have no evidence that it has been. It is marked by no events, and I should not know the days of the week, were it not for our dinners. Methinks I hear you say, "A very novel way of noting time"; but every Tuesday and

Friday we have bean soup, which I depend upon, and anticipate from one day to the other. It tastes more like what I eat at home than anything else we have; though everything is cooked in the best manner, yet there is that relish wanting which you never get anywhere but at home.

June 28, *Sunday.*— A delightful morning. To-day at one o'clock we crossed the line, just thirty-five days since we left America. Being Sunday, Neptune did not come aboard, we, however, treated the sailors. I felt somewhat homesick this morning. This afternoon I have been reading Mrs. Judson's Life. It is astonishing how much she suffered and lived through. How grateful I ought to be that I have so far been preserved from the dangers by which I am constantly surrounded! I pray that I may be grateful for the many blessings I enjoy, and that I may daily learn to put my trust in that Being who is continually watching over me. I hope that I shall not always live a useless life, but by a good example (if nothing more) I may do something for Him who has done so much for me.

July 4.— I suppose to-day you are aroused by the ringing of bells, the firing of cannon, etc., and perhaps you will be hearing an elegant oration from one of our most promising young men. I should like to know who is spouting to-day! I imagine you still in Salem, while I, though in thought free as air, am confined to one little spot, though constantly changing my place of abode. What a tremendous puddle this is!

July 12.— Rather a gloomy day. The sun sets at five now, which makes the evenings rather long. They accused me at dinner-time of having the blues. I must confess my thoughts have often been across the stormy deep to the peaceful land of America. Can it be wondered at, my dear sister? I suppose you are now going to meeting; it is nearly dark with us.

July 15.— A bright sun and strong wind to-day, going under single-reefed topsails for the first time. Neptune is angry to-day, and has given us a great lashing. Yesterday the water was calm and placid, and looked like a sea of glass, to-day it is tossing its white-capped waves in grandeur. The vessel looks like a skeleton, so many sails are taken in. I spent the day in reading. Impossible to work, the ship danced so. Fine sport to-day at dinner-time. Wish I were skilled in making caricatures.

July 20, *Lat.* 37.4 *East, Long.* 1.— Fine breeze, but quite cold. We are now so near the Cape. The wind is on the quarter; and the ship goes along so smoothly that below I should hardly know we were on the water, it is so still. I have been reading Scott's Life of Napoleon; finished it to-day. I have somewhat moderated my rage in regard to Napoleon, but still think him a man of the most inordinate ambition, and selfish in the extreme, and that all he did was for his own glory, not out of regard for France or her good. I think he had many good traits,— at least, his heart was not hard. I find in hunting for his virtues I am pulling up vices; but, however, I will let my judgment rest. This is evident: that he was the cause of many a tear, and made many widows and orphans. He was probably sent into the world for some wise purpose; but I cannot get over his divorcing his amiable wife, Josephine.

July 25.— Becalmed this afternoon, the water looks like a sea of glass. I have never seen it so smooth before. It is cloudy and dreary enough. This evening we could hardly tell the sky from the water. However, we have amused ourselves with one thing and another, and on the whole have passed a very pleasant day. Take us all in all, we are a very pleasant set, when we have a mind to be. We have plenty of good things to eat and drink, and plenty of books and work. Of course, we all have our dull moments. Have been reading and working part of the day, the rest of the time skylarking.

July 26, *Sunday.*— Roused this morning about seven by the cry of "Sail ho!" An English ship. About eleven she came alongside, and, to our joy, we saw a little world: it was a large English ship filled with passengers. We saw about a dozen ladies, and a great number of gentlemen, babies, servants, etc. It looked like a moving world, and you can imagine the pleasure it gave us to see so many human beings and so much life. We carried on a little conversation by means of trumpets, and the captain agreed to stay by us an hour to give us the longitude, ours differing somewhat from his. He lowered his boat soon after, and sent four of his youths on board the "Sumatra," three passengers and a mate, the latter the only decent one among them: the other three were dressed as fantastically as you can imagine. They appeared to think we looked on them with admiration, but, I assure you, they have been the subjects of many a joke. They and we, however, were very civil, and after taking a glass of wine, begging a pack of cards, inviting us to dine, and offering us anything they had on board, asking and answering questions, they bid us good morning. I must describe their looks a little, because we don't have such a chance very often. The first, then, that jumped on board was a long, lean-looking chap, supporting a huge pair of mustachios and whiskers on a pale and sickly phiz. He, for an Englishman, was very cordial; but we accounted for it by his being a Mason. He wore a drab-colored pair of pantaloons, blue coat, etc.; last, but not least, was his cap, which was made of leather, with a strap coming down and buckling under the lip, which gave him a very singular appearance. We have had many conjectures about that strap. He endeavored to look interesting; but Uncle W. thought by the looks of his fingers he must be a tailor. The second was fair to middling. His dress consisted of light pantaloons, a blue frock coat embroidered from top to toe with cord,— a military undress,— and, to crown all, a scarlet cap. I cannot give you any idea of that, it is beyond description; but the color was bright scarlet, and worn to one side, it looked singular enough, I assure you. He was cultivating a pair of mustachios, but as yet they were in their infancy. He likewise endeavored to leave an agreeable impression. The third was dressed in common style, but was a great buck. Indeed, they all were. We concluded they were military characters going out to join their regiment, as the vessel was bound to Madras and Calcutta. They were, however, very polite; and after mutual good wishes we separated, the "Roxbury Castle" moving on before us, much to the chagrin of Captain R., there is so much pride felt in beating another vessel. . . . By the bye, I have said nothing about the ladies. There were some very interesting-looking girls among them; and I should have liked to have gone on board their vessel. They were dressed very handsomely and looked very genteel. There were thirty-two passengers, beside servants and the crew. Judging by our own ship, where there are only six or eight, they must have confusion worse confounded at times, what with babies squalling, and one thing rolling, and another smashing. I tried to read this afternoon, but could not compose my aching head nor settle my mind enough to pay much attention. I know you will make sufficient allowance. Recollect our peculiar situation, nine weeks since we have seen anything like life before. I think I have given you as much as you will want for this day. Make much of it. Such an event does not happen every day off the Cape of Good Hope.

July 28. — Cannot see the (English) ship to-day. Fine wind, and we are going at the rate of seven or eight knots an hour. Now we have passed the Cape, we are looking forward to St. Paul's and Java Head.

This will be the most boisterous part of the voyage. If you want a good idea of the confusion, the troubles, the fun of a dinner when the vessel is rolling, read Silliman's account of his voyage to England. He describes it very well.

August 1.— We have passed the "Roxbury Castle," and Capt. R. is now happy. Fine wind, and we are going at the rate of ten knots at night.

August 3. — Wind right aft. After dinner I went on deck, and the face of the ocean exhibited a new scene altogether.

" I ne'er shall forget the wonder, the awe, the delight that stole
    o'er me,
  When its billowy boundlessness opened before me."

I never before have realized those "mountain waves" we have frequently heard of. It is really a grand sight, but it seems as if each wave must come over us. However, I did not feel at all alarmed, as I expected to; but one thing makes me hop again. That is, when she ships a sea or strikes one with her bow. It seems, for a moment, as if we were striking a rock, and must go down; and then the water splashes across the deck. To-day there was a whale at a little distance, about 50 feet long; and he jumped out of water with his whole body 30 feet in the air, as near as we could judge. What monstrous strength they must have, to lift such a body so high! It was really a grand sight.

August 4. — Seventy-two days since we have seen land, but we have had delightful weather most of the time. My dear sister, if you did but know it, it is a very rare thing to go round the Cape of Good Hope in the winter season and have such beautiful weather. We certainly ought to be very grateful.

August 7. — Seems like April weather in America, sunny and rainy. I suppose you are now melting, while we are wearing cloaks and mandarins. I went into the cook's office the other night. The fire was too pleasant to leave. It reminded me of our fireside at home, not from any similarity in the construction, but because of its warming effects. Excuse me for the comparison, but many a good thing has come out of that galley, I assure you, though you would not guess it if you were to see the cook. He is certainly a most forbidding-looking creature.

August 10. — Passed the islands this morning before daybreak, much to our regret, without seeing them. We had hoped to set our eyes on land, but must now give it up till we get to Java Head. St. Paul's and Amsterdam are not inhabited. St. Paul's is famous for a boiling spring, where the thermometer marks 240 degrees at times.

August 11. — Fine wind, pleasant weather, making our way swiftly towards Java Head. I cannot realize that I am so far from home. For almost three months now, we have been floating on from wave to wave, without change of scene, only of weather, — my prospects of happiness all lying in the future, which is hidden. I have built many a lofty castle and many a mud hut, as suited the feeling of the time. Hope arrays herself in bright colors at times, I assure you, and not infrequently do I return to my dear home and rest myself, contented and happy, surrounded by those I love, but I fear many a day will pass ere that. Adieu to gloomy visions. I do not allow myself to borrow trouble; but, if I could only let you know how comfortable and happy we are, it would be a great relief to me.

August 16, *Sunday.* — Another week gone, and still the same scene. Shall I tell you what I have done to-day? There is nothing else I can say. Well, I arose as usual, at half-past seven, ate a good breakfast of warm bread (and you do not get nicer at home), then, as usual, again walked the deck for about an hour. Imagined you all seated in the parlor, father just taking off his boots and preparing to smoke his cigar; mother sitting near, perhaps wondering where Harriet is (would that you could know how comfortable!) or perhaps relating some anecdote of that dear little Ellen's pranks; you, my dear sister, enjoying the society of your dearest friend, perhaps* (ha! ha!); grandmother attending upon her little idol, Charley; and the rest in bed. So, you see, I imagine you all happily united again in a comfortable house in Brooklyn. [Whither the family were to remove from Salem shortly after Miss L.'s departure. — *Ed.*]

Saturday, August 22. — Here we are, still beating about in the Indian Ocean, an immense waste of water, every day calculating how many more before we shall see land, which you cannot wonder at, con-

* The elder sister had been engaged for some time. — *Ed.*

sidering we have been thirteen weeks without that precious sight. We think now by Thursday we shall see Java Head. How refreshing the thought!

August 24. — Delightful day, fine wind as usual. This afternoon about five heard the cheering sound of "Land ho!" and I assure you I was on deck in a short time. Christmas Island (within four degrees of Java Head) had just opened to our view. It was thirty-six miles from us; but we watched it till we left it astern, about nine o'clock. If it had been in the daytime, we should have passed within six or eight miles of the island, and should have had a fine view of it. As it was, I should have thought it a black cloud, had I not known to the contrary. We shall probably see Java Head to-morrow night. Christmas Island is inhabited by that very interesting animal, the wild hog. It abounds, moreover, in cocoanut and lime trees. The sight of land made me think of the land I saw last, and gave me some unpleasant reflections. Three months to-day since I left home, and one year to-day since I went on the water for the first time (you remember that famous water party?). Little did I think then that I should be tempted to cross the ocean!

August 25, 26. — Fine day again. The weather is now getting very warm. At dusk it blew very hard and it was quite dark, so the captain thought it best not to run for land, but kept on and off. The next morning I turned out at six o'clock, and could see land distinctly in three directions, — Clapp's

Island, Bowers' Island, and the great island of
Java. You may judge of our felicity, after having
but one scene for three months, to be suddenly surrounded by islands covered with cocoanuts, pineapples, etc. I sat in the long-boat all day, hardly
taking time to eat, in consequence of which before
night my face was almost blistered. We entered
the Straits of Sunda in the forenoon with a delightful breeze, and had a very fine opportunity to
view the land, as we went very near the shore. It
was mostly very high, and covered with an impene-
trable forest, which looked very green. There were
many rocky bluffs and points, and I discovered
many pleasant little spots; but I cannot say that I
saw any spot on the island of Java, or any other, in
which I should like to take up my abode. I could
not help thinking what a graveyard it has been, and
still is, for all foreigners. We were amused with
the Malay proas out fishing. They are very slightly
built of bamboo, and I was astonished to see how
the natives managed them. They go out with the
land breeze in the morning, and return in the afternoon. We anchored off Anjer about sunset after
a delightful day's sail, as we were in want of fowls
and fruit; but before we had anchored, and while
we were going along with a stiff breeze, a boat
came off, and for the first time I saw the Malays.
There were three of them in their little nutshell (for
it was not much better), and such a chattering you
never heard. They offered their fruit, which we
agreed to take, and lowered a large basket to them,

while they held on by a rope. In a few minutes their little boat filled, and they all went under water. I thought, of course, they were gone, and it was out of our power to save them; but the men said it was as impossible to drown them as it was to drown a fish, and I was soon relieved by seeing them astern. Two of them were swimming and holding their frail vessel up, while the other one bailed it out; but the poor fellows lost their dollar, and we got the fruit, pineapples, bananas, mangoes, sweet potatoes, etc. However, it was not our fault. I suppose you will like to know what I thought of a Malay, and how my modesty could stand such a shock as seeing a man unclad; but I agree with Bishop Heber in thinking their color serves as a covering. They seem like a different race of beings. The faces of those we saw were bright and intelligent. They are very short, the men averaging five feet two inches, and the women four feet eleven inches. Their teeth, from the constant chewing of betel, become very black,—a thing in which they take great pride. A young man before his teeth get well blacked would be mortified to be seen by any one.

After we had anchored, the president at Anjer sent a boat off with the news-bag, the first mail since we have been out. We left Anjer about 10 P.M.

August 27.—About half-past four this morning I was waked by the dismal announcement that we must dress and go on deck as soon as possible, for we should drift on to the rocks in a few minutes. I was on deck in a short time, I can assure you, and saw the reef of rocks within half the ship's length of us. It was a dead calm, not a breath of air stirring, and the current so strong against us that the ship was entirely unmanageable, while we were drifting at the rate of two or three knots an hour. Had it not been for the current from Stroom Rock, we must inevitably have gone on to the reef; but to our joy we were spared this disaster. Our boats were all ready to be lowered, and we were still close by Anjer. The captain says our lives would have been in no danger, but I do not think it would have been very pleasant. The greatest danger in the Straits of Sunda and Gaspar lies in these strong currents, the many shoals, and the calms that prevail here. We have passed a number of uninhabited islands to-day, and have also seen the coast of Sumatra, about which I saw nothing interesting.

August 28. — Sailing sweetly through the Java Seas, out of sight of land, with a hot sun, but a good breeze.

August 29. — Little breeze this morning, but a favorable current, which is carrying us direct to Gaspar Straits. We saw the island of Banca this morning at ten, and before night we were safely through the dangerous Straits of Gaspar. At half-past eight we passed Gaspar Island, — a very good run, I assure you.

Sunday, 30*th.* — Fourteen weeks this morning since we left home, and we now find ourselves with a pleasant breeze and everything comfortable in the China Sea. Pretty warm weather, but that is quite pleasant, we have had so much cold since our departure. Out of sight of land to-day.

September 6. — Pleasant day, with a charming breeze. We are now thinking of getting ashore by Tuesday. I cannot say that I think of it with much pleasure, though I may be agreeably disappointed in the place.

September 7, *Monday.* — We are now in Manila Bay. Passed Goat Island about 1 A. M., entered the bay, and will probably anchor at sunset. Rained all day till nearly dark. About half-past seven we anchored, within hail of an American ship, which proved to be the "Sabrina," sailed six days before us.

September 8. — A pleasant morning, though it looks as though it would rain before night. I was up on deck early, and it was a pleasant prospect, I assure you. The Cavite (where ships usually anchor in the south-west monsoons) on one side and Manila on the other. The *caseos* look quite lively, with the natives going about from one to another. These *caseos* are dug out of trees, and have a covering of bamboo, under which the family live. In one the wife was rowing. I should not have known her to be a woman at first, as she had on nothing but trousers. The men are merely covered about the middle. I did not like their looks as much as the Malays. Their faces are not so intelligent. Manila looks pleasant from the Bay. It is a walled city, and we can hear the beating of the drums from the shore where the troops are stationed. After being examined by the custom-house officers and going through a variety of ceremonies, the gentlemen left us, and went on shore to seek accommodations. We were rather lonely till the captain returned about three. He brought the dreadful news of the death of Mr. Forbes and Mr. Monson, lost in a gale of wind in going from Macao to Canton. Uncle could not come off, as he was obliged to wait till late to get a permit for our baggage, and then the sea was too heavy.

PART II.

September 9. — We awoke this morning early, and found the rain was pouring down in torrents. I had just made up my mind to spend a dull day, and to amuse myself by writing letters, when Mr. Johnson called out that Uncle was coming. We jumped with delight to think we were so soon relieved. We breakfasted, and about nine started for Manila in a government boat. It rained hard, but there was a covering to the boat, so that we did not get wet. I really do not know what to say about Manila. You cannot get any idea of it from description. I am told it is like all Spanish towns, the forts, convents, and churches taking up a large part of the place. The roofs of the houses are covered with tiles. They are mostly of one story only, and some are very spacious. They have no glass windows; but they are made of pearl-shell in little squares, and some of them have Venetian blinds. The houses are all whitewashed, but are soon turned black by the climate, which gives the whole city the appearance of having been smoked, as by a great fire. An immense number of people live on the water in boats. We arrived at Mr. Russell's about ten o'clock. The boats go directly to the gate. The house is fine and spacious. The rooms are all on one floor, very high, and immensely large. We found a number of American gentlemen there, and after dinner I had a most delightful ride with Mr. R. on the Calzada, where we met all the nobility of Manila. It is the fashion to ride there every day about six. No ladies walk out. Our postilion stopped very suddenly, and Mr. R. told me that it was the hour of vespers, when every one is obliged to stop and say a short prayer.

Saturday, September 12. — Had a charming ride this afternoon with Mr. R. Rode in Spanish style, without my bonnet. None of the ladies wear bonnets. Manila abounds in pleasant drives, and on Sundays and feast-days they all ride back and forth on the Calzada till dark; but there are many pleasanter drives than this, I think. This afternoon we met a funeral. They bury their dead here without coffins, and carry them through the streets laid on a square board covered with a purple cloth. At each corner a torch is borne by four men, and then follow the friends, though there is no order in the procession. The mourners wore a sort of purple hood and scarf. The men carried children in their arms. There were several babes a month or two old. The burying-ground is quite picturesque in appearance, and the higher classes are buried in the wall, which is eight feet thick. They are put into small recesses, which are then built up with bricks and lime. By paying twenty-five dollars a Spaniard can be buried in the wall, but no foreigner can have a place in this ground. Everything we see here

makes us value more our own country and its privileges!

We also met two ladies on horseback. They have
curious saddles here, something like a chair. The
ladies were dressed in most singular style. They
had on red gowns, a white muslin kerchief on the
neck, and another thrown loosely over the head, with
a broad-brimmed beaver hat over it. They rode
very fast. We returned by the beach and the
Calzada, and saw a great many sights that would
have shocked a young lady in America; but I have
now got quite hardened

Sunday, September 13. — With the Spaniards it
is Saturday; for in going round Cape Horn, when
this island was discovered, they gained a day.
There is not much appearance of the Sabbath here,
as everybody is at work, and the noise is as great as
usual. After dinner I had a most delightful ride on
the Calzada. On our return we came near meeting
the Host; but, fortunately, Mr. S. was before us on
horseback, and turned back to stop our carriage, for,
if we had met it, we should have been obliged to
alight and kneel, which in the present state of the
roads would not have been very agreeable. We returned, and took tea with ten gentlemen. I have
improved so much now that I sit down to table without the least fear.

Monday, 14*th.* — The first thing I heard this
morning was the ringing of bells, and the military
crossing the bridge as they returned from mass.
About ten we rode out through the city to visit the

churches. The cathedral was not open. We went first to San Domingo. It is a pretty church, but rather gaudy. There were several women there who had just been to confession. They go away happy, thinking they are absolved from all sins, and ready to begin a new list! We then went home, and dined with eleven Americans. After dinner rode upon the Calzada and through the city, and on our return had some music and two Indian dancers, who danced the fandango, keeping time with the castanets. They were very graceful in their movements. After tea drove to the Palace Square to hear the music of the three fine bands, which play here every Sunday and holiday from 8 to 9 P.M.

Tuesday, 15*th.* — Had a delightful ride to-day into the country, which reminded me of home; but it takes away half the pleasure of riding into the country to go through the suburbs, which are very extensive, and filled with babies and pigs, which are brought up in the same style.

19*th.* — A pleasant morning, but rain in the afternoon prevented us from riding. Thunder and lightning in the evening, and the bells all tolling, as is the custom here in such weather. No prospect of our leaving Manila before next Tuesday. Uncle is getting very impatient.

Tuesday, September 22. — Left Manila this morning, and I really felt as if I were leaving home again. I have got so much attached here that I felt really gloomy. Our friends left us about nine o'clock, and I certainly have not felt so dull this three months. No wind, and we were beating about in the Bay all day, and at anchor all night. I never left any place but my home with so much regret, and shall always remember my visit to Manila with great pleasure.

PART III.

September 23. — Got under way this morning about three o'clock, but, as it looked very squally after beating about all day, and as the men were all tired out, the captain thought best to come to an anchor in Mariveles Bay, a delightful little bay surrounded on three sides by very high land, so that we feel nothing of the hard weather outside, but we are all low in spirits, and I certainly never felt more gloomy. I thought I would give the world to be on *terra firma* or somewhere with my friends.

25*th*. — Cloudy and rainy weather, but a good breeze, which makes some smiling faces, though it is discouraging to be three days getting out of this bay. However, now we have passed the Corregidor, we are in hopes we shall again have our luck. I have felt really homesick these three days past. How shall I support four years' absence? It is just four months to-day since we left.

26*th*. — Wind continues strong and fair, though it is rainy and gloomy enough. We have all been busy below, making preparations for landing again. There is certainly nothing like employment for making one happy. I have felt better to-day than I have for a week. We calculate we shall be in Macao in three days. I long, yet dread, to see this place, I have heard so many different opinions about it; but I am determined to take no one's opinion but my own.

Monday, September 28. — Sick all day. Squally, rainy, uncomfortable weather, and a heavy, irregular sea, which made us all sick. I was stretched on the floor all day, or in my trough, until four o'clock, when I heard the cry of "Land!" and never was it more welcome. To our great joy, we are now within a few hours of our destined port, and glad shall I be to tread again upon *terra firma*. We anchored off the Lima Isles. It blew very hard all night, and must have been very uncomfortable outside.

September 29. — A delightful morning. It seemed like one of our May mornings at home. We set sail at 6 A.M., and anchored off Macao Roads at 10.

Uncle and Mr. A. went on shore soon after, and returned about dark. Mr. Russell has a house and everything necessary prepared for us.

Wednesday, September 30. — This morning all busy enough getting our things out of the ship. There was a heavy sea, which made it very difficult for a boat to come alongside. Indeed, we were obliged to lower everything over the stern; and you would have been amused to see us tied into a chair and swinging over the stern of the ship. But we got along very comfortably, and saw many very amusing things on our way to shore. There is an immense quantity of boats all about, in which whole families live, — indeed, two or three generations. The women steer the boats, and frequently have an infant slung to their backs,—the common mode of carrying children among the poor,—and the poor little thing only has a shaking if it cries. They sometimes use their children very cruelly.

One idea of the Chinese amuses me exceedingly; that is, that a vessel cannot go without eyes. They therefore have a large eye painted on each side of the bow, which looks very singular; and, if you ask them why, they say, "Hi yah, how can see without eye?"

Macao from the sea looks beautiful, with some most romantic spots. We arrived there about ten o'clock, took sedan chairs and went to our house, which we liked the looks of very much. The streets of Macao are narrow and irregular, but we have a garden in which I anticipate much pleasure. In fact, there are two, one above the other. All the paths are of flat stones, and are as smooth as a floor. You ascend five flights of steps and come to an observatory, from which we have a fine view of the bay and harbor, and can see all over the town. Round the observatory there is a terrace, and there are many pretty plants. With this little spot and a few birds I shall get along very comfortably. I had no idea there was so pretty a place here, but I want some one to enjoy it with me.

Friday, October 2.— We had a number of calls to-day, and the English Company's chaplain called to see us. Through some mistake of the servant, we did not see his card till he had left; and I was much astonished, as there was nothing ministerial in his appearance. Indeed, I thought him a great buck, and treated him accordingly. I have had so many charges in respect to these youngsters that I do not know that I shall treat them as civilly as I ought.

October 7. — Finished my letters this morning, and went out to make calls, as it is the etiquette of the place to return calls very soon. We therefore took chairs, and called first upon Mrs. F. at the very end of the town, — a most splendid house and a romantic situation. It seems a perfect paradise. The house stands high. You ascend an immense flight of stone steps, and enter a veranda with a marble floor and filled with plants. You then enter the drawing-room, which is furnished elegantly. The rooms are large, and the house seems like a palace. There is a beautiful view of the town and the country around it from the windows. . . . We have received invitations to a fancy ball at Captain W.'s a week from Friday, and intend going, if nothing happens to prevent.

October 8. — Mrs. T. came over this morning with two large books of costumes for us to choose from for the ball. I shall not tell you what they are till we have worn them. Dr. College, the English consul, and a Mr. Millet, a droll chap, called; and what with purchasing dresses, receiving things from Canton,* writing letters, and so forth, we were kept upon the go.

Friday, 9th. — No one called to-day, but I have been very busy. I find quite enough to occupy my time. I long to go to walk, but cannot until we

---

* Mr. L. went up to Canton on October 1st.

have our chairs (which are being made in Canton) or some one to wait upon us. However, I have had a fine walk upon the terrace, which is a delightful place. In the morning it is beautiful, and the birds are flying through the house all day. We frequently see five in the hall and dining-room at once. There are trees round the house, in which they lodge, and there are some fine singers among them. I will credit you with considerable patience if you ever get as far as this in this journal. However, I think I should seize with much eagerness such a packet from you, and hope to one of these days.

Sunday, October 11. — Not having our chairs, we were obliged to stay at home to-day. I endeavored to spend the day as it should be spent, but you have no idea how difficult it is to keep alive one's religious feelings here or to pass Sunday in a proper manner. I read aloud one of Buckminster's excellent sermons, but had no sooner finished it, and was feeling somewhat disposed to be serious, than four or five people called. They make calls here on their return from church. You see there is no country like ours for religious principles. The Chinese pay no sort of regard to the Sabbath, but go on with their work just as usual. You hear their gongs every little while, chin-chining joss. This is a feast-day with the Catholics. Apew, our comprador (steward), came in this afternoon to ask if we wanted to see *a walky*. We could not divine what he wanted, but we followed him up to a terrace that looks into the street. After waiting some time, we at last saw a Catholic procession, and it was worth waiting for, though I cannot tell you what it meant or anything about it, except that the men were dressed in loose white satin trousers, with a sort of loose blue satin gown that came down to their knees, and they carried lighted candles. There were several little girls, rigged up with wings to resemble angels, and a fine band of music. The cannons all round the fort were fired, and the bells were ringing. It seemed, as you may judge, more like a festival than a Sabbath. [It was the festival of "the maternity of the Virgin Mother." — *Ed.*]

12*th*, 13*th.* — Very busy preparing our dresses for the ball. There are none but men tailors here, and we are obliged to cut and fit our own dresses, thinking the men would be more trouble than good to us, as it is so difficult to make them understand. When we speak to them, they always say, "Yes, sir," and make dreadful work talking; but I find I get along better than at first.

Friday, 16*th.* — The night of the ball. We went at eight o'clock to call for Mrs. F., and thence to the Whiteheads', where we enjoyed ourselves very much, and did not return till 3 A.M., the first time in my life that I was ever out so late. Everything was elegant, and the costumes were of all countries and ages. I shall give you all the particulars in a letter, and therefore will not trouble myself here. We had some fireworks in front of the house. One gentleman took the character of Paul Pry, and was very amusing.

Sunday, October 18.—We attended public worship at Dr. Morrison's house to-day. Were quite delighted once more to hear something good, and to pass our day more as we used to. There were only six people there, but the sermon was very good. They use the English Church form here altogether. On our return we found several cards, as Sunday is a famous day here for calling, but we intend to discourage it by making none ourselves.

I forgot to tell you of the walk we had yesterday afternoon. We went out with the coolie, and he took us all round the Praya Grande, over a great hill, and back through the town,—a monstrous walk, and for the first one it was terrible. It is so long since we have walked that it overcame us all. The streets here are intolerable,— hilly, irregular, and horribly paved. We met no one but Portuguese and Chinamen, who annoyed us very much by their intent gaze. On our way, however, we saw two of their women with small feet. I was perfectly astonished, although I had heard so much of them; but I never believed it, and always supposed I must be deceived. These women's feet were about the size of our little Charley's. [A boy of three.—*Ed.*] Only think of a full-grown and rather fat person having such feet! I thought she must be in torture, but she walked apparently with the greatest ease. Both women carried little canes.

The men here dress their hair most singularly,

having the front of the head shaved close to the skin, while the hair is allowed to grow long on the back of the head and is braided from the top, and you almost always see them with a queue of hair hanging to the bottom of their trousers. They take great pride in the length of their hair.

The Chinese are a most singular people. They appear to me a most united one, and will do anything for their countrymen. While I cannot find that they will ever accommodate a foreigner by beating down their own people, they will impose upon foreigners greatly if not closely watched. Our comprador is a very shrewd fellow, and speaks pretty good English. He wanted to know to-day if Mr. C. was not thirty years older than I am. I asked him how he knew how old I was. "Oh," he said, "I can see: I can savy." He made many other inquiries which amused me very much.

My dear sister, it is now over a week since I wrote last in my journal. I have had so much to do with company and visiting that my journal has been sadly neglected, but I will try and remember something of what has happened. I cannot conceive of people calling this a dull place. Tuesday we were invited to Mrs. F.'s, to take tea and walk in the garden. It is the most romantic place, is very extensive, and abounds in serpentine walks. There is a beautiful view of the sea, and immense rocks and trees, and several temples in the garden. In another part there is a cave in the rocks where the celebrated Camoens wrote his "Lusiad." A bust of him stands in the cave. It is a wild and delightful spot. What would I not give to have you here to enjoy everything with me! It is all I want now. Every wish is gratified excepting that one — which cannot be — to see my friends.

On Wednesday our good friend Dr. College called. He is the best man I have seen yet. Everybody loves him and speaks well of him. He has been truly kind to us, and we are under great obligations to him. It is a shame that he is a bachelor!

After six I walked on the terrace all alone, till all the posts looked like men, and it was so dark that it was not pleasant. I was thinking of home, sweet home, and was half inclined to wish myself there. I frequently do, my dear sister, though I may appear to you to enjoy myself, and I do; but there are times when one wants a comforter.

No letters for us by the Liverpool packet. What do you mean? How cruel! She sailed ten days after us, and not a word for any of us! Hard, hard, hard! Well, I shall do as I would be done by, and write as often as I can have that privilege; for there is nothing I enjoy so much as writing home. On Thursday we went to Mrs. F.'s, and I enjoyed myself very much. You would be astonished if you were to see your once diffident sis dancing the first quadrille, not without much urging. However, you must know that I am the only spinster in the place, and I am pulled about in every direction. [I have often heard my mother say that ladies were so scarce in Macao at the time, that they were obliged to take a different partner for each figure of the quadrilles.— *Ed.*] We had considerable singing and dancing, some fine glees, and a fine band of music. It was really delightful. We had a supper, which was rather tantalizing, as most of the company had dined there, and were not at all hungry; and we, who dined at three o'clock, were obliged to look at the niceties, the satisfied party being in the majority. We returned about twelve, not much delighted with our host, as he seemed inclined to tell every one that his wife was the daughter of a baronet, and was well-born and well-bred, which made him quite ridiculous; but we excused him by thinking that he had had a dinner party! Friday we had calls all the morning, and an invitation from Mr. Plowden to some theatricals this evening, several scenes from Shakespeare's "Merchant of Venice," etc. We went about half-past eight, under the protection of Dr. Bradford. The performances were fine. There was some good singing, and the young gentlemen acquitted themselves in fine style. We had a very good farce, called "Killing no Murder," and several other scenes from different plays. After the performances we had a fine supper. Between the scenes the gentlemen and ladies walked in the veranda. I like their manner of fixing the supper tables here. They have small tables holding about ten, which makes it much more social. The party broke up about two. I thought it impossible that it was more than twelve.

Saturday, October 24.——After dinner felt rather dull, and retired to our summer-house, which appears to be remote from society. I took my pencil, and for a little amusement sketched a slight view of the surrounding hills, which are very pretty. Would that I were more expert in sketching from nature. It is a delightful employment! From the front of the summer-house we have a fine view of the fort on one high hill. On another hill near by stands what is called the *Gear*, signifying Beacon. It is very high, and is a convent, I believe. Below we have a view of the town and the beach, the Franciscan Church, and the green where the ladies walk; and every Saturday evening a band plays there, which is pleasant. I can hear them from the summer-house. On the other side we have a little view of the sea, but a new house lately built intercepts our view very much. In the other direction we have a fine view of the harbor and the surrounding hills, with an ancient church and convent. It is really a delightful spot. I love it now, and if we remove, as we some expect to, I shall regret it much.

October 26.——This morning Captain Roundy called, and undertook to bore my ears for ear-rings. I, like a heroine, fainted away from fear, but the operation, I think, is rather unpleasant. In the afternoon Dr. B. called for us, and we went to Mr. Beale's, where we were cordially received by the old gentleman, and entertained beyond measure. He has an aviary filled with a most choice collection of birds. The bird of paradise is by far the most beautiful. You cannot imagine plumage more perfect. You have seen stuffed ones, but you can barely judge of the beauty of this bird, which is much too handsome for the temper it possesses. The next in beauty were the gold and silver pheasants. Their plumage is rich, and they seemed conscious of their beauty. Another singular bird is called the dagger-breasted pigeon. It has a slate-colored back and a white breast, with a spot of red directly in front, which resembles blood, and makes it look as though it had just had a fresh wound. I cannot describe to you the beauty of all these birds. They were too numerous. After we had looked at them enough, we walked in the garden, which is literally filled with plants and trees of the rarest kinds, and has a pond filled with a great variety of gold-fishes. About six we were joined by several friends, and went to the house and took tea made in the Chinese style. Each one's tea is put into a covered cup till sufficiently steeped, and is then drunk without milk or sugar. That did not suit my taste for sweets, I assure you. We left Mr. Beale's about seven, after engaging to breakfast with him on Wednesday.

Tuesday, October 27. — In the afternoon we all went to the Campo, a beautiful place some way out of town between two high hills, with the sea washing up on one side. I ascended one of the highest, and on looking round saw my party at a great distance below. They had not followed my rash steps, but I was not sorry to have gone. It was a perfect spot, and I shall try it again. Coming down, I was accosted by Dr. Pierson, who had very politely come up to my assistance. He thought I was in some danger of breaking my neck, but it wasn't the first time I had climbed a hill. Callers came in about eight, and stayed till twelve. I suppose you will think that rather a late hour, but it is not in this country.

November 1.—I suppose you are now enjoying a fire, but we still find it comfortable with windows and doors all open, most delightful weather. I wish all invalids could be transported here. This air could not help restoring them. Sir Andrew L. and Sir John C. and Mouqua, one of the Hong merchants, called after service. Mouqua is a great character. He had on his winter dress, which is rather singular. The cap is blue in front, the crown scarlet, with a blue glass button on the top. The whole dress was blue, of different shades. I asked why they did not let ladies go to Canton. He said, "Too muchy man want to look." He said, too, "Canton too small; no walky." He was very gallant, I assure you.

November 2.—A splendid morning, my dear sis, and I hope you have as pleasant a one. The bells are ringing. Mrs. C. is sitting by me, manufacturing a bonnet, and the Chinamen are jabbering below. I should admire to have you hear their jargon. There are no words to be made out of it to my ears. It seems to consist of low, guttural sounds. They are a stupid set of people, and spend most of their time in sleeping.

November 3. — The bells have been ringing and guns firing all day, because that villain of a Don Miguel is chosen King of Portugal, and to-night all the high places and churches are illuminated. The fort and the convent on the hill look very brilliant. Many of the Portuguese houses are lighted up, too. O Molly, I have been thinking about home all day; did not feel well this morning, and got low-spirited. What would I not give to see you! Good-night, my dear sis; pleasant dreams and sweet repose to you. Always remember me in your prayers, though far away. I need them more than ever.

November 5. — Called for Mrs. T. at two o'clock, and from her house to the race-ground, but without thinking that I should enjoy myself. I cannot tell you why, but my spirits seem to have lead attached to them. The race-ground is at what is called the Barrier, which prevents all foreigners from passing over that spot. The course is about three-quarters of a mile. It is a delightful place, and I was much amused by the novel scene. There was a temporary house of bamboo built for the ladies, and I assure you, my dear sis, it was very interesting to look upon the motley group below us. Chinese of all descriptions, dressed in their most singular costume, some with those large basket hats, many of them with nothing on their heads, but carrying a fan which they hold up to screen them from the sun. Some of them had bags on their backs about half a yard square, in which they put their babies. The poor little things were knocked about in the crowd as if they had been so many bits of wood. Portuguese and Lascars were mixed with the Chinese, and to hear the mixture of languages — none of which I understood — made me think of the confusion of Babel, and led me to wish that those foolish people had been content to live on the earth while they were permitted. Some of the races were very good, and some large bets were made. We returned about seven, and had a long discussion upon the merits of the English. We concluded that they had been extremely polite to us, but that it is necessary to treat them with some reserve, and that the men are a good-for-nothing set of rascals. Do not tell anybody, but all they care about is eating, drinking, and frolicking. [Marginal note by the journalist: "Quite a modest conclusion."]

November 8. — Awoke this morning wofully disappointed to find it only a dream that you, my dear sis, and my brother Abbot were here with me. You never were more plainly before my eyes! Aunt L. has just gone to church, but I thought I would not go. When I look at Mr. V. and think that the last time I saw him he was betting at a horse-race, or dancing with me, I lose all reverence for him or what he says. I resolved to stay at home and read my own sermon, and I think I shall feel quite as well satisfied as by going to church, and I sincerely hope a little better.

November 9. — Went to Lady C.'s quadrille party.

Wore a white muslin trimmed with yellow satin over white satin. Though the plainest dress in the room, it was as handsome as I wished. The ladies here dress a great deal, and we do not pretend to vie with the English ladies in anything but good conduct. I danced every dance, and had several engaged when I returned home about one o'clock.

[About this time the bright young spirit begins to catch glimpses of the darker side of this gay and seemingly innocent life, and snatches of the gossip of the little colony begin to come to her ears. After making a round of morning calls, she returns to write in her journal.]

November 12. — Have heard some stories this morning which will be a good lesson for us, and, I hope, make us more on our guard than ever. You have no idea how circumspect it is necessary to be in this place! This gossip concerns me only as it concerns the whole sex, but I intend to learn a lesson by another's experience. It is about a lady who has been staying in Macao for the last six months. Thank fortune, she has now gone! It really made me quite melancholy, and I longed to be at my dear home in the bosom of my family and those I love. I must make myself as contented and happy as possible, but it is a heartless way of living. There are but few here we can put confidence in. . . . I have no one to walk with, and it is not proper for me to go alone. However, I mount upon the terrace and walk there, and enjoy my own pleasant thoughts.

You may perhaps say, "She has got the blues." Pray make allowances for moods, and imagine me as happy as a lark. Ungrateful should I be if I were not, for there is not a wish of my heart ungratified, if it is in Aunt's power to grant it, but, alas! I am sure you would think I was happy and easy if I were to stand before you and let you gaze upon my round, fat visage. I assure you I look more like "the frigate" than ever, and feel quite anxious, as my appetite persists, and cold weather (the most fattening thing) is approaching.

November 14.—We all met at Mrs. M.'s for our water party. We went to the Isle de Verd, and there landed while tiffin was prepared, and after our refreshment, got under way. The scenery all around us was delightful. The sun was behind us on our return, just setting behind the hills, and shedding its softened beams upon the city of Macao, adding much to its beauty. As we approached, the busy scene before us was quite new and amusing. A vast number of the poor people live upon the water, and appear quite cheerful and happy.

November 16.— Aunt L. went out, and left me to keep house. While she was gone, four of the Macao beauties called to see me. Now I suppose you would like to know who they are. The first is Mr. Howard, a shrewd, quick-witted, sensible young man, and a handsome face withal; a fine singer, and affords considerable amusement at parties, as he possesses great imitative powers, and frequently gives us representations of all the great English actors. He wears under his chin a long black beard, besides black mustachios and whiskers. It seems like looking through a forest and discovering, at a distance, two stars, to look at his eyes. Seriously, though, it is an outrageously long beard, but it is the English style. The others were Mr. Clarke, Mr. Morris, and Mr. Alexander, all clever youngsters. I did my prettiest, I assure you, with so many beaux.

November 18.— At eight o'clock we went to the Albany, where we were received with every mark of attention. The entrance was decorated with flowers and brilliantly lighted, and in the centre hung a large oval piece of transparent silk or something of the kind, with the word "Welcome" in large letters on it, and also decorated with flowers, which had a very pretty effect. The drawing-room, staircase, and supper-room were decorated in the same way. We had some fine fireworks in front of the house besides the dancing, etc. Mr. Howard gave us some amusing reminiscences. I danced every time, and got into quite a hobble; for I engaged for four deep about the middle of the evening, and, when it came to the third, could not tell for the life of me whom I had engaged to dance with. Two gentlemen came, both claimed me for that dance, and both were equally urgent. I, however, danced with Mr. Card, hoping there would be time for No. 2; but poor Morris had to be deferred till the first dance of the next ball,— when that will be, no one knows. I do not tell this with the least vanity,

Molly. It would not be so if there were many ladies here, but you know they are scarce. There are twenty times as many gentlemen, only a little sprinkling of ladies. I have no rivals, as there is but one other spinster in the place. We left the party highly gratified with our evening's amusement; waited upon to my chair by Morris. Hope I have not offended him, for he is a pretty little fellow. It was about two when we got home. I suppose father will think that his daughter is in a fair way to be ruined; but tell him it would be considered very ill-natured in this place for the only young lady here to stay away (from a ball), and I must say it's the only amusement we have.

November 21, *Saturday.* — This evening we proposed walking in Mrs. Fearon's garden and taking tea with her. We walked up, and were overtaken by the charming Mr. Howard and Mr. Clarke. They left us at the gate, and we had a beautiful walk in that paradise of a place. It is large, wild, and romantic. It is a work of art, it is true, but it resembles nature so perfectly that you would think it originally formed in this way. The rocks and trees are immense, and there are several banyan-trees growing with their roots almost out of ground. I wish I could give you any idea of it by description. We then went to the house, where we were soon joined by many other people. Cards were introduced in the evening, which did not suit our Yankee notions. [The New England custom was then to begin the observance of Sunday at sunset on Saturday.— *Ed.*] We had a little supper, and returned in our chairs about ten, not altogether pleased with the evening; and we have resolved to avoid Saturday evening visits in future, not knowing what will take place among people who think but little of Sundays.

November 23.— Aunt L. received a note from Mr. Dent this morning, requesting to be allowed to accompany us to the play to-night. It was one of the drollest things you ever saw. I should like to have you know him. He is a pleasant creature. We had satin play-bills sent us this morning, which I shall send to you, that you may see the style in which everything is carried on in Macao. I assure you everything corresponds. We went to the play at seven, accompanied by Mr. Dent. You would have been amused, I am sure. Several of the scenes were painted by Mr. Chinnery, a famous portrait painter. The play was performed very well. Some parts were admirably done, but the most amusing were the female characters. Mr. Chinnery was one, and they could not have chosen anybody less fit to perform a female part; but, however, his ridiculous appearance made much sport. He represented Miss Lucretia McTab,* and Mr. Alexander was Miss Emily Worthington, a tall, lean-looking man, with a gruff voice; but she was supposed to be breaking the hearts of all the young beaux, and you have no idea how ugly she was! It was so inconsistent that we could not but laugh. After the play we had a farce called "Bombastes

* In "The Poor Gentleman," by Colman.— *Ed.*

Furioso." It was very amusing. After the farce, a supper, which lasted till nearly two. We had some fine singing, and enjoyed it very much.

December 2. — Letters from Canton, telling of a great fire there, two hundred houses burned. The Chinese will not put out a fire. They say it is "Joss pigeon (God's business), and no can." They are a most remarkable people!

December 8. —I forgot to say that I went to Chinnery the portrait painter's room yesterday. He had some fine likenesses there. He is remarkably successful. How I wished that I had a little of the needful to put into the man's hand, that he might take my beautiful phiz, that I might transport it across the great waters into your own hands, for I flatter myself you would like it! But there, what's the use of wishing?

December 9. — Went to Mrs. D.'s party, and had a very pleasant evening. Mrs. D. is a sweet woman, and she has a husband as pleasant. He is a great favorite of mine, and I think he likes me. Now you will say, "H. exactly, vanity of vanities!" Well, what is more, I *know* he does.

Dec. 25, 1829. — This evening we are to dine with the Company at half-past six, where we shall be as stiff as stakes, and, I suppose, shall not enjoy ourselves at all. These dinners are amazing stiff, but I shall rig myself in a white satin under-dress, with a wrought muslin petticoat, and a pink satin bodice to set neatly to my neat little form, and made by my own neat little hands. I shall then jump into my neat little chair, and proceed to the scene of action. I shall say all the neat little things I can, and discuss the merits of the several dishes in my own way.

Later. — At half-past six we jumped into our chairs, and were the first to arrive, which did not exactly suit our feelings. However, we were soon followed by all the ladies and whole squads of gentlemen. After conversing awhile, I was led to an elegant table, and seated between the elegant Mr. D. and Mr. V., the chaplain. Everything on the table was splendid, — a whole service of massive plate. There were about sixty at table. The dinner consisted of every delicacy, served in the most elegant style and with the greatest order. Every one brings their own servant to wait upon them at table. When the first course is cleared away, these extra servants all fall back to the wall, and the regular servants carry out the dishes, handed to them by the butlers. I think you would have been much entertained to look in at this immense table, with the long row on each side of these horrible-looking Chinese, and to see the different expressions on the countenances of those whose business it was to eat and those whose business it was to look on. I ate a piece of plum-pudding that was very nice; but it wanted something, — I suppose the home relish. What tasted most like home were the cucumbers, which really looked natural. It would be impossible to describe the various dishes. Suffice it to say that everything was as elegant as possible, and that there was everything that could be obtained that was nice and delicate. The time passed very pleasantly, and there was nothing stiff about it. Everybody appeared perfectly easy and at home. After dinner the lights were extinguished, and the long table was covered with blue lights.* We were all to put our hands into these blue flames, and pull out the raisins beneath. This is called snap-dragon, and is a favorite Christmas amusement in England. I thought I was in the infernal regions, and I never shall forget the frightful visages of some of the gentlemen as they held the plates up near their faces. The effect is astonishing.

To-morrow morning I part with my journal. I feel as though I were to part with a friend. Take it, my dear sister, and correct the errors if you can. It was begun to amuse at sea, and according to promise has been kept up here, but in a hurried style; for I have hardly a moment for writing, or I should have looked it over and endeavored to correct the sentences better. I hope next year to receive every day's account in a neat book like this, written by my dear sister. Good-by, my darling, once more.

* Dishes of burning brandy and salt.—*Ed.*

BOOK II. PART I.

January 1. — Our good old ship "Sumatra" passed Macao to-day with a smacking breeze. Received a few lines from Captain R. per pilot. [Captain R. was the bearer of the first book of the journal to its destination. — *Ed.*]

January 9. — Commenced Irving's "Columbus" this morning; find it very interesting. This afternoon Mr. V. called for us to walk. We went, not being aware that the wind blew very hard, and foolishly ascended a high hill, where, I am sure, it would have been much more safe to scud than to go as we did with royals and studding-sails set. Although I kept crying, "Stand by topgallant halyards," it was of no avail. We were beating against the wind, and, when we were at the height of the hill, my dress tangled round Mr. V.'s legs, and in trying to extricate himself he caught his foot in the trimming, which came very near throwing both of us over the precipice into the sea, and great would have been the fall thereof. But after much labor we weathered the gale, and arrived safely under the lee of the hill. Aunt L. and Mrs. C. were wise enough to turn back; but Mr. V. and I are much alike in one respect, — we both dislike turning back, and will persevere if possible.

[For many pages now the journal is a somewhat monotonous record of walks and calls and evening parties, with "Mr. V." turning up at all times and in all capacities, from the preacher of "an excellent sermon" to the partner in a waltz or a card party. — *Ed.*]

January 19. — Mr. B. just returned from Canton. Brought us the news of the steam frigate "Fulton's" explosion. Made my heart jump at first to think you have all got to go in a steamboat.* How I long to hear of your safe arrival!

January 24. — The comprador (butler) chin-chin'd us not to ring the bell to-morrow, being their New Year's Day. The Chinese have an idea it will call up Fanqui, or the devil. They fire crackers all day for the purpose of keeping off the evil spirit for the coming year.

January 25. — A great day with the Chinese. They all have a new suit of clothes, and keep a sort of holiday, going home to their families, to chin-chin Joss, etc. They are all obliged to pay their debts at this time. Most of the servants got a little too much luncheon this morning. Our comprador did not hesitate to say that he was "too muchy drunk."

28*th.* — The whole town in commotion to-day to celebrate the coronation of Don Miguel. For three successive evenings the town is to be illuminated. The whole place looked very brilliant. A temporary fort was erected on the green, where the Portuguese had a masquerade ball.

* From Salem or Boston to Brooklyn. — *Ed.*

February 3.— Dined at Mrs. T.'s with the secu-
rity merchants (Chinese), and never was more
amused than with the different observations they
made. They gave us a full account of their customs. Old Tinqua had the audacity to ask me how
old I was. He says he has five wives. No. 1 his
father and mother chose for him. "He no like No.
1. Too muchy ugly." No. 2 "he likey. He
choose her." He is sixty-two, but you would
never think him more than thirty-five. I thought
I was paying him a great compliment when I told
him so; but I hear that I could have said nothing
more displeasing, as they like to be considered
old.

February 6.— The East India Company have now
settled all their difficulties with the Chinese, and
the ships are ordered off to Whampoa, chop-chop (at
once). The captains, of course, are all off, too;
and there are many happy hearts and smiling faces,
for they have been very anxious to get away. Uncle
arrived from Canton very unexpectedly. We had
not seen him for three months.

16*th*.— Mrs. Baynes has this morning left Macao
with all her children for Canton. She went in the
Company's cutter. We shall now be all on tiptoe
until we hear the result.

February 21.— We heard of Mrs. B.'s safe arrival
at Canton yesterday. (Uncle went there on the
19th.) The Hong merchants, it is said, have
called upon her; but they always call upon the chief
on his arrival. They say, "In one or two days more

can see if that lady come up." It is uncertain
whether there is any law against it. Walked with
Mrs. A., who says an American ship has come in
with six passengers. We could not credit it, but
upon our return we were told by the servants that
six American gentlemen had been here, and had
gone to Mrs. Morrison's. We were then kept in
suspense a little longer, but after waiting patiently
about an hour, there came a note from Mrs. M., saying she hoped to have the pleasure of introducing
a batch of friends from our dear country to us in the
morning, but still no news from the ship. Who
she was, or what time she sailed, was still a mystery. I was anxious enough. [It must be remembered that it was nine months since the L.'s had
left home or had heard from there.—*Ed.*]

I begged Aunt L. to despatch a note, begging
for particulars; but Apew (the comprador) came in
with the desired information. The ship was the
"Roman," one hundred and twenty-five days from
New York, which was music in my ears. The passengers would call on us in the morning. I fancied
myself then reading heaps of letters. I went to bed
to dream of the pleasure that awaited me.

February 23.—This morning every minute was an
hour till the gentlemen came. . . . They could tell us
nothing of our friends; but one of them said he was
in Salem a few days before leaving, that it was still
standing, and things appeared to be going on as
usual. They assured us there were letters on board
for us, and that we should receive them in a day or

two. The ship had gone to Lintin, and you may judge of my anxiety.

24th.—A rainy day, and no letters yet. I copied the town signals this morning that I may know what a ship is when she comes in, as they are all made known by the telegraph.*

25th.—I arose this morning low-spirited and anxious for my letters. I sat down to read, but with every step I heard my head was out of the window to see if it were the desired messenger. I sat in my own room till it was time to dress and go into the drawing-room. Aunt L. handed me a few lines just received from Captain Lavender, in which he said, "I send you a box containing papers and all the letters which were sent." Judge of my distress when she told me no box had come. How I wished myself a man, that I might run to the boat and over-haul it! But in a few minutes in came the desired box. Now do you not think that patience has had her perfect work? Nine long months without re-ceiving a line, and then to have such detentions! But to proceed. The first thing I saw was my father's handwriting, and then I knew he was alive. I literally grabbed at the others, and hardly waited to see whom they were from. One after another was torn open. I wanted to read them all at once, and was vexed that I could not read faster. The ink of one was so pale it was impossible to read that first. Another had so much in it that I must leave that till the last. My dear father's and mother's letters were then carefully perused, and all

* Semaphore? — *Ed.*

the others in due time. Yours, my dear sister, were read last, but not with the least interest. They were a great treat to me, and carried me directly home. We are now anticipating earlier dates, as you mention sending by several ships before, and you may judge how happy I felt to know how well and happy you all seemed. I had been very anxious to hear of your safe arrival in New York, and how you had all got through the hot weather. How many thousand blessings have we all to be thankful for, particularly this last year! We cannot be grateful enough. Spent the evening in reading the newspapers and gleaning little bits of news.

February 28. — Sunday morning, but little like Sunday. No church. Read a chapter in my Bible, and so forth, and sat down in my own room to bring up my journal, which was nearly a week behind hand. After writing a few minutes, hear there is a youngster here who wishes to see us. I must go and hear what he has to say. Not dressed, but must make haste. It is now ten o'clock. Hope he will not stay long. . . . Here I am again. Have been detained two hours by that little *monk*. I do not know what his name is; but he has given us the whole history of his life and adventures, also a long history of the Indians of the north-west coast of America and the Sandwich Islands, — all of which would have interested me at any other time, but I was in a hurry to go to my room to write, read, etc. He tells us the ship "Tartar" has arrived, the only gratifying fact he did give us; but I made excuses for him. He is just entering manhood, is a little consequential, and thinks he is a beauty, I suppose. Well, he is a little, black-eyed fellow, the clerk of the brig "Active," now for Lintin.

Seven o'clock, Sunday Eve. — I have just returned from seeing a procession of this wretched set of people, the Catholics. If I could discover any signs of devotion in their hearts, I could tolerate them; but to see such mockery is beyond everything.

In the first place came six or seven men with muffled drums, and black silk drawn over their faces. They were all dressed in black robes. I do not know what they represented. Then followed others, bearing a banner with the cross and other banners with Latin inscriptions. One of the men in front was blowing a trumpet. Then followed about twenty little girls dressed as angels, with wings, hooped petticoats, and all sorts of finery. The little things were carrying banners in their hands. Then followed men chanting, dressed in black and white, without hats. Then came a car borne by four men, with the image of our Saviour bearing the cross. It rested on his shoulder. Then followed more padres, chanting. Then the military, with a band of music, then citizens, in their ordinary dress. The bells were ringing. There was no order, nor did the people, either high or low, appear to feel anything. They bore long lighted candles in their hands; but these they used as weapons of defence, thrusting them into the children's faces as they passed. Some of them were throwing stones and cutting all sorts of capers. An unruly mob mixed in with the procession, which destroyed all appearance of solemnity. It is now Lent, and they have many of these processions. When I see these things, I thank my God that I was born where they worship Him in a more Christian way, or, at least, in a place where every person knows what they worship, and where I hope that worship is more heartfelt than I think it here; but I will not judge! [Pretty well, after what our bigoted little Puritan has just written! — *Ed.*] I suppose you see more of these things now than when in Salem. Apew came to tell me that "the Portuguese Joss would make a walky" to-day.

March 2. — Have received another package to-day from my kind and faithful sister, giving me an account of the great emigration, also the robbery. Fancy a pack of thieves overhauling your love-letters! I should be afraid of seeing them in the next paper. It was rather a rude welcome to the city, but it will teach you to be on your guard.

6th. — Another cloudy, foggy, unpleasant morning. Have been reading Hall's "Travels in the United States." I do not think he does the Americans justice, nor do I believe any Englishman ever will. I feel quite enraged with him at times, and would fain throw his book by, but I am constantly hoping to find something to redeem it. He seems to think himself a mighty body, and I am sure he may justly be called an egotist. In some places he makes the Americans appear quite ridiculous. I hope I shall have patience to finish the book, but it requires a great deal.

March 9. — At one we met Mr. Otaduy at Mrs. A.'s, and took our first lesson in Spanish. Think we shall like it very much. It will serve to amuse and take up some of the time, which is rather dull, now we are so much alone. Ah, my dear sister, if I could now spend one hour with you all around the six-foot table, what would I not give!

10*th.* — We went to the new house this morning. It begins to look nice. It is very near the Cathedral, and the street was all in a bustle. They are mourning, or rather ringing the bells, because the Pope * is dead, which we heard a long while ago.

11*th.* — We have passed a delightful evening with Mrs. A., and on our return, to our great astonishment, found Uncle in the parlor; but the poor man had just arrived, and was quite sea-sick, so he has gone to bed. It quite startled me at first to see him. I thought he had heard some bad news, and had come down to tell us. I was so much startled that I did not appear glad to see him, but I am sure I am perfectly delighted. Good-night, my dearest sister, mother, father, and all hands.

March 15. — At one we went to Mrs. A.'s to take another Spanish lesson. Mr. O. thinks we get along very well, which is quite encouraging. Passed the pleasantest day we have had in a long while. After tea, sat down to my verbs, but Mr. Beale sent us "Devereux," and I took my work

* Pius VIII. died Nov. 30, 1830. — *Ed.*

while Uncle read. (I came pretty near killing a moschetto then,—knocked off his hind leg, I guess.) I have been reading a little of Hall's "Travels" since I came to my room, and find it rather tedious. I cannot think he does our dear country and good people justice. I think he is vexed that we are as well off as we are.

March 28. — Did you ever read Montgomery's "On the Deity"? If not, do read it. It is a most beautiful thing, and seems to lift you from the earth and makes you wish to soar above and be with Him "who was and is the Fountain Soul" : —

> " Hill, flood, and forest, mountain, rock, and sea,
> All take their terrors and their charms from Thee,—
> From Thee, whose hidden but supreme control
> Moves through the world, a Universal Soul."

I must make one more quotation, though you may think me quite too poetical : —

> " 'Tis sweet, when roaming by the wave-girt strand,
> To weave fond visions of our own far land ;
> Or dream, while faintly chimes the convent bell,
> On distant friends, and each domestic spell,
> And feel one spirit mark our lone career,
> And dwell in every heart to friendship dear." *

You know the blessings of this friendship, my sister; and I can fancy it. It is wanted in this place. Some friend who has a kind, congenial heart. Do not let George see this, or he would laugh at me, I know.

* "I think my ladyship was in quite a poetical mood at this time."— Marginal note, September, 1830.

After dinner, we strolled upon the hills and made a couch of the rocks. The sudden warmth of the weather takes away the strength, and makes us feel quite languid. We sat on the rocks musing till the sun had set behind the hills, after tinging the clouds with the richest colors and leaving the moon with a small share of her brilliancy to light us over the graves. You must know that, when we take our walks, we must always go through and over these graves, but they never give that feeling that we should have at home in walking through a grave-yard. I have often wondered why not, but I suppose because none of our friends, relations, or acquaintances, repose here.

29th. — After dinner went to our new house, and walked upon the terrace there till it was time to dress for Mrs. Turner's, whence we have just returned, having spent a delightful evening. We played our American game of "old maid," which seems to take mightily. Poor Blight had the queen three times, which quite worried him. He thinks it very ominous. We are to remove to-morrow. So I must be up betimes and pack up my duds, for nothing is done yet. So good-night, my dearest sister.

March 30. — I rose quite early, put my things all in order, and before two o'clock all the "topside," as the Chinamen say, was removed. And how do you think they manage it? You know we have no carriages of any sort, but everything is carried on men's shoulders, not as a man in America would shoulder an axe, but suspended from poles. It is astonishing to see what burdens they carry with apparent ease, — great heavy things, such as trunks, sideboards, etc. You never see a Chinaman carry anything in his hands, but always in baskets, jars, etc.

(*From a letter.*) — This house is much better finished and more elegant than the other, and much cooler, which is a great object in summer. There are six large rooms, quite sufficient for our small family. It stands near the Cathedral, from which we see all the processions, etc., start. The back of the house opens on to a large terrace, which gives us a fine view of the roads, and all the ships coming in and out, the hills all round, and the Praya. Downstairs there is a fine entrance hall, whence a flight of dark varnished stairs and a small entry lead up to the drawing-room, — a room that you would be proud of in America. It has a fine domed ceiling, ornamented with stucco-work, a handsome marble fireplace, and three French windows, opening on to the veranda, and thence to the terrace. The dining-room faces the street. Two doors open from the drawing-room into my room, also a fine large room with a domed ceiling. Next to mine comes Aunt L.'s room, very spacious, and built in the same way, and a very handsome little sitting-room beyond that. Plenty of "go-downs" (store-rooms), large bath-rooms, etc.

April 1. — Went to walk with Uncle, and met three Parsees, or fire-worshippers, on the way. They were dressed in white robes with a sort of red turban upon their heads. At one of the Chinese graves there were four men and children chin-chinning. Every year they visit the graves of their fathers and grandfathers, and returf them, building a fire on the graves, in which they burn Joss paper. They would bow, clasping their hands upon their breasts, then kneel and touch the grave with their faces, all jabbering in their horrid jargon. Returned home, arranged the plants, and sat upon the terrace till tea-time. A most perfect evening; the moon was shining as bright as day. This elegant bay stretched before us, with the little boats flying about it,—a most beautiful sight.

April 2.— 10 P. M. finds me in my spacious room, writing to my dear sister, and what shall I say to her for to-day? Shall I tell her I was cross this morning? Whether I do or not, I am very sure I was. You know it is an uncommon thing for me to be cross. Do not ask me the cause, for I am sure I cannot tell you; but I felt better before two o'clock.

I heard Mr. Wilkinson's voice in the drawing-room, and, "thinks I to myself," I'll go and hear what he has to say, and see if I shall not feel better; and before he left my usual good temper was restored.

After dinner looked out of the window, and saw one of the Company's ships with the sun shining on her well-filled sails. How I wished for Mr. Chinnery's talent for painting, that I might sketch for you the beautiful scene before me, the large and handsome church, milk-white, with a splendid flight of stone steps, and surrounded by trees and shrubbery. Just beyond, the fort, stretching into the bay. Beyond this again, you can see the roads, and the little boats skimming over the surface. In the distance two islands of high ground can be discerned, and the beautiful ship heading toward her much-desired home. A little farther in, is a little European boat flying along under full sail, and any quantity of Chinese boats are in sight. Now can you not imagine that we have a pleasant view from our terrace? And now here I sit fighting mosquitoes in my own room. Every half-second my pen is put into my mouth while I attempt murder. The coolies are "sleeping audibly" enough under my room. I never knew people snore so loud as they do. Aunt L. has frequently sent down of an evening to have them turned over!

April 5. — Did not walk to-day, as we were to have company in the evening. There were fourteen with ourselves, and a very pleasant party. We commenced playing "old maid" after tea, and then played Aunt C.'s game, which made much sport. Some one gave as a question, "When will Mr. Blight give the ladies a tea-party?" which was thought a grand move; and we all decided, after much sport, to give him the pleasure of our company on Friday evening. Old Chinnery, who is a monstrous epicure, wished to know if there would be a supper or what they would have to eat. The reply was, "Toast and tea, certainly, and butter, if it is to be had." The bachelors, you know, all keep house here, have everything in style, and plenty of servants, and it is but right that they should do something to amuse the ladies. Don't you agree with me? I wish you could join us in these delightful little parties. You have no idea how pleasant they are. The tea-parties at home are so much trouble that you cannot enjoy them, but here everything is easy. If anything is wrong, it is all laid to the servants. The hostess is not blamed, as with us. Every one calls for what they wish, and the servants make the tea and bring it in.

Good Friday, April 9.— This morning at nine, after much ceremony in the church, a procession was formed, with the cross coming first, the padres and friars following. Then came a coffin covered with black, and an image to represent the body of our Saviour just taken from the cross. Behind that, his mother and two other women. There were many banners and a long procession, a fine band of music, and I certainly never heard anything more solemn. They played softly and slowly, the drums muffled with black, the priests chanting at the same time. The streets were thronged with people, and all hats were off. I cannot bring my mind to think it right to perform this ceremony. It seems horrid to me to see an image made to represent so divine a person.

The church was hung with black, and at one end was a representation of Calvary. The Virgin Mary was also in black.

Sunday, April 11.— Was awaked from my sleep this morning by a band playing in the most spirited style. The music was fine. Another procession went from the church, and one man walking in it represented Christ risen from the dead. I could not help thinking how can any man that represents the Saviour ever sin more? Only think, what could have been his feelings when walking through the streets representing that divine person! It makes me shudder.

Last night we had a most refreshing shower. The drought had become quite serious. The Chinese have fasted and prayed for rain, and have hired the Portuguese to pray for them.

April 17. — This morning dressed ourselves for the purpose of sallying forth to call on the ladies just returned from Canton. First called upon Mrs. Fearon, who looks finely. Says Canton is a better place than she had fancied, but, notwithstanding, she is very glad to breathe the fresh air of Macao again, which, they all say, is much purer than that of Canton. They say the Chinese were very civil; that they gathered in crowds round the house when they expected them out, but filed off on both sides at their approach, and made no noise. Nothing but a little buzz of admiration was heard. Mrs. Baynes says that when she first arrived the people had boats stationed upon the water, and paid three cash to see the Fanqui women, but none made the least disturbance. I think the Chinese are much more civil than either American or English people would have been if a Chinawoman with little feet had appeared in our streets, dressed in the costume of her country.

Why, she would be mobbed and hooted at immediately!

April 26. — Well, my dear sister, to-night I have an event to communicate. This morning I was sitting in my room when Mr. Russell called me to the terrace; and what do you think was to be seen? Why nothing more or less than a Steam Ship [*sic*] flying through the waters, and displaying herself to the admiration of all, particularly those who know nothing about such things. It reminded me of home, although I had never seen many of them. You must know that it's a very odd thing in this part of the great world.

This steamboat, the "Forbes," sailed with the "Jamsina" for the purpose of towing her from Calcutta to China, she being loaded with that precious drug, opium. This vessel brings much news, among the rest the failure of an immense house in Calcutta, Palmer & Co., for over thirteen million dollars. Only think what a sum, ruining, I suppose, thousands. Last night I read till I dropped asleep the "Notions of America by a Travelling Bachelor," which are, I think, very correct; and, if he were an Englishman, as he professes to be (which I very much doubt), he is the best Englishman that ever lived, or else he has fallen in love with some of the pretty girls there, that he often speaks of, and wishes to curry favor with the blooming patriots. He is, I should think, the first one of his countrymen who ever did the Americans justice in a work of the kind; and so strongly do I feel that it would be impossible for one of them to overcome prejudice and national feeling that I cannot believe him an Englishman. (Afterwards heard that it was written by Paulding, of New York.)

29th. — Went to Chinnery's this morning, and finished some very pretty sketches copied from his. Uncle and Mr. Russell got their chop (orders) from Canton, and are to leave us to-morrow; and dull enough we shall be for a while. Oh, I cannot bear these constant partings! But there, fate decrees!

May 12. — Have just returned, at ten o'clock, from a dinner at the East India Company's. Have had a very pleasant time. Do you recollect what a dreadful thing I used to think it to sit down to table with half a dozen gentlemen? Times have altered since that, and I do not mind thirty or forty, or as many more as you choose! I thought before I went that I should find it uncomfortably warm, but the luxurious punkah was going, and kept us just cool enough. The critical moment is just when the ladies are about to go to dinner. The great point is to get between two pleasant people, but we, poor dependent creatures, have to put up with those who will put up with us. But I will not complain. I am generally very fortunate.

18th. — My twenty-first birthday. It happens to be St. Antonio's, too, and the church on the hill has been illuminated.

May 30. — You see I have lost some time here, but I have been on the couch all the week, having been threatened with a severe attack of fever. But, thanks to good and seasonable advice, I am now pretty much myself again. This little touch of sickness makes me feel what a blessing health is, and I feel much more grateful to Him who has bestowed upon me so long such perfect health, for with good health one has good spirits, and everything is pleasing.

June 22.— After breakfast received some things from Canton, among them a splendid comb, brought by friend Dunn, who has not seen a lady for eight years! He has come down to do his countrywomen the honor of being the first ladies he has called on in China. I was made happy to-day by hearing you were all well on the 16th of January. A letter was sent me to-day, and happened to come while there was a gentleman here. Politeness forbade my opening it, and I was obliged to keep it in my hands till he was gone; and the plague made a monstrous long call, too. I thought he never would go! The letter was from our dear friend Miss Gray, and told me that you had heard of us in November, which pleased me much. I feared you might have been kept anxious much longer, and to hear that you were all well was a great comfort. But the mystery is not yet unfolded how she alone could have heard of this opportunity. This single letter found its way to me by the ship "Timon" to Anjer, forwarded to Singapore, and, I suppose, put into the Company's packet, for it was sent by the Company's steward.

June 26.— A little schooner arrived here a few days since from Manila, called the "Fourth of July."

She is an American from Baltimore, was formerly a pilot boat. She went round Cape Horn, touched at Valparaiso, from thence to Manila, and is now here for a cargo of silks. She carries twenty-five tons. I think one must have some courage to go in her. She is not so large as the Company's cutter.

27th. — Sunday morning, hot, and no air. Just ten minutes past ten. Mr. V. has just sent his watch here for Aunt to set hers by. We were late at church several times, and he said he should preach at us if we did not come earlier. So every Sunday now he very kindly sends us the right time. I should like to have you know him. He is one of the oddest mortals that ever inhabited this globe, I believe.

June 28. — After dinner Mr. V. and Mr. F. called. I got into a scrape with the parson, and do not know how I shall get out of it. I believe I did not know what I was about. It is nothing very horrid, — do not be alarmed; but it is difficult to get along with these gentlemen. I meant to put the blame all on his shoulders, but I feel pretty well convinced that I was the transgressor. It was thoughtlessness on my part. However, I met him at Mrs. T.'s in the evening. He came home with me, and promised to answer a question next time, for we got home a little too soon. He goes out on a cruise this morning, and next time will not be till the end of the week. Oh, I wish you were here, my dear sister, that I could tell you all these interesting hobbles that one is liable to.

Fourth of July. — Our country's birthday. May there be many happy returns of the day to her, and may she always be blessed with wise and judicious rulers! One year ago to-day I was in the good ship "Sumatra," wondering where the next year would find me. Now the anniversary finds me peaceful and happy, surrounded with comforts, but lacking the greatest of all, my own dear friends; and often do I think that all the ease and comforts I enjoy are dearly purchased.

August 1, Sunday. — Went to Dr. Morrison's this morning; communion day there. How sincerely I wished that I could partake with them! but I do not know at present what would be necessary or how to join. But I mean to think more of it, and inquire, for I do most seriously think it the duty of every one, and a privilege, too, it raises such holy feelings. I left the church, feeling melancholy that I could not be a partaker. I returned home, and read one of Buckminster's sermons on the subject, which more fully convinced me that it should not be neglected.

August 2. — After dinner called on Mrs. Clifton, a lady that arrived a few days since. Mr. C. was sitting in lordly style, smoking a splendid hookah, which custom is brought from Calcutta. It was formerly the fashion for every one, ladies and gentlemen, to smoke them after dinner, but it is fast falling away, and now none but the determined smokers use them. It is certainly the most gentlemanly way of smoking, and makes a great display, as the hookahs are made of splendid materials. There is generally one man, or hookahbadar, to take care of the pipe.

August 6. — I wish I could give you the least idea of a Chinese procession that passed here this afternoon. It seems they are dedicating a new church, or Joss house, and it makes a great fuss in town, but, were I to fill page after page, I fear I should fail to give you any idea of it. In the first place its length, and its variety of objects, dresses, music, etc., were beyond everything. The dresses were many of them very splendid, or, rather, made of the most splendid colors and materials you can imagine, but loaded on in a style that cannot please the eye of any person possessed of taste. There were females splendidly attired, on horseback, and sitting astride; little boys rigged up in the most grotesque hats and dresses, carrying the most splendidly wrought banners of the richest colors. Then there were children suspended in air, so that they appeared to be standing on nothing, they were so ingeniously contrived. There was also a little Venus, coming out of her shell, and millions of other things that I am sure I cannot remember. And then the music! Music did I say? O heavens! If such discordant sounds can be called music, it must have been the height of perfection, for never was there such a noise, the horrid gongs beating so that we could not hear a person's voice, though ever so near. Oh, I must not forget the interesting pigs! Poor piggy was murdered, roasted, and lacquered for the occasion, and carried along on cars. There was one lamb, poor little thing, with its wool sheared off, and set up on a car as though it was alive. Then followed a pig all ready for cutting up, another roasted, and another lacquered. You must know at all the marriage processions, funerals, or what not, these poor innocent pigs are sacrificed. They were followed by cars filled with fruit,—presents to Joss, I suppose.

18th.—Calls from Mrs. Blair and Mrs. Montgomery, the new arrivals,—very genteel people. They bring us the latest Calcutta fashions. Such sleeves I never beheld,—complete frights! [These were the big sleeves of 1830, stuffed out with down pillows. See Chinnery's portrait.—*Ed.*]

August 25.—This morning after breakfast I was standing on the terrace, cleaning my birds, when I was handed a package of letters from home. It came so unexpectedly I was quite delighted. I instantly left my birds to the boy, and ran to my great chair to take real comfort in reading them. Yours, my dear sis, is not full enough. I want you to tell me rather longer stories. You just give me a few words, and leave it to my brilliant imagination to picture the rest. Now I think you are mistaken in its capabilities! I felt highly honored to have a letter from Mr. Eames. He is a good man, and I like him fifty per cent. better for it. I shall endeavor to answer it if I do not lose courage before there comes an opportunity. Am delighted to hear you are all well and seemingly happy. I only wish time and space could be annihilated, and I could be with you! Is it wrong, my dear, to indulge such a wish? Yes, I think it is. Cannot we be satisfied with so many blessings? Oh, ungrateful girl that I am! preserved through so many dangers, finding friends wherever my destiny has led me, enjoying the greatest of earthly blessings, the blessing of health, how can I complain! And how do you think we got these letters? They had a most mysterious outside. We could not think what to make of it, but we at last found out by sending to Mr. Sturgis. It seems the "Bashaw" arrived yesterday from England, having spoken the American ship "Galaxy," bound to Manila, in the Straits of Sunda, and took from her our letters; but we have not yet got the papers you mention.

August 30. — A hot northerly wind scorching our cheeks this morning. How different this wind is here in the summer season to what it is with us! Blowing over the land, it of course comes to us scorching, and it is astonishing to see what an instantaneous effect it has. The people here generally shut it out of their houses, it cracks the tables and dries up the furniture immediately; the grass looks as if a fire had passed over it. A few days of this wind would completely destroy the paddy (the growing rice.)

August 31. — The last day of summer! Is it possible? So we move on, my dear sister. We took our Spanish lesson to-day; and I wrote a letter in Spanish, which Mr. O. pronounced *muy buen.*

He was astonished, he said. You would be amused, I think, to take a walk with us and see the China-men. To-day, as we went along, there were eight or ten of them sitting about, some with one knee over another, some in Turkish style, some smoking their pipes, and all with fans in their hands. Indeed, you scarcely ever see a Chinaman or woman without a fan. Even the chair-bearers fan themselves as they carry their burden. They sometimes perch themselves on the highest hills and sit there gossiping. We see them after dark lying about in every direction, they take their mats out and throw them down in the best place they can find, and make a rock their pillow. They are not at all particular about a pillow, indeed, they never use anything softer than a bamboo one. Some of them do arrive at that luxury. It may be truly said here that nature's wants are few. Give a Chinaman plenty of rice and fish, a bamboo mat, and a small piece of cloth for his waist, and he can live; that is, in the summer. In winter they suffer much from the cold, and require a great many clothes, but in Manila, where it is constant summer, they want scarcely anything.

September 2.— A most splendid evening. I sat on the terrace enjoying it till after ten. Thought much of you this evening, and wished I could re-count to you the events of the day. They are not worth writing, but would just do for a little gossip. And now I have arrived at the last page of this val-uable book. I shall commence another instantly, and I will endeavor to make it more worthy of you; but small are my abilities. Would I had improved them more! If this gives you a moment's pleasure, it will answer the purpose of your devoted sister H.

PART II.

OCT. 27, 1830, TO MARCH 3, 1831.

[The journal from Sept. 2, 1830, to March 1, 1831, is missing; but a few letters and fragments of letters, describing the long-talked-of journey to Canton, have been found, and parts of them are inserted here. — *Ed.*]

Oct. 27, 1830. — You will see that we are still in Macao, and, for all that we can see at present, here we are likely to be; for the Chinese are making a great fuss about us poor harmless Fanquis (foreign devils), and say, and persist in saying, that "that lady" (meaning Mrs. Baynes) "must go down," but "that lady" is very obstinate, and will not go. They have threatened to send soldiers to take her away, upon which Mr. B. has had up a hundred armed sailors from the ships, and cannon placed at the gate of the factory. For the last fortnight we have been in a great state of excitement, but it is thought generally that it will blow over, and, though the Chinese will never consent to ladies going to Canton, that they will wink at it, and, as Mouqua told Uncle, "they will shutty eye and shutty ear." I should be very glad to have the English carry the point if it can be done without bloodshed, but time will show. [The attempt was soon made by the American ladies to follow the example of their English sisters, as the next date will show. — *Ed.*]

Canton, November 6. — Here we are in the Celestial city, in a fine house, with every comfort around us, but the Hong merchants are making a row, and it is doubtful whether we remain long. But I will go back to Macao, and begin my adventures from there, giving you the particulars of our passage up, the difficulties and troubles we had to reach the Celestial city, etc. It is a long story, so be patient.

Well, Uncle arrived in Macao on Wednesday, November 3, in the little brig "Terrier," belonging to Mr. Cushing, and which he had kindly offered for our accommodation, and on Friday morning we got into the "Sumatra's" pinnace at six o'clock, and went on board the "Terrier," the Chinamen all refusing to give us the least assistance, except one boat-girl, more courageous than the rest, who lent us a board to step on as we got into the boat, for which she was liberally rewarded with a dollar. There is no doubt the mandarins got half, as the system of "squeezing" is carried on through all ranks. We got under way at seven, the wind cold and piercing, and blowing strong from the north (which was dead ahead), and it was not long before both Aunt and myself began to droop, and were pronounced to be quite "under the weather." It would never do to say we were sea-sick. That would be too vulgar. We went below into a neat little cabin, finished off in fine style, where a nice breakfast had been prepared for us, but eating was quite out of the question, and we were very glad to find ourselves on deck again. We beat up to Lin-

tin, arriving there about two. It was thought best
to send another boat with us, that we might row up
the river, should the wind fail us. We accordingly
took the "Sumatra's" boat in tow, with four of her
men in it. Lintin is a small island with a very
high peak, and a fine anchorage for ships, where all
the outlaws (alias smugglers) lie, with their opium.
I counted about fifteen. The wind continued with
the tide till about four, when we were obliged to
"take in the muslin" and anchor just above Lintin,
as the tides are so strong that it is impossible to
go against one without a strong breeze. There we
lay until ten, — a lovely evening, but rather cold.
When night approached, it was very natural to think
about turning in, but when we asked "were there
cockroaches on board," the answer was fatal to our
hopes of a night's rest. While on deck, I said I
should not mind them, I could sleep anywhere,
and at nine I went very courageously below; but
when I looked into my berth, nicely fitted up with
red silk curtains, a tremendous one appeared at first
view, and, while endeavoring to kill him, half a
dozen more appeared, which quite cooled my courage, and in despair I took my pillow, and, with my
cloak around me, threw my weary limbs upon the
transom, hoping to forget the cruel tormentors. But
fancy was wide awake, and the moment I shut my
eyes she was bringing clouds of them before me.
Aunt L. at last composed herself on the floor, with
mosquito curtains around her, but there was no
room there for two. About ten the tide was again

in our favor, and we made sail, and commenced beating up the river. The continual noise on deck and the constant talking were very disturbing, and, just as wearied nature would begin to forget herself, the vessel would have to tack, and, as I did not much like sleeping head downwards, with the risk of a bump against the other side of the cabin, I must needs tack, too. So you may judge that hard was my lot that night. You may suppose we did not feel much the better for it in the morning. About daylight we again anchored, a few miles below the Boca Tigre, or the Tiger's Mouth, as the Portuguese call it, where we found the "Sylph," a schooner of about thirty tons, ready to take us the rest of the way. On each point of land here there is a Chinese fort, and, while we were waiting for the tide again, we might easily have been sent back from here, had the mandarin suspected our presence. So we both wore velvet caps and cloaks, to prevent their recognizing us as women. At noon we went on board the "Sylph," and passed the Boca in safety, passed a man-of-war, too, but they did not molest us. We were well armed. Had a delightful head wind till we reached Whampoa, too late to see the beautiful scenery and the fleet of ships now there. At eleven the moon rose in splendor, so that we had a fine view of the pagodas as we neared Canton, and the endless variety of boats. I forgot all my fatigue, and we stayed on deck, admiring everything. Everything was still and quiet, thousands and thousands at rest in a small space. It was more Chinese than anything we had seen before. The tea-boats are immense, and ranged along in such order that they form complete streets upon the water. There are also houses built upon boats, and forming streets. I have enjoyed it all very much, and have not yet repented that I came. We anchored about half-past twelve Saturday night, and came ashore without the least difficulty. Indeed, no one would have known that we were not "all samee boy" in our cloaks and caps, as we jumped out of the boat without waiting for arms. I said to Captain R., "Now I will walk directly to the factory"; and I did go straight to the door, I knew it so well by description. The porter opened the door, and for the first time we entered a Hong in the Celestial city of Canton. And now you will perhaps wish to know what a Hong, or factory, is. Perhaps you will fancy looms about; but it is nothing more nor less than a range of houses built one back of the other, and entered by arches, with a passage under the houses to get to each. We have the advantage of being in front, where we can see everything that goes on. The rear houses are like prisons, as there is nothing to be seen from them but the walls of the houses in front. There are four houses in this Hong. Ours was empty, but — [Here the letter ends, the last sheet having been lost.]

November 15.—These despicable Chinese, who are not worth our notice, have the power to disturb us all. They yesterday issued a chop saying that

trade would be stopped "if one Low did not immediately remove his family to Macao." Now it is so
provoking that the Company* ladies, because they
are a body and can bully them, are permitted to stay,
and we, poor creatures, must go. You have no
idea of the knavery of these fellows. As an instance, I will just tell you what old Mouqua told
us a few days since. He said that, when Mrs. B.
came up, he told the Viceroy that her husband was
very sick (which was false), and that she had to
come up and take care of him. When Mrs. T. came,
the Viceroy sent for him again, and he said that she
was Mr. B.'s cousin, "and he so sick he wanchy too
much to see her." Now, he says, that we have
come, "I no can talky sick any more. Now I know
not what talky."

We do not feel convinced that this chop is from
the Viceroy, but suspect it is a forgery of the Hong
merchants, and we shall have to go back to Macao,
while the English ladies stay here and enjoy themselves. Mr. L. says it will be attended with great
éclat if the trade of an empire is stopped on our account; but the upshot of the matter is, if the trade
is stopped, we shall have to budge.

November 17. — We are still here, and all they
wish us to do now is to say when we will go. They
say if we tell them three or four weeks hence, and
then are not ready, "putty off a little, that have
mandarin fashion,"— good-for-nothing creatures that
they are!

* East India Company.

November 27.—About dark it grew rather cool, and a fire was proposed; and you have no idea how cosey we looked, with our carpets down and a blazing coal fire. Our circle round the "wee bit ingle" was composed of Aunt, Uncle, Messrs. R., H., L., and B., and my own dear self. After a social cup of tea, Mr. Russell left us for the office, and shortly came back with budgets of news. The "Ann Amelia" had arrived from England, bringing Mr. Marjoribanks and others, to supersede Mr. B. and his assistants. So they are turned out, and lose their sixty thousand dollars for this year. It seems the directors at home disapproved *in toto* of the measures of last year, and this is the consequence. It is thought very severe here, as all did what they thought for the best. I feel very sorry for Mrs. B., as she will feel it a great mortification. I hear she is to leave Canton in a few days, and will probably go to England by the first ship. After the first surprise was over, a walk was proposed, as it was a delightful moonshiny night. We walked in front of the factories without exciting much observation. We then went up Old China Street, through Bouquiqua Street, and down New China Street. We were discovered to be Fanquis there; and lights were called for, that the Chinamen might look at us. They kindled up fires in an instant to behold our fair faces, and we had quite a rabble round us before we reached the front of the factories again, though they were all perfectly civil, and made no noise, but only showed a little curiosity,

of which they have a share in common with their
fellow-creatures of more enlightened parts. But,
when we reached the open square, the "gallant tars"
that were promenading there espoused our cause,
and scattered the mob in quick time. After they
had dispersed, we sallied forth again, and went to
Mr. L.'s house. You have no idea how elegantly
these bachelors live here. I don't wonder they
like it.

It is now decided that we are to leave Canton on
Tuesday or Wednesday next. They grant us a chop-
boat to go down in, and in my next letter I shall be
able to give you a description of a chop-boat, and
of the inner passage to Macao, which is said to be
very pleasant. We should have been very happy
here for three months if they would have let us stay,
but they will not. All the Chinese outside say that
Chow Tuck (or Governor Le) has "lost face" very
much by letting the English ladies remain and
sending the Americans down; but there is no reason
in it, and I hope they will get paid for it one of
these days. They say that a message has gone to
the Emperor, and he will settle the business, but
there is an insurrection in the upper provinces, and
I doubt whether his Majesty ever hears of it.

Macao, Jan. 8, 1831.— We have had the last
week an immense quantity of news, such as the
death of King George IV. (June 25, 1830), and, *via*
Mexico, news of the abdication of Charles X., his
flight to England, and the revolution in France;
also, most wonderful of all, Lafayette's being at the

head of the National Guards again, after such a lapse of time. We hear that this revolution was a bloodless one, but the news came in such a round-about way that we feel very anxious to get direct particulars. It is thought that Spain and Portugal will follow the example of France, and throw off the yoke, too. I believe I have written you since the revolution here, — I mean in the affairs of the Company. You may remember what a gay season we had last year, and the cause, a little difficulty with the Chinese, which obliged the Company to keep a great many ships here, and cost them a pretty penny. Upon hearing this, the directors were quite enraged with the chief (Mr. B.) and his staff, and immediately ordered him and others to be superseded by Mr. Majoribanks, a shrewd Scotchman. All this made a great alteration in the politics of this place. Mrs. B. is a heroine, and bears it all beautifully. She is a charming woman, and a pattern for all wives. Mr. B. is a nervous, sickly man, and, I believe, a great sufferer.

The weather here is delightful, and since we returned from Canton we have enjoyed it highly, for, I assure you, we got completely tired of company while there. By the bye, I daresay you know the terms that the Americans in Canton have been on with the English for the last two years. I am happy to say that under the new administration all differences are settled, and on Christmas Day they had a general meeting at the Company's, and a most delightful time, — a splendid dinner, a great deal of speechifying and good-fellowship. The new chief is very popular, and I hope all will be pleasant in future.

Now for "the woman pigeon." The Chinese succeeded in getting us away, as they attacked us on a vulnerable point. Had they stopped the American trade in general, they would have had all the gallant youths fighting for us at the city gates, but they only stopped that of our house. I hear the last report was that the Emperor's answer had been received, forbidding *any* lady to visit Canton henceforth. Whether this is true or not we have our doubts. At any rate, the Viceroy has not seen fit to issue the mighty chop publicly, but will, it is thought, when the Company leave. The Chinese are very cunning, and know very well what they are about. Uncle has not been down since the first of December, when he came with us; and we do not expect to see him till February or March.

January 25.— I long to know what you think of our trip to Canton. I daresay you will think we were wrong to attempt it, thereby breaking the laws of even the Chinese; but I assure you there is no comparison to be drawn between the Chinese and any other nation in the world. They will not allow any innovation upon "old custom," and will ding those words into your ears forever if it is not for their interest to violate it, when it is quite a different thing. Another thing they acknowledge is that they "cannot talky reason," and must be "bullied." Every one advised Uncle to make the experiment of taking us up, and they were very shrewd, and knew just the tender point to touch, — the stopping of the trade of the one house. So we were obliged to give in. Not that I wished to stay in Canton any longer. Three weeks answered my purpose very well, but I could not bear to let the Chinese know they could do anything with the Americans. For my own part, I was not well while there, and I am sure Aunt L. was not. It is very delightful to have our friends round us, and I would put up with many inconveniences to be with Uncle and a few others who live in Canton, but to be constantly subject, morning, noon, and night, to visits from people we care nothing about, but are obliged to treat civilly, I assure you, fond as I am of society and company, it was too much for me. On our return to Macao it seemed more enchanting than ever. The lovely weather and the quiet were really delightful; and since my return I have employed my time much to my own satisfaction, which is very comforting.

Poor Mr. B., being a feeble man, has taken his troubles and disappointments quite to heart, and last night was at the point of death. Mr. Dunn took passage in the "Canning" for England, after having been feasted, toasted, and cheered to his heart's content. He has the good wishes and good will of all who have ever known him in Canton. He is very fond of good living, and will have everything of the nicest kind, and is as particular in laying a cloth under the table to make it match with the stripes of the carpet as ever Mrs. Ropes was.

March 3. — We have received orders from the Governor of Macao to leave this place. He says he has received them from the Court of Lisbon. Now this is so counter to the treaty of the nations that the reasons for doing it are not understood. He says he shall not resort to force to drive us away, but, I assure you, it is not very pleasant to be threatened from one place to another. We were sent to Macao by the Viceroy of Canton, and, if the Governor here tells us to walk, we shall just have to apply to said Viceroy for permission to remain. People say the government of Macao is only nominally Portuguese, and I do not think there is much danger of our being sent home. Soon after we arrived, Uncle called on his Excellency, as is customary, and told him what house he had taken, and the Governor told him he must apply to the Court of Lisbon or Goa* for permission to stay here. He wrote to Lisbon; but it will probably be three years before he gets an answer, when I suspect we shall be ready to go home. So much for orders, which do not trouble us much.

In the last few days I have seen considerable of a Mr. W., who came out in the "Fanny" from Philadelphia, a very "clever" and pleasant young man. He leaves this afternoon, however, for Canton. He has a long tongue of his own, yea, verily! Philadelphia turns out some great talkers!

* Portuguese headquarters in India. — *Ed.*

BOOK III.

WELL, my dear sister, I am beginning another book. I wish I could be sure that you read them with interest. My last I sent off, I think, on the 25th of February,* to go by my friend Mr. Russell. Since I sent the last, I believe nothing particular has happened, except that I have been introduced to another American gentleman, who came out in the "Fanny" from Philadelphia, a very clever and pleasing young man. [Spoken of in the last Canton letter.— *Ed.*] He was introduced by Mr. B. on Sunday morning, being too diffident, he says, to come alone. He managed, however, after the first time, to come again to walk with us, and to stay to tea. He is an immense talker, but always talks well,— wise, witty, or grave, as suits his hearers. He is not handsome, but has a most intellectual face. He draws very well, and immediately took me under his protection, and became my teacher.

March 1.— After dinner we went to walk. Got into a bit of a scrape ; something about walking with Mr. W., not worth telling, however. Mr. W. spent the evening with us,—a clever youth.

March 2.— This morning a party of nine, including Mr. V., Mr. W., and myself, set off for the Lappa.

* This was the lost volume, before mentioned.— *Ed.*

We had a very delightful sail and a walk on the other island. We visited the Joss house, which is situated in the most picturesque manner on the declivity of a high hill, among a great deal of shrubbery and some fine trees. The river runs before it at a little distance, and at one side, quite near, is a fine fall of water. The people were excessively civil, and gave us tea and all the oranges they had. They brought out some cakes, and something else, a sort of nondescript, Mr. Davis called it "pig-pye not sufficiently disguised." The junks of fat pork were much too apparent. We sat on the steps of the Joss house and partook of our frugal meal, and, having rested our weary limbs a little, we began our journey home by a different route. All were highly pleased with the excursion, and even Mr. Davis, who before he set out, thought it "the complete assassination of a day," acknowledged that he felt repaid. He is a great student, and feels every moment lost that is not spent with his books, I believe. He is what the English call an exceedingly clever man, and can make himself very agreeable. He and his wife wished me to dine with them, but I was too much fatigued, and went home. Took my books, and studied a little French. Mr. V. came in to bring my handkerchief, and stayed till seven.

March 3.— Mr. W. called to take leave. He goes to Canton this afternoon.

8th.— This morning I have been reading the papers father sent. I should like, when you do send papers, to have something besides advertisements. I do not think much of your *Long Island Star.* A few words from my dear father on the margin of one of them was worth all the rest.

10th.— Mrs. Davis came in after dinner to say that Mr. V. went out in the cutter yesterday morning, expecting to be back in an hour and a half, but he has not been heard of since. They have despatched several boats, for the wind has been blowing quite a gale. Went to walk in the afternoon with the Davises, and found a new place. Went through a village where we were assaulted or barked at by a thousand dogs, which, with children squalling, made quite a bedlam. Were very glad, on our return, to hear that V. had got back, having been in a most perilous situation. They came as near as possible to being lost.

March 19.— Mr. V. spent the evening with us. I wonder what you would think of Mr. V. as a parson. He is one of the drollest creatures I ever met, and keeps us laughing all the time. He is a good man in his way, but has little of the gravity of a clergyman.

20th, Sunday.— I am now going to prepare for church. I must write a letter to-day to Mr. W. Goody, what a job! He wrote me a very amusing one the other day, when he sent me some drawing materials. Now I must do my prettiest. I suppose I shall have to begin " My dear Mr. W.", as he took the liberty to say " My dear Miss L."; but that is so common here that it means no more than " my dear sir," when a challenge is sent. As it rained after dinner, I did not go to walk, but read one or two sermons, and then H. K. White's "Remains," which never fails to make me melancholy. I got quite dull before tea-time. Went to bed feeling that I should have no spirits to go out to breakfast to-morrow morning, but there is no knowing what an hour may bring forth. I am happy to say a night's sleep often softens the asperities of one's feelings, and calms one's troubled thoughts.

March 21.—Awoke this morning with a weight on my spirits, why I know not, but, however, was persuaded to go to the race-breakfast with Uncle and Aunt. Had a very pleasant time. Went to the race-course in a boat; a very delightful morning, no sun, and just cool enough. Races very good. Came home and went to drawing, am quite mad now for this delightful amusement. Dressed, and went at seven to the Company's dinner. V. handed me to table, I sat between him and Mr. L. If I could have chosen, they would have been the ones. Came home about ten, but I won't tell you, my dear, how out of humor I was or the cause of it, till I see you face to face. Then I will tell you all my little annoyances and troubles. I went to bed almost resolved never to go anywhere again while I was in Macao, but I suppose this resolution is made to be broken, and in the course of a week I shall be quite reconciled. But once in a while I do retire in disgust from everybody, and think that the rest of my exile shall be spent in poring over books; but I do like society, and soon I am again drawn into it.

March 24. — My dear sister, I would give sixpence to see you. I am not yet myself. I have got dreadfully out of humor. I have not now the happy disposition you say I have. My books of late have not had the interest they once had, but I hope to find myself again in a few days. Adieu.

I left off here in a very gloomy state, and deliberated which I had better do, — read over my old letters (my constant resource) or take a dose of salts! Having finally concluded that indisposition was the cause of my gloom, I dissolved the salts, and was just standing before the glass in my own room, thinking how interesting I looked with the glass half up to my mouth, making faces and shuddering involuntarily, when Aunt L. came in, bringing me three home letters. (I assure you the salts were instantly put on the table for future consideration.) I read them again and again. They were old, but just as interesting. They might have been up here two months ago, but were sent by a slow-sailing ship. Never mind, they came just at the right time, and I felt six per cent. better after them. Went to walk with Mrs. A. after dinner. Met Mr. V., and had a most delightful walk. The evening was quite perfect, and we went up the steps of the cathedral, and listened for some time to the rich tones of the organ. Oh, I do so delight in hearing it! It carries me instantly back to our church in Salem. Now at this very instant they are probably seated at the pine table in the western side of the orchestra [query, *choir? — Ed.*] singing away, as Eliza writes me they meet every Friday evening to practise.

March 28.— A warm day ; find a white dress very comfortable. Summer is coming upon us. Pulled out old dresses to-day, and find the great sleeves worn last summer will have to be cut out. Oh, dear, what a job ! What slaves to fashion we are !

April 3, *Sunday.*— Went to church this morning, Easter Sunday. Mr. V. gave us an excellent sermon, the sacrament was administered, and I felt a great desire to stay. I did not, but I sincerely hope before another time I shall have made up my mind to fulfill our Lord's last request, and to join in celebrating that rite which was instituted to remind us of our duty, and to draw us nearer to heaven and the presence of Him who sacrificed everything for us. Yes, my dear sister, I hope it will be a new era in my life, and that by performing this one duty I may be led on step by step till I arrive at the perfect knowledge. Mr. V. came in after dinner, and I had a long talk with him in the veranda. He says he will lend me some books to read, which he thinks will quite satisfy me on the subject.

6th.— Reading the Life of the Duke de Berry. I am quite in love with his character. What an unfortunate family they have been ! After dinner went to walk with the Davises, and young Daniell joined us, and, just before we reached home, old Daniell. You cannot imagine a greater contrast than these two brothers. One all fun and life, the other so languishing, so romantic, that the sound of anything gross or commonplace shocks him. It is really as good as a play to see him and Mr. Davis, who is very blunt,

and sometimes not so nice in his observations. Poor
Matt looks horror-struck, and, I suppose, wonders that
the ladies do not crush him with a look instead of
doing nothing but laugh to see the effect it has on
him.

April 10, *Sunday.*—This morning V. sent me
several books, giving some explanations of the Trinity,
and a kind letter with some observations on the subject, pointing out some passages which he thought
would convince me of the truth of the doctrine of
the Trinity and the Divinity of Jesus Christ, all of
which I shall peruse with attention, and pray to God
to enlighten my understanding. . . . I read the "Companion to the Altar," and feel convinced that I could
conscientiously partake of the Holy Communion,
although I cannot bring myself yet to believe in the
Trinity. How much I wish I could converse a little
with my dear father! Arguments strong on both
sides quite puzzle me; but can it be so important to
our salvation? Would our heavenly Father have
left anything in such hidden mystery, had it been so
very necessary to us? Would He not have explained
it to us, if of such vast importance?

After dinner went to walk with Mrs. A., and met
"old Daniell," who said he had come up to see what
that red thing on the hill was. (My bonnet!)
Coming home, he wanted to know what church I had
attended at home or to what sect I belonged. I
told him I had been in the habit of attending a Unitarian church. He would hardly believe it. Said,
"You are *not* a Unitarian, or how can you go to our

church?" He seemed to have a great horror of Unitarians. He said they were as different as possible from the Church of England, and, indeed, the only sect that did not come within the pale of their Church. He said they did not believe in the Divinity of Christ, nor of any of his institutions, the sanctity of marriage, of baptism, or anything. I told him they were an altogether different sect in America then; that I had been baptized, that they did believe in the sanctity of marriage, and that the sacrament was administered every month. He was quite astonished. Says the Unitarians are not called Christians in England. In short, they are there, I should think, what we call Deists, which are as different as possible from Unitarians. I endeavored to explain the difference, as well as I could, but could not recall the proper term for their Unitarians at the time. How I wished, at that moment, for all Mr. Upham's knowledge on the subject!

April 13.— I forgot to tell you that after reading Lord Byron last night, and then taking the expenses of the day, I filled up the paper with poetry, which has just afforded Aunt L. a good laugh. She says she shall send it to Canton. Perhaps it will adorn a column in the Canton *Register*. She told Mrs. D., who has given me the name of Byrona. Mr. V. came in and brought me a beautiful rose, which about ten o'clock inspired some more poetry, I think of a higher order. Have some hopes of myself. Think in the course of time I may be a POETESS!

23*d*.— After dinner V. came in, and how you will

laugh when I tell you what he brought me from Canton. You might guess till you were tired, and would fail, I think. It is an article which is thought very important when accompanied by something else, and which often makes a great change in a person's life; but, without the article that should accompany such a gift, I do not think it very important. It is, however, very pretty, and will serve as a remembrance and cause many a smile. I would not have it known here for anything. Guess if you can. I will leave you in the dark for the present. Mrs. A. came in, and saw this article lying on the couch. She said, "I think this should never be seen in the drawing-room, nor should it be in the possession of a young lady."

April 28 *to May* 15.— [Journal "sadly neglected" on account of much letter-writing. French, Spanish, and drawing, with a little sewing and many calls made and received, served to fill up the time, with constant visits from "V." On May 4 she writes : "I had a severe attack of the blues, and had just seated myself on the veranda to relieve myself with a few of those drops 'that from the eye relieve the heart,' when V. came in, and his cheerful company soon dissipated them." Again, on the 10th "V. spent the evening with us. We sat on the veranda and had a pleasant chat. He is my best, and, indeed, my only friend among the English." May 16 the journal begins to be a little fuller again.— *Ed.*]

May 16.— The Chinese are commencing their impositions again, tearing the Company's walls down, destroying their shrubberies, etc. The Foqua, now the next in authority, has been larking round in Canton, went into the Company's room, ordered the king's picture to be uncovered, and said he would sit in his presence,— one of the greatest indignities, according to Chinese ideas, that could be offered. They seemed to be carrying things with a high hand. Some of the committee have gone up to see what can be done.

May 18.— Again my birthday. Felt rather melancholy when I awoke this morning, for in my dreams I was in America. F. and A. in this morning; say the Company are excessively anxious for the renewal of their charter, and they think there is now no prospect of it, as every member now in the House of Lords has pledged himself not to renew it.

May 20.— After dinner a ship arrived from Calcutta, bringing four ladies,— two spinsters, I hear. Quite a happy event for the gentlemen, for I believe they are tired of the ladies here; and we were proposing the other day that we should change ourselves in some way for their benefit. But these new damsels will delight them for a while. Poor things! I pity them!

May 25.— Went to call on the new arrivals, — Mrs. Malden, a widow, and two Miss Williams, one considerably advanced, may be decidedly called an old maid, and ugly enough, the other about twenty. They are half-caste, and quite dark. I hear the young one is to be married to Mr. Mendez, whom we should call black; but he is a pure-blooded

Portuguese, and, if ever so black, is considered above a half-caste. Mr. D. joined us on our return, and told us of the absurd edicts the Chinese have issued, which it is quite impossible can ever be carried into effect, such as saying that no foreigners are to go into their factories, and, indeed, are not permitted to go out, nor are they permitted to have Chinese servants, except one coolie at the gate, to see that no improper person goes in. They may have two coolies to work and one to bring water, but they must not be the companions of foreigners, who are crafty and deceitful, and not to be trusted, with many other like absurdities.

29th.— For the first time approached the altar, and partook of the holy sacrament. May it be the commencement of a new life in me!

June 7.— Mr. W. made us a flying call after dinner. Came down from Canton this morning. Did a week's talking in ten minutes.

June 8.— If I could tell you all the funny things I have heard this evening, I think you would laugh. The ends of my mouth have several times been unusually familiar with my ears, for you must know the very sensible and facetious Mr. W. dropped into tea with us, and he did his prettiest to be entertaining, and succeeded. [Between "V." and "W." things began to be rather complicated, one being sure to turn up if the other were absent; and on July 6 is this rather significant entry.— *Ed.*] :—

July 6.— After dinner walked out with Uncle. We were joined by Talbot and V. The latter offered his arm first, and I had to take it. I shall have to cut him yet. Uncle shakes his head, and says it will not do.

July 10.— After church Mrs. Davis came to tell us that a nun was to take the black veil that afternoon. So at four I set out with her for the chapel of Santa Clara, a neat chapel belonging to the convent. The entrance is rather magnificent. After reading "Matilde," one is apt to fancy all ceremonies will be like that one (described in "Matilde"). I had prepared myself for something very imposing, but was exceedingly disappointed. Indeed, I might have known that it would be so, for some of their most solemn and imposing ceremonies are performed with the least degree of real solemnity. We had a good stand near the altar, and could see the whole. At the appointed hour the lady walked into the church, accompanied by the padres and the boys with lighted candles. She knelt before the altar; and an old padre (a wicked-looking creature) chanted something in Latin, and was answered by the other padres. The lady then mounted another step; and he chanted again, and sprinkled her with holy water or incense, then gave her an immense candlestick decked with all kinds of tinsel. She took it and walked out of the church, and was then lost to the world. The band played a dancing tune as she entered the church, to remind her, I suppose, that she must leave the folly of the world behind her now. From the chapel she went into the nunnery. At the end of the chapel is a grating, and there was a great rush there to see the end of the ceremony. But never (I hope) shall my curiosity lead me into such a scrape again,— to see a Portuguese nun, at any rate. There was I in a crowd of these nasty people, black, white, and gray, and could not move an inch. Fortunately, Mr. V. protected me as well as he could.

But, after all this squeeze, you will wish to know if I felt paid for it. I am hardly satisfied that the account was balanced, but I will tell you what I saw, and you shall judge. We at first saw the nun behind the grating, dressed as in the chapel, in her splendid dress of white lace trimmed with pink satin over a white satin under-dress, diamond necklace, head-dress of diamonds, fingers covered with diamond rings, and a white veil thrown over her head. She casts all these aside, renounces the world and all its vanities, has her hair cut off, and comes again to the grating. The padre chants again, and the organ plays, with much singing, which being all in Latin no one could understand. She then embraces and salutes all her sister nuns, ugly old creatures, who are behind the grating, covered with their long black veils. She then puts on the dress of the nunnery, which is of something dark blue, with a rope round the waist, covers herself with a thick black veil, face and all, and is seen no more. To make all this very interesting and touching, you will fancy her young, beautiful, and engaging; but, lest it should make too deep an impression on you, I will just undeceive you on that point, and tell you she was excessively ugly, and, it is said, not under thirty-two years of age. I suppose she despaired of ever getting a husband to please her mind. She gives $1,500 to get in there, and conceals her charms from the world forever. The gentlemen made no attempt to rescue her. The nuns are there as novices for a year and a day before they take the black veil, and during that time they can return to the world if they please ; but, if at the end of the time they conclude to remain, the bells send forth a merry peal, and there is great rejoicing. I assure you I was most happy when the ceremony was over, and delighted to find myself in the fresh air.

July 14.— A very hot day. Thermometer 89 degrees at four o'clock. After dinner Talbot came in, and we went to walk. He is an excellent young man. You would be amused to hear him and King rejoicing at the chance they shall have when they go home, having seen a census for 1830 for Massachusetts, giving fourteen thousand more females than males! They think they will have their pick. It's rather desperate, I think.

July 19.— Mr. S. called this morning, introduced by Mr. Bull ; quite an interesting youth and a good muster * of an American. He is one of the Boston aristocrats, and perhaps would not speak to us at home. However, they are very gracious here, and very polite. He and Mr. B. dined with us.

22*d*.— Our party for the water proposed for to-day. V. came for us about half-past five, and we went down to his house, and waited till about six, and

---

* Specimen or pattern.— *Ed.*

then went off. We had a most delightful party of about a dozen. The night could not have been more perfect,— still water, and just wind enough to move us steadily through it. Had a band of music, and everything good to eat and drink. We anchored for tea, and with a delightful breeze reached Macao about 1 A.M.,— rather late hours, but several of the party wished then that we were six miles out. The town felt like a furnace when we came on shore, after enjoying the pure sea breeze. By the bye, we came on shore in a sampan rowed by two Chinese girls. As Wood says in his " Sketches of China," "These boats are *manned* by a brace of Chinese *ladies*."

August 4.— A budget of letters arrived for me about two. I have seen accounts of the great "revivals" in the papers. I cannot say, my dear sister, that they give me as much pleasure as they do some people. I think it is generally too great an excitement, that it is apt to vanish like the dew. There are many, in my opinion, who, after having felt the power of the Spirit as they term it, and made a profession of their faith, are too apt to think the work done. But I pray that it may leave lasting effects on the minds of all. Our little Willy seems now quite impressed. I hope it will last ; and, if he so early tastes the goodness of God, he will be a happy as well as a good man.

8th.— The guns have been firing all day, the bells ringing, and the flags flying at half-mast, mourning for the old Queen (of Portugal) who died two years ago. They never move here until they receive official notice.

10*th*. — This evening finished "The Water Witch," the last forty pages the only part worth reading. Went to a dinner party at the Company's, a very pleasant party, but I cannot say I enjoyed it much, as I was obliged to carry into effect some new and good resolutions, — which was very hard, and cost me a pang then, and almost a sleepless night. Poor V.! I've had to cut him, — not from any inclination of my own, but to satisfy the people. They will talk so. How I should like to be within speaking distance of you, my sis, that I might tell you all my little troubles!

August 13. — A pleasant morning, for a great rarity. The direct ships are arriving almost every day now, and bringing the faces we saw on our arrival. Went to Casilha's Bay, and admired the view. Sturgis and Sullivan, two wild Bostonians, joined us. It was as much as my dignity could do to keep them in order. They appeared to be trying to see which could make the prettiest speeches. I laughed at them, just to let them know that I did not swallow it all, otherwise think I should have let it pass by in silent contempt. I have got to be such a matter-of-fact personage that this stuff annoys me. However, they were only in fun; but I did not happen to be in a funny humor. Mr. Alexander showed me his sister's miniature to-night. How much I wished I could show him yours! He, poor fellow, idolizes this sister, and, like myself, was never separated from her before. I always encourage these young chaps in talking of home or their sisters, for they are too apt, unless their affections are deeply rooted there, to become indifferent. It shows a good disposition in them when they speak affectionately of their brothers and sisters.

August 15.— Had a letter from Uncle this morning, who says that Mr. Shillaber is in Batavia, and his sister Caroline with him. Only think! one of my schoolmates. I got up from the breakfast table and despatched a letter to her instantly *via* Singapore. It seems good to hear that there is one of my young acquaintances so near. I shall now indulge a hope of going to Batavia. How much I should like travelling in Java! Rather an unpleasant situation there for a young lady, I should think.

17th.— Had another letter from Mr. S. to-day, urging Aunt L. to spend one monsoon in Java. She means to send for Caroline to come here. How happy I should be to have her! and I hope we shall one of these days.

About six Mr. V. came in, and I said all I had to say to him, and now I hope I shall be plagued no more. He stayed about an hour,—as long as he dared, he said.

September 4th.— Sunday morning again, and what has become of the last week? It makes me tremble when I ask myself how much better am I than the week before. What knowledge have I gained, or how have I improved the time? A frightful answer for the past week, I am sure, for I must confess, without hesitation, that it has all been wasted. I have read scarce any. I have been vexed and annoyed with trifles and events that I could not control, and perhaps have been led to judge wrongly of those who appear friendly, and perhaps have made some harsh observations. Oh, dear suds! how prone we are to be led away by the feelings of the moment, when, if reason were called to our aid, we should save ourselves many a pang! I often ask myself why I was born, and for what purpose was I sent into the world. I am tired of doing nothing. Would that I could be placed in some scene of action where I could do good to some one! But there, prosing enough for this morning, I'm thinking.

(*Monday.*— I seem to have been in a sad state yesterday morning, but I feel better now.)

September 17.— Took tea with Mrs. Grant. Mr. H. came in about nine, and sang his farewell song, bade us good-night, and left for Canton. A very quiet party, nevertheless several mighty things occurred, which will only be written upon the tablets of the memory. Every day I exclaim, What a funny world this is, and what funny people there are in it! You may laugh at the idea of seeing anything of the world in Macao, but, I assure you, we see an infinite variety of characters.

September 18.— This morning was spent in self-examination, to see if by any means I could think myself worthy to approach the altar, and in remembrance of our Saviour commune with his Christian disciples. Oh, my dear sister, would that I could meet with you and those that are dear to me, with those that I trust are far worthier disciples than any that we find in this distant and irreligious world! How I long to hear from you all, to know what progress you make in a religious life, to know if the effects of that great revival are lasting or whether it was a momentary excitement! I rather dread these general excitements, my dear, but I pray that their effect may remain.

20th.— I shall have a summons to breakfast in a minute and a half. The coolies and Nancy are dancing about our rooms now, clearing up. I daresay it would seem very odd to you to see two men coming to clear up and sweep your room, and such sweeping! "A lick and a promise." They cannot imagine the use of doing the same thing every day. They say: "Suppose make clean to-day, all same dirty to-morrow. What for so fashion clean?" They think it a great waste of labor. However, they are pretty well drilled now, and know what they must do. It has become a habit.

September 23.— A typhoon threatens this morning. The wind is blowing a gale. Oh, dear suds! what a stormy day! The wind increased till about two, when the tide coming in made the sea quite tremendous. We could see it from our windows washing over the tops of the houses on the quay. It has completely destroyed the Praya Grande, rooted up ten-foot pieces of granite, and thrown them into the halls of the houses. A little boat was anchored out in front of us. At last, they cut their cables, thinking it was their only chance, and let her drive. It was a dreadful sight. It seemed impossible that she could live in such a sea. We watched her till it seemed as though with the next wave she must dash on to the Point. I have since heard that with the assistance of Captain W. the men were all saved. The boat was completely dashed to pieces.

September 24.— Nothing but a scene of destruction this morning. Our veranda is quite unroofed, our mats all gone. Where is the quay? Gone, completely demolished! Houses without roofs, a large piece taken quite out of the Company's, from the roof to the ground, and immense masses of granite thrown up. Several Chinese houses at the end of the quay quite levelled, the Peña church much damaged. On the other side, on the point near the Franciscan church, lies a large fishing-boat, a complete wreck. Out in the roads is the hull of a large ship that only a few days since I saw come in with her towering masts filled with canvas. Now they are levelled to the hull, not a stick left standing. This is what meets our eye; but, alas! I fear that it is not all. I hear that during the gale masts of ships with numbers of men clinging to them were floating about, the men calling for assistance, but the ships could give them none. I am afraid we shall hear of much more damage.

September 30.— A dreadfully rainy day. The rain ceased about dark, but the wind began to blow, and we feared another typhoon. The Chinese call it "the Typhoon's wife." However, we went to Mr. L.'s this evening, and danced till after twelve. I cannot say I felt happy, for I received a note just before

I left that made me quite miserable; but I danced every dance, notwithstanding.

October 1.— Replied this morning to my note of last evening, which cost me a sigh and many tears. Not but I think it right to do as I did, but I cannot bear to be unkind, and I fear it will be thought so. But it cannot be helped,— there must be an end. After dinner I went to see Mrs. A., then to Mrs. T.'s. There I met Mr. V., the one my note was sent to. He was civil, but I could see a change in his manners. Poor soul, I am sorry for him!

3*d*.— Seven gentlemen, including Mr. V., called this morning to say adieu. (The Factory leave to-night for Canton.) Poor V. was barely civil to me. Oh, dear, if one could only explain one's feelings and motives! At five Uncle left us for Canton. I went to see Mrs. A., having heard she was not well, and, when I came home, found a note in answer to mine of Saturday. It occupied three pages of fine writing, describing me as the most unkind creature in the world. I wrote a short note in return, asking for a few moments' conversation with him, but it only reached him just as he was sitting down to dinner at G.'s at seven o'clock, and they all left for Canton directly after dinner. But not till he had written a kind note, dated ten o'clock. I referred him to Uncle, if he could not see me. He trusts we shall meet under more auspicious circumstances. I think we both feel happier.

October 6.— This morning I was sitting in my own room when Assow (one of the Chinese servants) came to me. He said: "Miss *Haya*, Company's butler wanchy see you. I have talky he master have go Canton; but he say no wanchy see master, wanchy see that lady called Miss L." I went into the drawing-room, and told Assow to ask him up. To my astonishment, he came and handed me a letter which Mr. V. had requested him to deliver in person. (Not very important.)

October 13.— Read "Paul and Virginia" in French to-day, and worked on my rose-colored gingham dress. Resolved that I would endeavor not to grumble any more. We have got into a dreadful habit, or I have, of complaining. It is the fashion here, but I have resolved to-night to be out of fashion, for it is wicked when we have so many blessings to repine because we have not more. Ungrateful creatures!

15*th.*— Had a long and important letter from Uncle, deciding a case. Spent the evening at Mrs. T.'s. My reflections before I went to bed were not pleasant. I am sorry to say that I find out every day how deceitful people may be in this world. I hardly know, my dear sis, whether all the experience I have had this last year will be for my good or not. It has been bought with much pain, and I must say my opinion of human nature has been much lowered by it. It requires much patience and submission to get along in this place. You would be startled if I could relate to you many of the scenes I have witnessed. Do not think this has anything to do with Mrs. T. She is a woman of the strictest principles and excellent feelings. If I am not deceived in her t , I think she will be the friend, after all.

24th.— Had a letter from Uncle to-day, saying that Mr. Shillaber and his sister had left Java for Manila and Canton. She, poor girl, was quite ill. I long to have her come here. I should be so happy to do all I could to make her comfortable. A ship is a dreadful place when one is ill.

October 27.— Went to Captain W.'s this evening. Mrs. T. had the kindness to dress my hair for me. Wore white lace over white satin. I danced seven quadrilles, and got home at one, quite tired out. Was introduced to several gentlemen from the sloop of war. One youth looked so astonished when I told him I was from America. He seemed to wonder I was not a savage, or at least I thought so. I was quite amused with this person.

29th.— Mr. Millet came in after church, and entertained us with the history of his travels in Java and the wonderful parts of the island that he visited. Speaking of the fruits, the mangosteen is thought the most delicious fruit in the world, he says, and he limited himself to a hundred a day, which he could eat without the least harm or feeling at all cloyed. I wish I could impart to you all he told us,—of the fountains of mud thrown up into the air, of the splendor of a volcano, and the wonderful plain of fire. He says that this spot of ground about ten feet by five will immediately burn a piece of paper or anything else that comes near it. You can see a sort of gas coming out of the ground and rising to the height of five or six inches. In the night it looks quite brilliant. It is held sacred by the natives. He says

Java is the most perfect country to travel in. At the place where he stayed for two months the temperature only varied from 75 degrees to 80 degrees, which is quite perfect. How I should like to travel there!

November 3.— A rainy day. Mr. Bradford spent an hour with me, and we talked politics. He brought me his sister's letter, giving the scandal of Washington, the real cause of the dissolution of the cabinet. It seems there was a lady at the bottom of it.

17th.— Mr. V. in this morning. I had a long *tête-à-tête* with him. He spoke in the highest terms of Uncle. Rode on horseback after dinner. V. joined our party. I was sorry, because it will make a fuss in Canton.

December 12.— My dear sister, my book is now drawing to a close, and it has been sadly neglected. Caroline Shillaber arrived on the 7th, and I received a large package from home by the " Franklin " at the same time, the only two things worthy of note that have happened since the last date, I believe. I send you this book, my dear sister, hoping it may interest you ; but I hardly dare flatter myself that it will. I have no more books like those I have sent, shall have to take to Chinese paper, I suspect. I have nothing new to tell you, except that I ride horseback every day, and like it much.

(From a letter.) Caroline and I get along finely together. Her health is very good, and she is a sensible and well-informed girl, really an uncommon girl. She is only about nineteen, and has the quickest perception and the best judgment of any girl I ever saw. She has a quick temper, but good sense enough to control it, and a pair of piercing black eyes which keep the gentlemen at a goodly distance, though those who know her generally like her much, at least any she takes a fancy to, which is not every one.

December 15.—This must be my last date, and I must close my book and send it off. I find it very pleasant having a companion, I can assure you; but I cannot make a walker of her. She has been so used to a carriage of late that walking fatigues her, and I must confess it requires a year's practice to run over these rough paths and hills. I have become quite celebrated in that way, for I go over the hills as I should over a level.

Well, my dear sis, wishing you a Merry Christmas and a Happy New Year, and all the best blessings of Heaven, I shall close this book, seal it up, and trust it to the waves. If it serve to show you that your sister, though absent, is still the faithful one she was, it will answer my purpose. Love to all.

From your ever affectionate sister,

HARRIET.

BOOK IV.

February 1. — And now, my dear sister, I can have a little more conversation with you, as my dear Uncle has furnished me with another book. As usual, I make no promises that it shall be more entertaining or useful than the last; but it shall contain a faithful account of the way I pass my time, and perhaps sometimes a few observations on what I have been reading, etc. At best it cannot be very amusing, for one day almost certifies another. [A curious expression used frequently in this journal. — *Ed.*]

3*d.* — Went to the barrier, where Mr. W. joined us. He began talking at one o'clock, and kept it up till ten, with scarcely a response, except a laugh, from the rest of the party!

6*th.* — Received a note about half-past two, which ran thus: —

> The humble petition of W. W. W.
> This sheweth:

That the petitioner humbly solicits the pleasure of carrying *arms* with Miss L. this afternoon, and the petitioner would ever humbly pray, etc.

I answered it in due form, and had a very pleasant walk with the petitioner. He is a young man of splendid talents, and can be excessively agreeable.

7th. — Messrs. W., G., I., and B. took tea with us. I read a little Spanish with Mr. Ibar, and had a pleasant evening. Mr. W. and Mr. G. started for Canton about eleven, with a head wind. When Caroline and I were sitting cozing over the fire after they had all departed, she disclosed to me a secret, which so discomposed my nerves that I did not sleep till near four. I was, however, much entertained, as C. began to talk in her sleep, upon which I had a very funny dialogue with her. At last my shouts of laughter, which I could contain no longer, awoke her.

12th. — A cold, dismal day. A note from Mr. W. to-day with some caricatures. Met Dr. College at Mrs. T.'s, to whom I made sundry complaints, and prescribed for myself some bark, which he said he would send me, kind creature that he is. He said he must say I did not look so beautiful as I used to. In fact, I am looking more like a tallow candle than anything else; but I told him, if he did not restore the roses, I would not forgive him so ungallant a speech. [My mother's complexion was so brilliant in her youth that some of the gentlemen, who believed in an interesting pallor for "elegant females," used to say to her, "Really, Miss L., you are positively in rude health." — *Ed.*]

February 17. — Gloomy, cold, and rainy weather. Walked after dinner with Uncle, Mrs. D., and Mr. B. Just as we got on to the beach, we were joined by Mr. V., who had the impertinence to offer his arm. Oh, dear! well, my politeness, I fear, will have to suffer a shock yet; for I will be rude, if words politely given and looks are not enough. Hyyah! I will *not* walk with him! Excuse this soliloquy, but my thoughts went on to the paper unconsciously.

18*th.*—We had a long discussion on romance this morning with Mr. B. and Dr. College, who is the most matter-of-fact person in the world.

. . . Find by the help of Peruvian bark, which I take twice a day (at the expense of horrid contortions of my visage), that I am regaining my color and strength, and consequently my spirits; for I am convinced that, unless one is well, they cannot have good spirits,—in this place, at any rate.

February 25.—Another year of your life has passed, my dear sis, and with this day commences your twenty-fourth year, I think. If you are not married soon, you will get into the old maid list. We are both of us growing old. Well, you know, and it is almost useless for me to say, that my best and kindest wishes for your happiness ever attend you, and that all the felicity this world affords may be yours, is the sincere prayer of your absent sister. Perfect happiness is not a resident on earth, so do not expect it. I flatter myself I am quite a philosopher. . . . Spent part of the afternoon with Mrs. T. I would I were near enough to you to tell you a thousand things that daily annoy me and destroy my comfort. I think you would hardly recognize me as your heedless and wild sister; for I have become so tamed, so thoughtful, that I astonish myself.

[Nevertheless, her future husband's brother, who did not know her till after her return from China, said of her in a reminiscent mood, "My, but she was a lively one!"—*Ed.*] I suppose it is age, in a measure. I have learned thoroughly to bear and forbear, and will recommend myself as a good wife for a quick and high-tempered man. I think I should manage him beautifully!

March 6.— Mr. Ibar came in this morning, and read Spanish with us. Says I pronounce very well. We read one of Moratin's comedies. Very amusing and well written. Called "La Escuela de los Maridos." The style is elegant, and for delicacy far exceeds most English comedies. In fact, there was not an idea in the whole that would rouse a blush in the most fastidious. V. came in after dinner, and wanted us to walk; but I told him we should not walk. So we lost our own walk, for we had fully intended to go. We were very anxious to go as soon as he went away, but we were influenced by Aunt L.'s prudence, and now I am glad we were. There is nothing like having a steady person to conduct one. Many an error she has saved me from.

13*th.*— Dr. College in this morning. Stayed two hours. He is a "darling." The best Englishman I ever saw. He is truly good at heart. I believe there is no nonsense about him. Went to the R.'s in the evening. I wore my pink gauze over white satin, Caroline blue satin under white lace, and Aunty purple silk. A very large party. Danced all the evening. The chief of my amusement was tormenting Mr. H., a demure, steady, serious-looking fellow, but handsome and very gentlemanly. Never was known to dance. At Mrs. Grant's I made a "dead set" at him, and asked him to dance a quadrille with me, which he declined doing. He got well roasted for it, but he was incorrigible. He said he was a wretch, and never deserved to be forgiven, and was ready to do any penance.

March 19.—Rainy morning. Messrs. H. and W. in. We domesticated them. Caroline and I were drawing; and they spent half the morning with us, cutting our pencils and waiting upon us. It is very pleasant, I assure you, to have them drop in so.

20th.—Walked with W., who took tea with us, and at eight left for the (Canton) boat. This evening a note from Ibar, saying the "Gen. Hamilton" has arrived, having on board Captain and Mrs. McCondray. Hyyah! it does not take long to "catch a wife." Only about a year since he left, and here he is back again with his *sposa*. I long to hear whom he has married, and all the news, which I hope is good. Expect this will set some of the other bachelors on tiptoe.

22d.—After dinner we had handed to us our packet of letters per "Gen. Hamilton." I was delighted, I need hardly say, and happy to hear you were all well as late as October. I am quite encouraged about writing in my journal, now you tell me it interests you. Suspect I shall be more "copious" than ever. A little praise sometimes does an immense deal of good. Your description of getting home after three months' absence pleased me much. What will it be when I get home after five years!

Although my letters made me happy in a degree, yet I was quite ripe for a good cry. However, I shed but few tears, and concluded it was better to laugh than cry. So Caroline and I soon found a subject, and we kept it up till nearly twelve. We have several capital subjects in Canton for a joke, and we expend all our wit upon them when we are so inclined.

March 28. — Read French aloud to C. this morning. A translation from Cervantes by Florian of his "Galatée," extremely sickening, being full of lovesick swains, who are ten times more silly than lovesick damsels. Threw it by in disgust, and took up the far more rational and interesting work of Washington Irving, which is written with his usual elegance and drollery. He seems to have a great partiality for old-fashioned words, which he draws in in a very funny way, — may be called quaint.

29th. —Our morning reading soon interrupted by old Millet, a stiff old bachelor, who is conceited in the extreme, and fancies he must be right and every one else wrong, of course; but, to give the d—l his due, he has been very obliging and kind to us. Soon after came in a bundle of books, notes, etc., from W., which amused, petrified, and astonished the addressed, and left them in doubt whether the youth had taken leave of his senses or not. Sent some poetry, too!

30th.—Mr. Ibar came in, and we abused our beloved President Jackson and his whole cabinet. Find from I. that it was known all over Macao that I ate lobster salad at Mrs. D.'s on the 27th, and I suppose in Canton, too, ere this. Have just returned from walking, and C. is setting Aunty into convulsions, telling her of our capers. You may remember how I used to rave about a certain doctor at home. Well, there is another doctor here,—*parfait amour!* We met him on the Campo on horseback. We stopped by mutual consent, chatted, petted the horse (instead of his master), and made him promise to call to-morrow to see Aunt L., as she is not very well. However that may be, we shall have the call. Aunty says we shall not go out; and we say, if Uncle does not come down and take care of us, we will not behave. V. spent the evening with us, and we teased Aunt L. to give us a ball. She has half consented.

April 3.— Mr. I. came to read Spanish to us this evening; and just as we commenced we were interrupted by Captain Little, just from the Sandwich Islands. Every one gives sad accounts of the missionaries there. I have heretofore endeavored not to listen to them, thinking they were prejudiced; but this Captain L. I should depend upon. He says the natives are being converted, from the simple and, as it were, innocent life that God in His mercy intended them to lead, to idleness, drunkenness, and treachery and deceit of all kinds. They (the missionaries) have treated a little band of Catholics there as no Christians certainly had any right to treat their fellow-beings. He says the accounts they send home are very incorrect, and so it goes.

April 5.— This morning C. and I adorned ourselves to pay some visits. First called on Mrs. W., who "had a litty sick, and no could see." Then on Mrs. G., who also "had a litty sick." The influenza seems to be travelling through Macao, and very severe in some cases.

8th.— This evening a Captain Whitney was ushered in, a brother of Uncle's old friend, J. W. Aunty had gone out, so I felt myself bound, as a dutiful niece, to entertain him till her return. I began the acquaintance with sundry sage questions and remarks upon the weather, contradicting him now and then for the sake of conversation, till in about half an hour we were good friends; and before Aunt L. came home we had discussed the merits of China, Manila, Java, Bengal, Lima, Valparaiso, the Sandwich Islands, and the missionaries, who, I am sorry to say, do not win either the respect or love of their fellow-men, or, at least, their countrymen. No one that comes from the Islands speaks well of them, though for my part I make great allowances. We passed a very pleasant evening, and gained considerable information respecting the manners and customs of different nations. I could not help audibly wishing that I was a man, that I could take up my bundle and go where I pleased. Felt half inclined to fall in love with some captain or supercargo, and put it in the agreement that I should go wherever I wished or wherever he did. I do hate this dependent system!

April 9. — This morning sent out invitations for a party that Aunt L. intends giving on Wednesday. Received two annuals, a present from Mr. W., with his compliments, — so ceremonious it alarms me. Oh, dear, what animals men are! They are certainly incomprehensible. I do think I have had some odd specimens to deal with. When I can tell you, my dear sis, all the funny bits I have in store for a *tête-à-tête* in "our" little chamber, you will laugh and wonder. Now I am sitting scribbling here, waiting for the hour to arrive when I may dress for Mrs. Daniell's, for at half-past eight we are to go. Is it not absurd to introduce London hours into Macao?

11*th.* — Busy as a bee all day, making preparations for our party. Had everything turned out of my room to make a supper-room of it, because it opens into the drawing-room and is quite magnificent. Got everything elegant and in good order, but was tired enough before the company came. Never mind that, however, must dance all night. At eight we were all adorned and ready. Aunt L. wore a China gauze over white satin, C. pink aerophane over white, and my ladyship blue crape over white satin. Our hair was dressed with natural flowers that some youths sent us for that purpose. Ibar was master of ceremonies. He said he was not well, but for the honor of Spain he must do his best, and he made everything very agreeable. We had Mrs. D.'s piano, and Mr. and Mrs. P. played and sang beautifully at intervals. Had the guitar, too, and four Portuguese musicians, to the grinding of whose fiddles we danced. I danced every dance, and when the party broke up, about half-past one, I could have danced as much more. I had got just enough excited to forget my fatigue. We had a handsome supper, and everything in style, I assure you. We mustered about forty,—four American ladies, English, Spanish, Portuguese, French, Swedes, Scotch, and I'm sure I don't know what others. We made the Scotchman dance a reel, and I joined in myself.

April 23, Easter.—At the church of San José the altar is dressed in black, and no light from heaven is seen, till suddenly the black is withdrawn, and flowers drop from above, and the joyful tidings of the Resurrection are made known. I must say the Catholics are much more strict in their outward observances of religion than any others, but I cannot say how far the heart is concerned. However, it is not for us to judge. How few there are of any sect who act up to what they know to be the duty of a Christian! Went to church this morning, and the sacrament was administered. I hope my thoughts and prayers were directed aright.

April 24.—A very hot day. Went to the factory about nine, and danced all the evening. Was very much fatigued. I felt in wretched spirits, and must confess that though it was a very brilliant and gay party I enjoyed it but little. Not one there that I cared about pleasing. Do you understand that feeling? I do not suppose you can, as when you go to parties you always have the one you love there. There was one person at this party, too, who will not behave as I wish him to. He is most unmanageable.

30*th.* — A melancholy affair I heard of the other day has just been made public, and what do you think was very near taking place? A *duel,* yes, a duel in China, in this little family, as it were. The two unhappy editors [Mr. W., of the *Courier,* and Mr. K., of the *Register,* both of Canton.—*Ed.*] have been sparring for a long time. It was begun by the *Register,* and the *Courier,* having all the ability and talent on his side, was able to drive the *Register* completely from his ground. The latter (finding he was nearly beaten in argument) thought to put the other down by treating him with "silent contempt," upon which the editor of the *Courier* made some remarks which caused Mr. K. to call on Mr. W. and demand an apology, which Mr. W. refused to make unless Mr. K. would do the same to him; but no, nothing would do but an "unqualified apology." Whereupon, having refused this, Mr. W. received, and immediately accepted, a challenge, and, as his privilege, appointed time and place. Mr. K. made divers objections to fighting in Canton, and finally went off to Lintin, where he has stayed till this time, and Mr. W. is honorably exonerated from the duel. Everybody says that he has behaved like a gentleman, and Mr. K. has not. Much as I hate duelling, and much as I think it should be shamed and put down, I do think there are some cases in which a man must fight, in the present state of society. This is the talk of the place now, as you may suppose. As it did not end seriously, it makes some fun.

May 1.— Spent a very pleasant evening at Mrs. P.'s. Two young Calvos there, just from Paris, real French in appearance, manners, everything. They gave us some specimens of the Galopade, the new dance. It is very horrid, I think,— at least I should be very sorry to be obliged to dance it. After dinner we all had to sit down and sew over our gloves for the evening; for you must know we can never put on a pair here without having first sewed every stitch of them, which is very trying.

May 4.— Mr. Ibar and Mr. H. in this morning, talking over last night's party at the Company's. Felt stupid enough, as I generally do. I say it is the reaction after excitement, but C. will insist that I did not laugh all the evening. Can you believe that I, the greatest giggler in the world, could exist a whole evening without laughing? Just before dinner commenced "The Enthusiast," by Miss Jewsbury. Very beautifully written. The young Enthusiast is a great genius, and from her childhood wishes for fame. Poor thing, she has her wish, to her heart's content, but in possession finds fame an empty bauble, dearly purchased and unsatisfactory in the extreme. There are a great many fine sentiments expressed, and many feelings I have often had myself; but I cannot say that my thoughts and wishes lead to that point, — fame. The character is much like Caroline's, I think. Had a letter from Mr. W., with four lead-pencils, and his statement of the late affair, which I may perhaps send you. The pencils, he says, are what Mr. Chinnery would call "positive black butter." This same Chinnery is a droll genius.

May 5. — Came in from our walk and had a large packet of letters handed to me by Aunt L., who said Captain Roundy was somewhere. I did not stop to hear where, but rushed to my own room for scissors and a light. Saw a letter from Captain R. first, in which he said, " I send your sister's miniature!" Think of my having a resemblance of you in my hand, my dearest sister, and not opening it first! Never mind. C. says, "Now do be moderate!" I endeavored to be; and at last I extricated it from its snug bed of cotton, where, with your own dear hands, you had placed it. I unclasped it. The first look did not satisfy me. I saw no resemblance to what I fancied my dear sister. I looked again, and caught it. The tears came in showers then, for I saw the same dear face; and now I have looked and looked till I think it a good likeness. Yes, it is you, my dear. I have kissed it again and again; but at first it looked to me dead, and even now I long to make you smile upon me. You look so *triste*, and in the night so pale. Still, the more I look, the better I like it. Aunt and Caroline think it like. I laid it by to read my letters, but ever and anon my eyes wandered to the picture. It looks as Miss Ward [their old schoolmistress in Salem. — *Ed.*] said hers did, "as though she was looking at some refractory young nymph in the school-room"; but it is so delightful to see anything like you! On the whole, I am satisfied, though I wish I could make you laugh a bit. That sedate phiz of yours always makes people think you a great deal more thoughtful than your sister, when, in fact, you are not a bit. Have read my letters, and thank God for His watchful care over you all. To hear that you are still all alive and well is a great comfort. I have left your picture on the drawing-room table, and long to have daylight come, that I may see it to better advantage. Now I must bid you good-night, my dearest.

May 6. — Rushed out of bed the moment I awoke, much to the amusement of C., and laid hold of my picture, hoping I should find it still more like; but there is the same look in the day. I do not think it so good-looking as you are, my dear. It is much too grave, even for you, and the head has a cant on one side, which makes it look as though you had a stiff neck. Who painted it? I don't believe he talked with you, did he? I am persuaded one great duty of the painter is to keep the sitter in conversation, that the expression of the countenance may be caught.

14*th*. — This morning proposed a party to the Lappa. The party, or some of it, assembled at our house at half-past three. The "King and Queen" were detained by a visit from a mandarin. Aunt L. said, "Well, I hope Mrs. D. will give the mandarin his *congé* quickly, and not keep us waiting." Whereupon a lady said, "Do they always give them *conjee?*" (which is a sort of starch, often used here for food.) I shouted at once, but upon second thoughts sobered my face, and rushed on to the terrace, where C. joined me, quite ready to add her laugh to mine.

We had a long but very pleasant walk on the Lappa, though rather rough and hilly; but the hills were so green and the scenery so varied that our travellers told us we might fancy ourselves now in the highlands of Scotland and then in the beautiful scenery of Wales. The springs of water on this island are delicious, and a clear stream was running by our side most of the time. Now and then we came to a fall over the rocks, which I instantly bid my imagination picture to me as the falls of Niagara in my own dear country,— a stretch of imagination, to be sure, but that we can afford now and then. We found many beautiful flowers. The weather was very pleasant, as the sun was obscured, but no one was sorry, I assure you, on ascending the last hill, to discover in a little valley a table handsomely set for twenty-six people. A beautiful stream was running at one side, which was recommended to me as a looking-glass. We all dined well, and then had to descend, to get over the worst of the walk before dark. This was the only drawback, that we had to hurry too much. We sat down at the foot of the hill, a stream of pure water running at our feet, the full moon shining clear overhead. Altogether delightful and romantic, and some of the gentlemen sang, and very well, too. I was chosen captain of that half of the party. The plodding part had made straight for the boats. We had a most delightful pull home. The moon was so bright and the water so smooth that to prolong the time we went round the Point, and landed at the Praya Grande. Mr. Ibar gave us an amusing account of his adventures, and his gallantry to one of the ladies of the party. In some parts of our walk we had to go through paddy-fields. There is generally a ridge hardly a foot wide to divide them, and this place, in the dusk of the evening, unless one takes precious heed to their steps, is rather dangerous to walk upon, especially as it is often worn away. Mr. Ibar says one poor lady fell into two paddy-fields at once, so you may judge of her situation. There she was, seated on the ridge like a man on horseback, and up to her ankles in mud. To hear this told with all the gravity of a Spaniard was enough to make one laugh, and laugh we did. He said, to rescue her from her unpleasant situation, he jumped into one field, and, covering himself with mud up to his knees, he extricated her, and was much pleased with himself for his gallantry. A moment after I had heard a cry of "Mrs. R. in the paddy!" One of my *preux chevaliers* rushed into the paddy beside me, for what purpose I then had no idea; but it seems he saw the sad situation of Mrs. R., and determined I should not share her fate.

May 18.— Perhaps you know that my twenty-second year expired last night of a natural death. Only think how old I am growing! Upon my word, I am fast getting into the detestable list of old maids! Never mind, it will be all the same a hundred years hence. To-day I commence my twenty-third year. I wonder what will be my feelings at the close of another. Shall I go on in the same quiet way, or will circumstances have entirely changed? Shall I be as happy as now, or shall I be miserable? I sometimes wish to look into the book of fate, although at the same moment aware that it is in infinite wisdom that it is concealed. Oh that I could only know the consequences of certain actions, which would soon be performed if it were not for doubt! Well may we say with "The Nonchalant," "Doubt is the Alpha and Omega of our existence"; but one thing is certain, the more I think, the more I am involved in perplexities. Why have we desires for knowledge so far beyond our possibilities of gratification? Is this only the first stage of our existence, and are we to go on progressively from one world to another till we reach the perfection of knowledge? Or what are we to be in another world? These questions I want answered; but where am I to go for the reply? We know not, must be the answer to all. All may think, conjecture, and suppose; but none can know, and the more we know the more ignorant we feel. The more we search, the deeper are the doubts, the more incomprehensible is our existence, the world, and the Maker, the Great First Cause, the Ruler and Governor of all.

May 20. — Read "Decision" (by the author of "Father Clement") aloud to Caroline. Do not much like it. True religion is, I think, deep, silent, spreading a mildness, contentment, and cheerfulness over all our actions, subduing our temper, correcting our evil passions and propensities, the still small voice growing with our growth and strengthening with our strength. I do not think we are to give up the pleasures of life, but only to enjoy them with moderation.

23*d.* — Have just had your picture in my hand, my dear sister. I wish you would smile; but you look more *triste*, if possible, than you did three years ago to-day. Just three to-morrow since we left our dear home, to tempt the mighty deep and seek a home in foreign lands. I pray Heaven three years more may not pass before I revisit those shores!

May 31. — Lieutenant Pinkham and Mr. B. of the "Potomac" and Mr. Warrener dined with us. The lieutenant was the best of the three in appearance. For goodness of heart and morals, sincerity, etc., I should say the schoolmaster would bear the palm; for he is about as green and unsophisticated as need be. He is a genuine Yankee, caught in the country, most probably. He wandered through Mr. B.'s house, returning ever and anon to express his delight at everything. He says he had often heard of

"Eastern magnificence," but he had no idea of it before. (Now you must know that Mr. B.'s house is one of the plainest in the place, very comfortable, but no elegance about it.) He is a very pious young man, it is said, but knows little of the wickedness of the world. We have several good jokes at his expense, but I shall not note them, for my sister would say I was getting scandalous. Well, I confess I am a very naughty girl, but I am sure in my heart I have not a spark of ill-will. You know I always liked a good joke. Mr. B. is a Salemite, and as vulgar, fat, and greasy a muster as I should wish to see.

June 15. — Caroline sick this morning. We sent for Dr. College, and he spent two hours with us. Promised each of us a cashmere shawl and a lace veil when we were married. He is as good a man as there is going, I believe. Read a review this afternoon. I try in every way to gain some information, but I am sometimes discouraged. It is so hard to learn when one is old. I wonder whether the knowledge we gain here will be of any use to us in another world. I think it must; for what is the use of acquiring knowledge if it is to be buried with us in the grave? I should like to know if we go on from world to world, still progressing in knowledge. Sometimes I think it must be so, and then — I am lost in wonder, and must stop; for who knows anything? Raining torrents, sheets, floods, all night, with heavy thunder and lightning. Seventeen inches of rain, I am told, in forty hours, which is quite tremendous.

June 17. — Went to church this morning. A great many there. Being Trinity Sunday, we had a sermon suited to the occasion. Some good sentiments were expressed, but most of it I could not comprehend.

Dr. C. and Mr. S. in after church. Had a long chat with the former, who says he has never heard any one speak ill of me since I have been in the place. Do you not think that a compliment? But coming from him, I believe it. I suppose they think I am a good-natured, harmless crittur! But what matters it? I care not. After dinner went in my chair to the Peña, where I had an hour and a half of delightful meditation. The scene all round was fitted to inspire calm and tranquil thought. I hope I am not to pass many more years in this uninteresting place, — not but that there is more tranquillity here than, perhaps, I shall find anywhere else; but it is a sort of quiet that does not suit my mind or disposition. I am restless. I want something to rouse me from this seeming lethargy. The present is a blank. The future is all uncertainty. The past has some bright spots. But, alas! not much that is satisfactory to look back upon. Would to God I could withdraw the past two years from my life! I sometimes construct schemes for happiness, and think with real pleasure of my return; and can there be any mistake in the joy, the delight, I shall experience in again being with my dear parents, brothers, and sisters, by whom I know I am loved, in whom I never can be deceived?

June 29. — Reading some Salem papers all the morning. It seems so natural to see the same old names; quite carries me home. I see they are going to make people fly between Boston and Salem by means of railroads. Oh, the march of intellect! March of bodies, too, double-quick time, I think.

July 5. — Spent the evening at the Company's. A dinner party, and stupid enough. Not one there I would have walked across the room to speak to. Is it not delightful? Walked in the veranda with Mr. King, talked of one thing and another, argued whether it were better to read novels and live in an ideal world or to devote our minds to base lucre! I raved considerable, talked of the days of chivalry, and wished that the brave and chivalrous spirits of the past could be put into the men of this age, without all the horrors of those times. From that I got to my own uselessness. I would not include the whole sex; but I told him I was a mere cypher, etc. He said I drew a sad picture, and looked very grave. I told him I might make him look grave, but it was, nevertheless, true; that I had the will to do more good, but lacked the opportunity. He said he differed from me. He thought we had the ability and the chances, but not the will. I told him I thought I was sure of the will, but I might be mistaken. I suspect he thinks I am a strange fish, but I can't help it. He seemed astonished. I hear poor V. has been very sick, and very much alarmed, but not without reason. I hear he makes a great many good resolves, which I hope he will keep, and that he may be able to say, "It is good for him that he has been afflicted." I fear there is great need for reformation in him as well as others.

[About this time there are many references in the journal to the attentions of a certain Mr. J. P. S. and to the jokes made upon them. "On the 15th we went to dine with him," Miss L. writes, "his birthday. Forty, he *says*, — but never mind. He has a magnificent house, and everything pleasant in it. He is *very agreeable*." The girls called him "Uncle Jem," and he seems to have been a daily visitor. Some days later we find the record of a walk to the Peña, when "Uncle Jem was *very agreeable*." Underlined again.] Wonder if he is as good as he seems. Oh, dear! I am dreadfully suspicious [but justly so, it proved], unhappily so for my own comfort; but, oh, this heartless, deceitful world! People laugh and look quizzical at the old man. Not that his age is at all objectionable to me. I believe I am a great hypocrite, for I treat people delightfully when I ought to frown upon them, and all for why? Because I am a girl, and must not put on airs. O ye married ones! The privileges that are yours for having taken unto yourselves helpmates! You may command, entreat, obey, if you please. You can make a little world of your own, and live within yourselves. Well, unhappy spinsters! I say throw off all this unfeeling general attention, centre it all in one, and then there will be some chance for your happiness!

July 13. — Came in from the terrace directly after

dinner, when Caroline was taken with fever and ague, I never saw anything so sudden; she was quite cold, and shook like a leaf, then followed violent fever. We sent for Dr. College, who gave her some quinine. I sat alone upon the terrace all the evening, musing. Had the blues. Had a good crying spell, and feel better.

14th. — Caroline better. Dr. C. came in, and he made me both laugh and talk (though the others had failed to do either). He made me a curious proposal, which I do not intend to avail myself of. I do not mean he offered himself. He is a queer creature, but every one likes him. I hardly understood his drift this morning. If the conversation could have been written, it would have made you laugh.

July 16. — Languid, listless, and lazy to-day. Its events have been unusual, and excited feelings of many kinds, but of too private a nature for this book, — events that might under other circumstances have affected my remaining life, but now I trust not.

17th. — This morning had an unpleasant duty to perform. How much one has to do at times contrary to one's inclination! I have had to appear selfish and hard-hearted to-day, and yet, — but then — Oh, my dear sister, that I were with you!

July 18. — Dr. College comes in every day, and chats with us. C. is not yet quite well. Mr. P. spent the evening with us, and amused us very much, giving us an account of all his loves, about twenty of them, and he is but nineteen! Had a note from Blight, saying Mr. W. was in Macao, — his health the plea; but I suspect it is all fudge. They do anything to get down here now and then. He called to see us to-day, looking very well.

21st. — Mrs. M., Blight, and W. took tea with us. I had a delightful evening, talking seriously with Mr. W. He is a pleasant creature, and one of my best friends, so sensible, so witty, and so amusing.

24th. — W. and I had a long discussion this evening upon metaphysics. Spent a delightful evening talking like rational beings, — a thing we do not often have a chance of doing here; but W. knows everything, and is a most delightful companion. Has great talents.

25th. — A lovely evening, and we all went to the Peña. Mr. W. and I talked, and Caroline and Blight went into a pine forest, if you can fancy such a thing in Macao. I felt in very good spirits; but all at once such a change came over me like a flash of lightning, and I could not raise my spirits again all the evening. 'Tis a very odd and most unhappy feeling, but I cannot shake it off. I have it often, and cannot account for it in any way. It sometimes seizes me when in my gayest humor, and I know no cause or reason why. I have been dreadfully stupid all the evening, and puzzled and perplexed, so, as it is now after twelve, I will go to bed, and endeavor to sleep off this depression.

July 27. — Nothing new to-day, my dear sister, that I can put in this book. Were I near you, I could a tale unfold. This is a strange world. I wonder why it is some persons love us for whom we care not a straw, and, when we are dying almost for something to rest our affections upon, the right one will not come along!

31*st*.— Half a dozen people dropped in and took tea with us this evening. A very pleasant party. Had a singular conversation with Mr. W., which I may have occasion to reflect upon many times in the course of my life. Well, the recollection will always be pleasant. He is a youth worth talking with,— high and noble feelings, good principles, and first-rate sense, with extensive information. A friend to be proud of, for he would be an ornament to any society.

Now here I am on the last page of another book. I hope you may find this more interesting than the others, but, if not, excuse it, and, if there are any sentiments expressed that are not pleasing, forgive me, and believe ever yours,

HARRIET.

BOOK V.

August 1.— What an authoress I am! My fifth book! Fancy them given to the public! *O tempora, O mores*, what an amalgamation! How many more shall I write in China? I hope not many, or it will be the same thing over and over again. I must change the scene, or my readers will withdraw their attention, I fear, for the writer grows lazy and inactive for want of stimulus and something interesting to relate.

2d. — The "Union" left to-day at half-past twelve for Canton, carrying Uncle, Mr. W., and several other friends. There is a northerly wind, which feels like fire upon one's face, the barometer falling, and every symptom of a typhoon; but they will go, and think they shall get there before it comes.

3d. — Blowing a regular typhoon. You may judge how anxious we were about Uncle. A dismal day enough, and then to think how many poor creatures will suffer! I do dread these gales. Fortunately, we heard about dark that Uncle was seen above Lintin yesterday, so we made ourselves easy for the night. Went to bed early, for it blew dreadfully, and I felt half sea-sick, the house rocked so. You will laugh, but the house really had an unpleasant motion, and being entirely shut up on every side was quite dreadful.

August 4. — Moderated this morning. Lost some of our mats and tiles, but suffered no material damage. Two gentlemen called this morning besides V., who says the damage in the inner harbor is very great, and dead bodies are floating about in every direction, ships driven on shore, houses unroofed, some utterly destroyed, and everything horrid. Everybody dreadfully anxious about the " Union."

5th. — About ten Aunt had a letter from Uncle, for which you may judge we were very thankful. He despatched a boat as soon as he got on shore to relieve our anxiety. They fortunately got inside the river, but were excessively uncomfortable, and arrived only yesterday morning. Had three anchors down, and lost one. The gale was felt very much in Canton.

8th. — Captain Dumaresq called this morning, the captain of the "Martha." He lost a mast in the gale. The "Don Quixote" returned dismasted. The "Spartan" went out to sea the morning of the gale, and picked up the crew of the "Fair American," — forty-four out of at least sixty, mostly Malays. She sank off the great Ladrones, was just from Java, and went down before they could save a shirt to their backs, — a narrow escape enough. The losses and accidents are beyond count. Every day we hear something new. There is hardly a green tree or shrub to be seen about the place. Everything looks as if a fire had passed over it.

August 11.— After dinner had just made myself comfortable on my couch when the boy brought me your interesting letter, per "Louisa," enclosing the very pretty card of the new firm. [Miss L.'s sister's *fiancé* had gone into partnership with her father.— *Ed.*] I am delighted to hear you are so happy and prospering. Your letter was quite satisfactory. It carried me home at once; and I can now imagine just how you live, what you talk about, and how you look. I suspect you will begin to think of getting married now. I shall hate to have you do it, though, before I get home.

August 13.— There was a procession from the church this afternoon. An image of a female was laid on a state bed, very richly dressed, and carried round with banners, the Host, etc. I asked Josepha what it was, but was quite shocked at her literal translation from the Portuguese. She said "God's mamma had died that day," and they were burying her in effigy. It is horrid.

Have just had a *consu* in Caroline's room. [Apparently, an abbreviation of "consultation," and used instead of "confab."— *Ed.*] I always go and sit down at her door to brush my hair, and there we talk sometimes till one o'clock. We discussed beauty and accomplishments to-night, and concluded that sensible men looked for something more than beauty in their wives, and for our own comfort agreed that beauty gained a great deal of admiration, but very little sincere love. Intellect is the thing nowadays, however. How different from the days of chivalry! I'm sure we should feel no interest in a hero now, let him be ever so gallant, if he knew neither how to read nor write. But it's half-past twelve, and I must e'en to bed.

August 16. — The direct ships in, and huge packets from England just coming ashore. I almost wished myself an Englishwoman, that I might participate in the general joy. Well, I saw, and reflected on what I saw, and came home and felt a sad depression of spirits, arising from different causes. Oh, what a trying world this is! I wish I could ever know that what I do is right. I am in a maze of perplexity. This has been an eventful day indeed! [But she gives no reason why.—*Ed.*]

August 18. — Began Walter Scott's last novel. Find it dry and uninteresting at the beginning. I hear they paid him a splendid compliment in Italy by giving him a masquerade ball, and confining their dresses and characters entirely to his novels. I hear a Mrs. Trollope has been ridiculing the manners and customs of our good country tremendously. Blight and Forbes spent the evening with us. I got in high spirits.

22d. — This morning I was lying on my couch reading, and the boy brought me an anonymous production in the form of an acrostic, which, if you will not call it vanity, I will copy for you. I suspect who may be the author. He endeavored to conceal his handwriting, but did not succeed. (Afterwards heard that this foolish effusion was written by a Mr. ——, of the "Don Quixote.")

" There is a winning charm of gentle nature
   O'er all thy being like a perfume thrown,
Making each beauty, both of mind and feature,
   Inseparable,— not to be singly known.
Something there is that as an unseen power
   Subdues the wonted current of our thought,
Leaving the heart all passive. But one hour
   Of thy sweet converse, and the soul is fraught
With feelings of a cast, oh, too, too deeply wrought!"

Soon after receiving this, I got a letter, which put the verses out of my head.

August 26.— A "bevy of beaux" spent the evening with us. I wish I could venture to take off every one, and put them down in their true colors. Oh, what a book I should have! To note down all the funny things said in this house, and the inconsistencies of men! It would be as good as a play. This summer has been the most amusing one I have ever passed in Macao,— big with events! Since their departure* Carrie and I have been thinking what different ideas and feelings we have now from those we had when we left home. A few years makes some difference in our feelings, and we see the same things in quite another light on an acquaintance with the world. I often sigh from the bottom of my heart to think I have become reconciled to things of which the bare mention would once make me shudder. Wicked, wicked world! Why were we created? Now, my dear, good-night. There's no use in thinking.

August 28.— This morning we sallied forth to

---

* Of the gentlemen, not the events.— *Ed.*

make some calls. Went, among other places, to Mrs. P.'s. The mistress of "the Palace" was agreeable, and her amiable son gave us a tune upon the "accordion," a new instrument just come out; dare say you have seen it. Rather pretty. — I am plagued. Had a letter this morning, which I answered short and sweet. Hope I shall have no more from the same source.

September 1. — The "Sylph" is in, seventeen days from Calcutta, shortest passage ever known. Brings accounts of lots of people coming here. Fashionables, too, so our gay season will soon commence. I don't like Calcutta people, though. They only abuse the place and make every one dissatisfied. Mrs. Davis came in, and we had a long talk about that Mrs. Trollope's book, which all the English are crowing over. It is as much as we can do to fight for our country and our refinement. I believe the sole motive for publishing this book is to put down the spirit of emigration to the United States, and to drive the people to Canada. Mrs. Trollope certainly writes with great spirit, but her going over with Fanny Wright is enough to show the class of people she visited. She tells many truths, but much that is false, or, at least, her facts are so embellished, or discolored, that there is no such thing as recognizing them. I will not pretend to say, nor do I believe, that there is as much refinement in America as in England, but I know there is decency and civility and elegance and luxury, if not to the same extent as in

England. But they (the English) will have their laugh, and they well may, if they will believe every word that is written by every person who chooses to wield the pen.

September 6.— Letter from home to-day, which disturbs my peace, for it tells of the death of Caroline's mother. I have not yet told her, nor do I intend to. She will probably have letters from her brother to-morrow or next day, which will mention it. Poor, dear girl, how she will feel it! And yet she has great firmness, and will bear it well, perhaps; but it is an awful thing to lose a mother, and so far away, too. Heaven forbid it should be my lot! I feel sad and sick at heart.

September 7.— C. got letters this morning from her brother, but, as he says nothing of the sad event of course I shall not mention it till I hear further. Walked after dinner, and had a very pleasant *consu* upon the hill with Mr. B. and Dumaresq. It was a lovely evening, and we talked of love and matrimony, etc., in general, of flirtations, nunneries, travellers, and stayers at home, foreign and American ladies, and, in fact, our subjects were very various. B. is a great enthusiast, and fancies woman to be all that is good and lovely. His anticipations of happiness are very great, and his expectations of pleasure in this world exalted. Ah, poor fellow! I did not undeceive him, or forewarn him that disappointments await him at every turn. No, they will come soon enough.

October 1.— Fine cool morning. Made Uncle a

pen-wiper, a very pretty muster. Went to walk after dinner. It feels like autumn weather at home, and we find our bonnets quite comfortable now. We have not worn them before for some months. You would think it very bold, I suppose, to go walking about without bonnets, but it is exceedingly comfortable, I assure you. I put my new cottage bonnet on to-day, and admire it very much. The crown is rather small, but the ribbon is splendid. A gentleman told me he did not hear the sermon yesterday, my bonnet attracted his attention so much. He said it reminded him of home. About ten V. came in, and bid us good-by. He leaves for England next month. It is not pleasant to say farewell to any one, particularly one whom you have been intimate with. He leaves Macao to-morrow morning.

October 6. — Had a pleasant trip to the Lappa this afternoon, and only one adventure. In crossing a ridge, my foot slipped, and I went half-way up to one knee in thick mud. With an effort I pulled it out, but in such a condition! There was no sign of my silk stocking or my purple silk shoe. I thought I had better dip it in the brook, and the cooly who was carrying our provisions seemed to be of the same mind, for he put down his baskets and jugs, came down to the stream, and with the greatest monchalance possible took up my foot and washed all the mud nicely off with a cloth. He brought the shoe and stocking to light, but left me in a dripping state, I assure you. This was a piece of gallantry I should never have suspected a Chinese to be guilty of. We have come to the conclusion this evening that he was some lover in disguise, for gallantry and kindness are not understood by the Chinese in general.

October 13.— Sat with Aunt L. all the morning, and had a very interesting conversation with her. She is a sterling woman, and the better she is known the more she must be respected. I never saw any one who would bear close inspection so well, or who was so strict and conscientious in the performance of duty. Aunt L. had a letter from Canton, of which you will undoubtedly hear more anon. It took up my attention till two, when I finished the rest of the morning writing to Uncle. In the evening we all got letters per "Tremont." Nothing new but the disgraceful time in Congress.

October 17.—This morning I finished a dress, and spent an hour with Mrs. Macondray, who says there is an order issued to take away all Chinese women-servants from the foreigners. As they are generally wet-nurses, this is a very cruel thing. Oh, these mandarins are too barbarous! The moment they see a fellow-creature making money, they begin to "squeeze" him, as it is called. No doubt this order is to extort money from the nurses.

18*th.*— At home all day, reading history. I do love history better than any kind of reading, and I should much sooner go to sleep over a novel than a history. In the evening we were escorted by H.

and S. to the opera, where we heard the opera of "Cinderella" very well performed in Spanish. The music was very good, the scenery pretty, and the acting very amusing. Cinderella was not very beautiful, being a boy of very sombre hue. In her home dress she reminded me of Harriet G. The company was chiefly Portuguese, and no beauty among them. The opera was wholly under the direction of Mr. Pavia, who deserves great credit. He wished to let his townswomen know what an opera was, and, having travelled all over Europe, and possessing great musical talent himself, he undertook the task, and succeeded very well. We really were very much amused. Got home about half-past twelve. There was a farce after the opera, which was rather tedious.

October 20. — D. just in from Lintin. It is currently reported there and elsewhere that I am engaged to D. and Caroline to S., and all for why? Because they have been seen walking with us a few evenings. Poor creatures! I wonder any gentleman dares to walk with us, for report engages us to every one; and, if they happen to break off and not walk for a day or two, why then they are *juwaubed*, or, in plain English, refused. We are quite independent of such reports now, and only laugh at them. We warn new-comers of their danger, and find out if there is any one to be made jealous at home; for these reports do not rest here, but take wings to America, and often rebound.

22d. — Got letters from Uncle this morning,

which discomposed me for the day. After dinner, however, I received letters from home, per "Panama," which turned my thoughts in another channel. Thankful to hear you are still all well.

October 23.—Went into Aunt L.'s room, and had a long talk. Sat there from ten till one, settling the affairs of the nation. I don't know that I ever felt more wretched. Had a letter from Canton while I sat there. What a world of trials and disappointments this is! Money seems to be the one thing needful, the *sine qua non* of existence. Oh, romance, where dost thou dwell? Our dearest and fondest hopes are often dashed for want of the filthy lucre, our fairest schemes defeated, our plans broken, and even our affections have sometimes to be sacrificed for the want of it! [The Mr. W. so often referred to as so clever and so charming must be the person whose addresses were not received favorably by the wise uncle, who knew him to be a man of irascible temper, little steadiness of character, and with neither fortune nor prospects, with nothing, in fact, but his brilliant talents to recommend him. Miss L. fully acquiesced in the wisdom of her uncle's decision later on, though it was hard to bear at the time. We can realize, however, that the blow was not altogether a crushing one, when we find her on the evening after this most melancholy morning amusing herself with the incipient mustache of one of their visitors.—*Ed.*]

We had a stupid evening. My whole amusement was watching one of our beaux and making fun of

him, for he is nursing a pair of horrid *mustachios.* [*]
His face is white and sickly. He is about as
large as a knitting-needle, and the most conceited
puppy you ever saw. To make himself look fero-
cious, he lets the light hair grow all over his upper
lip, to which he has to pay great attention, else he
stands a chance of chewing it. It is quite amusing
to see him poke it on one side, that he may find
room for his food. He caught me several times
looking at his manœuvres and almost laughing. He
almost hated me before, and he will quite now, I
suppose. He goes by the name of "Don Whisker-
ando."

October 27. — Walked over to Mrs. M.'s, and
while there Mr. M. came from Lintin to take his
wife up, and urged me to go with them. I asked
Aunt, who thought it a good opportunity; and, as I
longed to change the scene and get out of Macao for
a while, I consented to go very gladly. Wrote a
long letter to Uncle on special business, which I
shall probably write you in a letter.

28th. — Got up at five o'clock this morning. The
party for Lintin breakfasted with us at six, and we
got on board the "Martha," anchored in the roads,
at eight. The "Martha" is a fine little ship, and
reminded me very much of the "Sumatra," and our
departure from home, excepting the feelings. It
was a beautiful Sunday morning, just like the one
when we left our own dear shores. There was very
little motion, but nevertheless I was so unromantic

[*] At this time the New England prejudice against a mustache or beard was very
strong. — *Ed.*

as to be sea-sick. Towards night Mrs. M., being very delicate, went below, leaving as *triste* a trio on deck as you ever saw. My head ached most dreadfully, and there sat B., H., and my ladyship, all as deeply wrapped in our own meditations as we were in our cloaks, and not a word was spoken for some time. The breeze strengthened, and at eight o'clock we anchored at Lintin. We were whipped into the long-boat, and were soon put aboard the beautiful bark "Lintin." I do not mean by "whipping," my dear sis, that they took a rope's end to us; but we were put in a chair and hoisted over the side, the most genteel way of getting there. The "Lintin" has a fine round-house on deck, and excellent accommodations. The Peak of Lintin was close beside us, and about twenty-three ships around us. A very pretty sight, I assure you.

October 29. — After dinner we went on board the "Red Rover." I expect to be quite a connoisseur in ships before I leave here. A lovely evening, and a beautiful moon. Captains Mackay and Lockwood brought their little band of music, which sounded very well, and we danced a quadrille upon deck, and the gentlemen waltzed.

30*th*. — Went on shore with our party in the afternoon, and had a pleasant walk. The Island of Lintin is rather barren, though there are some fertile spots, and the rice plantations on the level ground look very pretty. We went through the village, and saw women, pigs, and children all eating and living together. The great, fat, dirty pigs have the *entrée*

of all the houses, to say nothing of fowls, etc. Saw
the stuff they make grass-cloth of being prepared.
It is a large stalk, which they dry and beat till the
fibres all separate.

November 1.— Captain Howland of the "Florida"
dined with us. Went on shore after dinner, and
walked half-way up the Peak with him. Poor man!
he was quite exhausted. Sailors are poor walkers
on shore. They have so little practice. A most
lovely evening. About ten received letters from
Macao, and one from Canton, of which you will
probably know the purport one of these days. It
made me *triste*, I assure you, and disturbed my
night's repose. There was some advice in Aunty's
letter which is very hard to follow, for it goes much
against my inclination, but I must follow it, I
believe, and I hope it will prove for my good.
Nevertheless, it is very trying to the feelings.

November 3.— After dinner we were whipped into
the long-boat, and pulled round among the ships.
The sun had just set, and the moon appeared to have
borrowed an unusual share of his light. My star
was shining brightly above us, the waters were still,
and it seemed impossible that a cloud could ever
appear to obscure the brightness. It was too lovely.
I was lost in thought, and longed to soar somewhere
— where I cannot. It seems at such times as
though one ought to be able to divide the material
from the immaterial and not be chained to so small
a sphere! However, the material must be attended
to, and gets much more attention generally than the

immaterial, for, in spite of myself, soon after we got back to the "Lintin," I sat myself down to a huge bowl of bread and milk, which relished exceedingly. Then I was weighed, and I find this mortal body weighs one hundred and fifteen pounds, which is seven pounds more than I ever knew myself to weigh. But it is the first time I have been weighed for five years.

November 9. — Have had my breakfast, and here I am in the cabin, leaning out of the transom, looking ever and anon upon the blue waters and the forest of ships around us, and endeavoring to think what has happened during the last week. The incidents are few, though many things happen that I do not put in my journal, partly from laziness and partly from prudence.

November 13. — A lovely morning. A smuggling boat alongside, such a sight you never saw. They muster generally about a hundred men, and when alongside they generally take the opportunity to "catchy chow-chow" (to eat); and they form in little groups of four or five men each, round five or six little messes of fish and oysters cooked in divers ways. Each man has his bowl of rice in one hand and his chop-sticks in the other, which they dip into the public bowl, and thence into their mouths (having none of the delicate ideas of more refined people), and then shovel as much rice into their mouths as they can possibly crowd in. They sit on their feet, and are dirty and ugly. They are generally of the lowest class, and as to morals I will not say. If they have a moment's leisure, it is spent in gambling; and I generally see them, as soon as they have crammed down their food, with either cards or dominos, and playing with all the interest possible. It is a curious sight to watch the expressions of their faces, — if by chance they have any expression at all other than one of avarice and love of gain. You may see one lying on the side of the boat smoking his long pipe, with apparent indifference to everything in this world and the next. I often wish to ask them what they do think or if they think at all. Was half-inclined to be melancholy and sentimental to-night, but thought it was not worth while, so ate my bread and milk and commenced some home letters. I think there is less variety here than at Macao, no events. We lead a quiet and steady life, and, indeed, I find it best suits my disposition of late. I am getting old and sedate; not so fond of gayety as when all was bright and fair. When I was young and unsophisticated in the ways of the world, I was easily amused, and believed all gold that glistened. [This *blasé* philosopher was then twenty-three years old! — *Ed.*]

November 19. — We were invited this morning to go on board the Company's ship "Orwell," just anchored. We were delighted with her. She is nearly as large as the frigate "Potomac." Her accommodations are very fine, and such ships may well be called "floating castles." There is a great deal of style and etiquette to be observed on board. Mr. M., who is going home in her, retires this year with a fortune, I suppose, dearly earned by twenty years' residence in this country. He has grown old and gray-headed in the service, and with his fixed habits he is no doubt unfitted for living happily and comfortably in any country but this. He leaves China without a sigh of regret, however. We stayed on board an hour and a half, had a nice tiffin, and returned to our little bark, which is very comfortable, though a mite compared to the "Orwell."

20th.—This morning a circular was issued for a party to ascend Lintin Peak, about fifteen to eighteen hundred feet above the sea. At one o'clock we started from the ship, seven gentlemen and myself, with about fifteen attendants carrying provisions, and a band of music. We proceeded up the hill. The sun was rather hot, and the roads rough and steep, but we reached the top of the Peak at half-past two. I have the honor of being the first lady that has reached the summit. I could have walked a good deal farther. We acquired very good appetites on our way up, and were glad to shelter ourselves from the sun behind an immense mass of granite, with which the summit is crowned, and, assembling round a table formed by Nature for the purpose, drew forth the contents of our baskets and had quite a sumptuous repast, the music playing at the same time. Altogether we should have made a most interesting group. Having finished our meal, we made preparations for descending, after having admired the view, which is very extensive. This island, as well as all the others with which these

seas abound, is excessively barren and capable of
very little cultivation. We descended on the opposite side, where the grass was very long. Some
of the gentlemen sat down and slid from the top to
the bottom of the first ridge. About half-way down
we came to a little cottage, just big enough to hold
the ancient Darby and Joan who were busying
themselves about the door. Their faithful dog and
some fowls seemed to compose their worldly stock,
with a stool and a mat. They kindly invited us to
enter their humble dwelling and eat some rice,
which is the one thing needful here. We politely
declined, and the old woman of about seventy
handed me a stool, and I sat down under the shade
of a tree to rest myself. The old woman seemed
much pleased with me, and my hands especially
attracted her attention. She saw that my gloves
were ripped, and she looked at them with an eye
of pity. As they were flesh-colored, I fancied she
thought the flesh itself was torn. When I pulled
the glove off, her astonishment was very great.
She chattered something in Chinese, and tried to
put my glove on, but could not succeed. She then
wanted to put her hand upon my face, to see if that
were covered in the same way, but I did not like to
have her touch me, and made signs to that effect.
She showed me her hands, that I might see how
clean they were, but I gave her my gloves, and bid
her good-by. I moralized upon her situation, and
concluded that she was just as happy as if she had
been rolling in luxury and refinement.

We arrived safely at the ship about six, after having had a delightful time. The gentlemen of our party took tea with us, and, having the band, there was dancing, and, more from bravado than anything else, I stood up in a quadrille. But for once my strength was gone. I sneaked away to the cabin below, and reposed my weary limbs upon a couch.

November 21.— Before I was out of my cabin this morning, Mr. M. came to my door and said he would take me to Macao to-day if I would like to go (instead of to-morrow, Thursday). So I packed up my duds, ate my breakfast, bid Mrs. M. adieu, and in less than an hour was on board the "Flora," a fine little schooner, and on my way to Macao. Being so long an inhabitant of a floating habitation, I was not at all sick, and enjoyed our sail much. Sat on deck all the time, and felt a little stiff from yesterday's walk. About two we arrived in Macao, and I found Aunty and Caroline well, and delighted to see me. It is really worth while to go away for a time for the pleasure of returning. Our house looks so magnificent after my being cribbed up in a cabin that I do nothing but look round in amazement at its vastness. Had a great deal to do, putting my things to rights, and talking, too. Aunt L. says everything smells of cockroaches, and I should not wonder, for there were many in my cabin. I never went into it without having to sing out to the steward to come and kill two or three and sometimes more. So I just tumbled everything into the wash.

November 24. — Had letters from Canton and Lintin which disturbed my peace of mind, and obliged me to act decidedly and against my inclination. How often that is the case!

November 26. — Sent off a lot of home letters and another journal. In the evening we got into an argument about "fatalism," Caroline against me and Aunt L. half inclined to be. None of us convinced. I went to my room and read till twelve. Having Beattie on Truth upon my table, I took it up and exactly agree with him upon the subject. If we are not free agents or have not some power over ourselves, how can we be accountable creatures? And, if we are not accountable creatures, why are we to be rewarded or punished for our good or evil deeds? And, while I believe in a wise and good God, I must believe we are free agents, and, although we cannot always discover the justice of everything, yet we believe in it. But what can we know? At least we cannot decide.

29th. — Caroline got letters from her brother this morning, saying he had taken passage in the "Cowper," and may be expected at any minute. Went out early after dinner. I never saw a more lovely night, so clear, so purely bright. As a correspondent of mine says, "We look upon the stars, flashing and sparkling like 'a jewel in an Ethiop's ear,' and sigh to think how much happier may be the tenants of those distant spheres; we long to leave this earth to revel in the happiness of another, too often without thinking that the star we gaze upon with such inexpressible longing, instead of the habitation of the happy, may be only the prison of the condemned." This was in one of his melancholy moods. Can you guess my friend, my dear sis? Would he could have been with me to-night, he is so rich in ideas, and so keenly alive to the beauties of nature! He can amuse, distract, and entertain; he is gay with the gay, and grave with the grave. In a mixed company you would think him the greatest rattle that ever existed, but take him by himself, let him feel interested, then he shines. Will it ever be my lot to be with him? I fear,— anxiety, hope, and fear are the predominating feelings now. To-morrow must bring me a letter, then my fate may be decided. Well, whatever it is, I will bear it patiently. I have had examples of patience and fortitude before me, and I will copy them in every situation.

November 30.— Wandered about in a very unsatisfactory manner most of the forenoon; my mind is in such a state I cannot read,— in fact, I can do nothing at all. My ideas all seem to have vanished, my thoughts are all centred on one point just now. Went to walk early after dinner, the sky so intensely blue it seems as though we could see beyond the stars. I cannot describe my feelings on such an evening; it appears to me that I must have the feelings of a poet, though they will not come out in words. No one can feel more inward delight than I in looking at beautiful scenery on such an evening; it seems to lift me from earth and make me think of heaven.

December 2.— This morning received the long-desired letter from Canton. It was all I could wish, but my mind was so much discomposed that I could not go to church.

December 6.— This morning I received a large music-box and a letter requesting my acceptance of it from Mr. D. It made me quite wrathy, as he has gone, and has left me no chance to return it till he comes back. I wish he had it in his cabin. I was admiring his disinterestedness this morning, but Aunt L. and Caroline do not seem to think it deserves that name. Well, I dinna ken. I am no great believer in disinterestedness myself!

December 7.— Some person or persons attempted to get into our house last night, and took a very unpleasant method, too, for they burned the door halfway up. They must have got over an immensely high wall. Fortunately, the smell of the smoke betrayed them, but the thieves were not caught. We were very glad they did not burn us up. As all the gentlemen are in Canton, they would have had no opportunity to show their gallantry.

December 8.— A rainy, drizzly, cold, gloomy day, spent as usual. Mrs. Underwood sent her cards, P. P. C. to-night. I have kept my resolution this year, and have hardly become acquainted with any of the strangers. If you do get interested in them, the pain of parting probably forever overbalances the pleasure you receive from their society. So they may come and go, and I will care not; in fact, I sometimes say I never will decidedly love another person, male or female, but I daresay I shall, for I have a strong propensity that way!

December 10.— Mr. Inglis called this morning. A very pleasant man, but very much inclined to be satirical. He has seen a great deal of the world, travelled all over Europe, America, and India, and, I suspect, is a little bit disgusted. I think he has not much respect for the fair sex; thinks them very pretty playthings, but not fit companions for lordly man! Ahem! He was once desperately in love with an American lady, a Bostonian, his first and last love! He speaks highly of American ladies, but the ladies in India he cannot abide, and, indeed, they are but toys. They are designed by their parents, from childhood for the India market. They are taught to dance, sing, and play, that is, they are taught to tinkle upon some instrument, and are then fitted up and sent out in ship-loads to be disposed of to the highest bidder. You will perhaps think I am joking, but it is a fact. From people who have lived in India I have heard the most melancholy description of such marriages,— more than half of them turn out unhappily. The climate makes Englishwomen unfit for anything, and they lead a listless, vain, and useless life. There are exceptions, of course, but this is the general rule. A beautiful young woman has just left here, who possesses great genius for music, plays and sings divincly, has a good husband, and one who dotes on her, but, alas! with all her outward beauty, who would envy her either that or her accomplishments to have the name she bears of being a flirt and ten times worse than a flirt! I was told to-day that her husband was obliged to fight a duel on her account in India, and there is now a gay young gentleman with her who is her slave. 'Tis strange that a woman who has a good husband, one who is worthy of all her heart, cannot be satisfied. To possess the greatest of earthly blessings and yet to so abuse them!

December 14.— This morning Caroline was made happy by the arrival of her brother, so long expected, how I wished he were my brother, too! It made me long still more to see some one I loved, some one in whom I feel interested. Though I was delighted to have Caroline made so happy, yet I never felt more wretched. Oh, Molly, you cannot know the feeling of loneliness that comes over me at times. I sometimes feel that I should be happier with those who cared nothing at all about me than not to have my own. Well, patience! I wonder how Job would have behaved had he been sent to China! But I will try and exert myself; I am ashamed of myself, I ought to have more energy, and I will, so *allons*.

22*d*.— Strange and incomprehensible! The man whom above all others I thought perfect, or rather the one whom for the last three years I have thought incapable of a dishonorable act, has sunk in my mind to the level of the rest of his sex. And yet I suspend judgment, for there must be some mistake, it cannot be true. If it does prove so, I shall never put faith in mortal man more. I cannot bear to be mistaken in this person, who has been my model for nobleness of character, and goodness of heart. It cannot, it must not be. Yet every circumstance is against him, every appearance condemns. We did not walk, for all our feelings were absorbed in this event, speculating, conjecturing, wondering, and completely *égaré.*

23*d.*— No light upon the subject until noon, when the sun appeared from behind the clouds, and all was cleared up. I thought it would prove so; how careful we ought to be in judging a person! Here everything was sacrificed to the highest principles of duty. It was almost impossible to see through the veil, but fortunately everything is cleared up, and now we understand it all. It should teach us to be slow in condemning.

24*th.*— A year ago to-night we were about going to the Church of San José. What a change a year has made! My friend Mrs. Cartwright was here then, but I fear she has now gone to her long home. Mr. V., who was also here, is on his way to England, and then how our feelings have changed! Now the bells are ringing, and the people are again assembled, saying mass and singing, and to-morrow will be a day of rejoicing that Christ our Saviour was born.

December 25.— A rainy, unpleasant day, nothing pleasing or attractive about it. One thinks of the happy family groups assembled round "the festive board" to-day, and sighs for such a scene. Now I hear the clock striking twelve, the witching time of night, but I do not want to go to bed. I have just left Carry's room. We have been anticipating the time when we shall be ancient spinsters,* having become almost disgusted with the *genus homo*, and almost determined to live a life of celibacy. We were thinking of living together and doing all the good we could. However, I think, if it is not Hobson's choice, I shall yet espouse some poor unfortunate man, just to be the torment of somebody's life!

December 26.— It seems I went to bed in a particularly Christian spirit last night, by the conclusion of my last page. Terribly cold! I do not like cold weather in this country; great barns of rooms, great cracks under the doors, and floors that you can see through; the carpet does not seem to do much good. It is so rainy now that we cannot get a walk, and our limbs are almost stiff with the cold. It makes me shudder at the thought of encountering our winters, though I know you have more comforts at home. The Chinamen all look as thick as they are long now, they have so many clothes on. The Portuguese, many of them, go to bed and lie there. Mr. Inglis in this morning, giving us the history of several widows who have been on here. Upon my word, I do not wonder that men get disgusted with our sex, they do behave so, particularly the ladies in India. It is enough to sicken one of marriage, I think. I sigh and groan in the spirit, as tint after tint of the romance of my youthful days is obliged to become extinct. Caroline and I sat over the coals till nearly one again; it seems like the ghost of last winter to be sitting in the same place in the same way. At this hour one's thoughts seem to flow more freely,

---

* MARGINAL NOTE.— *March* 20. How soon she has deserted me!

and, if one has a congenial companion, it is very pleasant. Have begun "Rob Roy," and compare my friend Caro to Di Vernon. Think in spirit and independence she is very much like her,— in fact, many traits of her character are similar. The brother and sister are very much alike.

December 30.— It's awful cold, and, though the thermometer is only about 40 degrees, yet to our feelings it seems nearer zero either because the cold has come so suddenly upon us or because we were so thoroughly heated last summer. Went to Dr. Morrison's this morning, shivering and shaking. Heard a very good sermon, requiring us to review the past and make good resolutions for the future. May I attend and remember! Another year has gone, and again the question returns, am I any better than at the close of the last? Alas! I am still in the balance that is found wanting, my account is always against me. Mr. Shillaber (Caroline's brother) and I had quite a philosophical discussion, such a one as I hate, on subjects I never enter upon if I can help it, for we end just as wise as when we commenced. He reasons deeply and thinks deeply, which is dangerous business, I think. And yet why was the power of reasoning given us, if we were not to use it? Is it wrong for us to use that power to its full extent? And, if we do, where shall we find ourselves? Who can answer even these simple questions?

Jan. 1, 1833.— I must begin with the compliments of the season. I suppose you are receiving your bevy of beaux to-day with your cookies and wine.

How I should like to be there and share in the sport! Our little Josepha went round this morning, with her kind wishes, to the maidens of the family, rich husbands and long life; to the married, wealth. The Caffres were all dressed in the most fantastic way, parading the streets, singing and enjoying themselves. They seem the happiest creatures in existence; animal pleasures alone constitute that happiness, however. I have just got thoroughly heated through, and have left the drawing-room to Caroline and her brother. It makes me almost envious, and I sigh deeply for a brother, too, that is near me. I am almost heartsick of this kind of life, I dare not think about it. I sigh and smile, and all say, "How complacent and serene you always look!" I sometimes long to answer,—

> "The ray that tips with gold the stream
> Gilds not its depths below,"

but I do not wish any one to know how I feel and the effort to conceal it is best for me. I should feel better if I could look into the heart of one person, I think; if I could but know the cause of certain actions. But, alas! perhaps I shall never know, and perhaps from misunderstanding I may be always regarded as heartless and deceitful.

January 3.— Took to my French grammar this morning, and studied till I became thoroughly sick and cross. Nothing disturbs my "serene" temper more than a grammar. There I sat all the morning, hammering verbs into my head, which seemed to resist the pressure with unusual force. Oh! if I had children, all this should be drummed into them when they were susceptible to such impressions. It is so provoking, when I can take up any French book and read it without difficulty, that I cannot conjugate a verb without all this trouble. I got sad and *triste*, perfectly dissatisfied with myself and my capabilities, and think myself the most stupid of creatures. I wonder that any one has any pleasure in my society. Indeed, I do not believe they would for any length of time, and I think I will never marry, lest my husband should get sick of me. I am unfortunately fond of gentlemen of sense, and could not abide one wanting it. I cannot, therefore, marry a fool, and a sensible man would soon be sick of me. Therefore I think it would be most wise and sensible of me to join the venerable class of spinsters. Now, my dear, I know you will think verbs have a very bad effect. *C'est vrai*, but they must be learned. After dinner I read "Rob Roy," and, having finished it, I regained my spirits in a great degree.

January 6.— Have been to church this morning, my dear, and heard an excellent sermon read by Dr. Morrison. The subject was that the chief end of our existence was to do good, certainly not to enjoy, for the trials and troubles we are subjected to in every stage of life prove that. I thought his reasons and arguments very good, but, if this is the purpose of our existence, how few fulfil it! ... I know one person here who does, and that is Mr. College. He is continually going about doing good; he makes every one love him, he is so universally kind and obliging, and exerts himself to make all happy who come in his way. We call him "the sunbeam," for everything smiles when he approaches. His greatest pleasure is in doing good, and his face speaks the goodness of his heart. . . . I think Dr. Morrison is right, and that we should be happy if we exercised the best feelings of our nature. The fatalist will say, what if other feelings overbalance these, then what can we do? I am not a fatalist, and believe that, though we cannot control events, we can control our own passions. If I did not believe this, how could I believe in a wise, just, and benevolent God? But there, I leave the subject.

January 8.— This morning I studied a little, and then went to Chinnery's room. There is a great attraction there now, a picture of my friend, which I was strongly tempted to pocket. It is a perfect likeness. I shall probably never see it again, as it is going to America. Well, I do not know why I should wish to, he is nothing to me.

A Dr. B. from Philadelphia took tea with us; he bowed and scraped like a Frenchman, talked, and made himself very agreeable. After he was gone, we began to think how different people who come from the civilized world are, to residents here. They talk so much that it quite fatigues us old residents, for here we get in the habit of saying only what is necessary. It is quite dreadful, the stupid, lazy habits we acquire. Caroline says that, when she first came, she thought all the ladies were terribly stupid. The fact is, we lose interest in everything. I am afraid I should be quite stunned at home for the first month. I would consent to be killed, however, if I could but get there; how can I endure two years more!

17th.—Studied all the morning, a cold rainy day. We have most intolerable gloomy weather now, coals scarce, and wood bought by the *catty*, very dear; what would you think at home of buying wood by the pound?

20th.—Shall I say it is cold again? Here I am, sitting in the drawing-room on a little footstool in front of the grate, one side is roasting, and the other shivering with cold. C. has just come in, and wants to know if you will invite her to your wedding if she is in America, and if she may be bridesmaid? When are you to be married, my dear? I should think you would be tired of courting, and yet I know not how mother would do without you, you dear little creature! I suppose you are trusting that I shall come home a venerable spinster, and be just fit *pour ménager.* The first is most probable, but the second not, for, when I do come home, I suspect you will condemn me as a drone, and turn me out of the hive. I must confess I never desire to see a kitchen again (you know I never had a *penchant* for the place), but, in any other way, that I can make myself useful, I shall be most happy. I do not think I shall ever be espoused, and besides there is nothing gives me more real happiness than making others happy, so that shall be my aim when I come home. If I cannot be a pattern of conjugal felicity, I can be a model for the heretofore despised class of old maids. After all, it makes very little difference whether women are married or not. If they are, ten to one they repent it, and, if not, they are independent, and can do pretty much as they please. After their hearts get callous, and their feelings too often thrown back upon themselves, it matters little whether they are married or not. One should be very unsophisticated to marry, I think. If they become old enough to look behind the scenes, ten to one they never marry.

January 23. — This morning we made an alteration in our system, we are going to have dinner late, and walk before dinner. Breakfast at nine, tiffin and a cup of tea at two, then at three go out to walk and come back before sunset, and dine at six. This is the plan for cold weather, and we like it very well. Took up "Patronage" after breakfast, and finished it. It's very interesting, and the best of Miss Edgeworth's that I have read. There is a great deal of talent displayed, some fine characters, and some which give a very good idea of fashionable life, which, for my own part, I never wish to know except in novels. Wrote several letters, and in the midst of writing received a soliloquy from a Bachelor who professes to have been jilted by his faithless ——. A droll affair, to be sure. It was addressed to "Mesdames H. L. & Co., at the Palace of Sans Souci, Celestial Regions." In reply to which we wrote a long note, but I do not think it worth copying. The "tender passion" seems to exhibit itself in the most wonderful manner in these regions. It has afforded us much amusement, I am sure.

January 28.— Received a letter from Mrs. M. this morning by Captain L. who has just returned from the Coast and the Sandwich Islands, and called to see us this morning. He is a very handsome man, only too thin. His face answers to Byron's "Conrad," in "The Corsair," I think. He says that reports reached the Islands and the Coast that I was to be married to three or four people. I told him I thought one quite enough. It is amusing to find what a notorious person my ladyship is; really I ought to be very vain. He says my fame has reached from pole to pole, and all, forsooth, because I happen to be a spinster in a distant land. I might have remained in America to the end of my days, and never have been known beyond my own fireside. And even now, should I take unto myself a spouse, I should forthwith sink into insignificance. Well, it is the fate of spinsters to be a subject of speculation. I am almost sick of this notoriety, and heartily wish I could see some one worthy of being — I won't say worshipped, — but there is always something in every one to make me get sick of them! I fear I shall never be suited. I feel that I am in a very "bad way," my dear, and am afraid I shall be a misanthrope before long.

January 29.— Received a letter from a gentleman in Canton, very interesting. He gave me his opinion of me and my character frankly and candidly, told me some of my faults, and also my good qualities. He was partly right, I think, but no one knows me so well as I do. I answered this letter at once, and pointed out the causes of the faults mentioned. I returned my thanks, and hope I shall endeavor to improve upon the hints.

February 1.— Warm day, doors all open, and a little rain. Mr. Sam S. in this morning, and I played battledore with him. Mr. College came in about two, and we had some rational conversation. He is a pleasant creature, so frank in his manners that you cannot help liking him; he is thoroughly English, somewhat aristocratic, and fond of old customs. The English resemble the Chinese in this respect; even though their reason tells them they are wrong, they stick to old habits. We talked a little about Unitarianism. He is prejudiced like all others, without knowing at all what it is. To me a creed seems a small part of our religion.

2d. — Felt miserable this morning; spent most of it in the interesting employment of weeping. Had a little misunderstanding, which I have at last happily settled, and it will be a lesson to me for the future. How experienced I am becoming! Well, experience forms the character. I have been a most thoughtless child, — have acted too much from impulse all my life, now I am going upon reflection. I see the error of my ways, and I will try to improve.

February 4. — Mr. B. came in this morning, and we played battledore. I was reading over your letter last night, and find that you kept it up two thousand times, which beats us all hollow, for our battledores and birds* are constructions of the Chinese, and the bird goes anyway but the right.

5th. — This morning Caroline, Mr. S., and I sallied forth to see the world. We made the circuit of Macao, C.'s first calls for some time, and besides there is something brewing which will astonish the public.

6th. — To-day my friend Mr. College offered himself to my Caroline, and she has accepted him; I have given you his character before. She will make him an excellent wife, there is strong affection on both sides, and will, no doubt, be happiness. She is capable of being just what she pleases, and I have no doubt will be all that he can wish. They have my best wishes, for if I cannot be happy myself I have no objection to seeing others so, — indeed, I am not so selfish as not to delight in the joy of my friends. But, notwithstanding, it does make me feel melancholy and more lonely than ever to see every one having some one worthy of loving, and poor I, no one. I seem doomed to this, and so I must bear it patiently and seem happy, lest those around should think me envious. Well, if I can't do better, I'll do all I can to promote the happiness of those near me. Perhaps my turn will come, but I see nothing in the future worth living for, nothing that I most wish for, that there is the least prospect of my obtaining. I should like to shut myself in my own room, and die a sort of temporary death,

---

*The word "shuttlecock" does not seem to have been in use at this time. — *Ed.*

4

till the time comes for us to leave this detested place.*

We dined at home, and spent the evening in talking, and thinking of the electric shock the people will have to-morrow. No one in the place, outside of our own family, had an idea of such an event.

February 7. — Mr. Latimer came in this morning, and I had the pleasure of electrifying him. His astonishment was great, and I enjoyed it much. College is beloved and respected by all, there is not a dissenting voice. He is not a negative character, liked because he does no harm, but positively beloved.

Latimer forthwith despatched a boat to Canton, to set the news afloat there, which will no doubt suspend all business for a time! The bachelors will feel they have lost one of their most worthy fellows, and the married men will rejoice at such a convert, for he had foresworn matrimony, till Miss S.'s charms overpowered his resolution. It would have been a shame that such a man should not have married, and happy must be the woman he marries! Well, it will never do for me to go on at this rate, or you will think I am in love with him myself, but no; you must understand that I admire him, and hope I know how to appreciate his character. I feel for Caroline as a sister, and would be as glad to see her happy as to be happy myself.

College came in while Latimer was here, and the congratulations were very fine. L. is one of his

---

*You must not mind these azure spots in my book, they come and go. — *Marginal note by the writer.*

best friends. College appeared "shut up in meas-
ureless content," and looked perfectly complacent
and happy, as though he would say, "Let him laugh
who wins." A rival was thunderstruck this morning at the announcement.

Twelve o'clock, and I have just come into my
own room to give you a few of my thoughts. Do
you know, my dear sis, what it is to feel alone? It
is to be in a far-off land, separated from your kin,
in a place where the society is too small, the interests clashing, petty feuds existing, where the voice
of friendship is seldom heard,— in a word, where
all are strangers to each other.

Then here is my friend Caroline. In the first
place she has a brother who idolizes her, who enters
into all her feelings, her wishes are laws, and not a
sigh escapes unnoticed, and now she is to be doubly
blessed in being permitted to marry the man of her
choice, and one who is worthy of her whole heart.
I would not deprive her of the smallest particle of
her happiness, but I cannot help feeling like one

> "Who treads alone some banquet hall deserted,
> Whose lights are fled, whose garlands dead,
> And all but me departed."

That is, I feel as though I was the only one without
some one to feel with me and for me. I must still
be what I am, the receptacle of cold and unmeaning
compliments, the cypher — nay, worse, for a cypher
adds value to the other figures, and I do not,— a
girl who is the object of speculation and criticism,

a girl who is expected to walk in the steps of a
chaperon, and because she does not happen to be
married has no right to give her opinion, and, indeed, is of no consequence. Yes, my dear, this is
to be alone. I have preached till my hand aches,
but I think I feel a little better, knowing that there
is one at an intolerable distance who will read this
with patience, and hoping that one of these days I
shall have the felicity of rejoining our own family
circle. That hope supports me now, and in those
days of happiness I shall look over this, perhaps,
and wonder that I could ever have felt thus. I
must fight against these feelings, I must

> " Be resigned when ill betide,
> Patient when favors are denied,
> And pleased with favors given."

This is said to be wisdom's part, so I will try, but,
alas! my nature is social and formed for sympathy,
and I cannot alter my nature.

February 10. — The first thing I heard this morning was Uncle's voice. He came quite unexpectedly,
and is looking pale and very thin, but says he feels
pretty well. Mr. College, Mr. S., Caroline, and I
all went to church this morning. C. walked be-
trothed, I told her. The English always think it
necessary to go to church before they do anything
else after any event, such as marriage, *accouchement,*
or the like. They have some odd prejudices, and
I think often "strain at a gnat and swallow a
camel." Spent the afternoon talking to Uncle, (it

does seem good to see him again) and reading him one of Buckminster's excellent sermons, speculations upon the future life. It agreed perfectly with what, since I have reasoned at all, I have thought of a future state, that is, that we go on from one world to another, gradually progressing. It cannot be, I think, that any one leaves this world in a state fit for perfect blessedness; we are none of us perfect, nor are any all evil, and I firmly believe that we shall all be rewarded according to our deeds, and the use we make of the talents committed to our charge in this world.

February 12.—This morning I received very unexpectedly a letter from my friend in Canton, to which, after mature consideration, I replied as I have told you by letter. Oh that I could look into his heart, and see its workings! I have become so distrustful of words now, that the warmest expressions fail to convince me.

The "Red Rover" brings the news of the death of the Duc de Reichstadt,* so there will be no danger from him any more,—indeed, I believe he inherited nothing of his father's spirit. Uncle is troubled with a racking cough, which I do not like. He has had it for some time. He is obliged to go up to Canton again to-morrow, a flying visit after an absence of five months.

College came in this evening as usual, to *bebe cha*, as the Portuguese say, and Aunt L. and I very sagaciously left the room, that is, we had sagacity enough to suppose we should be more agreeable in

---

* Died at Vienna July 22, 1832.—*Ed.*

another one. Well, I hope they will be married soon, for I do not like this turning out business.

February 17.— Walked along the quay after service, and into the Franciscan church, a very neat, pretty place, beautifully situated, as is also the monastery attached to it. They were in the act of filling up the grave of a person just consigned to the dust. They always bury their dead in the churches, and the manner seems to us very shocking. The body is carried through the streets exposed in the coffin, it is taken into the church and put into the grave without the coffin, it is first covered with quicklime, and then the earth is beaten down hard upon it by the black boys. When the flesh has decayed, the bones are sometimes taken up and burned. No female friends ever follow the funeral. The padres chant and read prayers in the church, and the bells ring most furiously from the time the person dies till he is buried, which is generally in a very short time. The priests, as in all Catholic countries, exact large dues from those who are able to pay for their prayers, and are very extortionate to the poor, I am told. Mr. College, who knows more of them than any one else, told me the other day that he was called to visit a woman who was very ill, in fact had quite lost her reason, owing to her father confessor, who thought it necessary to punish her for the heinous sin of saying the English were very good people, when some of her friends attacked them. He told her she must confess to him all her sins from the time she was seven years old. She being then forty, the poor woman thought it impossible, I suppose, and it preyed so upon her mind that she actually went mad, and Mr. College says it will no doubt be the death of her. (She has since died.) Is it not horrible? Many such instances of oppression occur, and it seems dreadful that the priests should have such power. I wonder when this Catholic religion will be done away with. By degrees I think it will be; the mild spirit of Christian charity is growing in America, and it cannot fail to spread. I should like to look upon this little planet two thousand years hence, and see what mind will be then, see if people will not think for themselves, and consider themselves the keepers of their own consciences, and God their only master, their best judge. How different the world is now from what it was in the fifteenth century, and shall it not go on toward perfection? I prophesy it will! We, or others, shall see these Chinese exalted in the scale, their turn must come, I think; the barriers must be broken down, ignorance must give place to knowledge, and slavery to freedom. Women will then be exalted; what a state they are in now, poor degraded beings! Mere toys for the idle hours of their masters, crippled and tortured merely to please them. As I was walking this morning, I saw a poor creature toddling along on her little feet. I am told that the agony they have to endure is beyond conception; they commence swathing the feet at the age of two, and for years they suffer excessively, all to gratify the mother's pride. I am told the men do not like it, although they think it necessary for their *first* wife to have small feet. I was one day talking with a very intelligent *comprador* upon the subject, who seemed to think our custom of nipping in the waist was quite as barbarous and cruel as to pinch the feet. [Sensible man! — *Ed.*] In fact, it seems to be a matter of astonishment to them how we can "catchy chow-chow" (or eat), which would certainly be a greater grievance to them than not being able to walk. A short time since there was a wedding in Canton, young "Minqua" was married, and the gentlemen were all invited to call upon the bride on the wedding-day. They were all rejoiced at the opportunity, a very rare one, and went. They were asked to sit down, and the lady was tottled into the room, supporting herself by putting her hands on the shoulders of her two bridesmaids. She walked around and courtesied to the gentlemen, who were not permitted to stand up to receive her. After having gone through this ceremony, she was backed out of the room, looking highly delighted that she had finished her task. She was very richly dressed, and had strings of pearls hung all round her face, coming from the comb behind. She was painted, and looked pretty. The presents were all displayed, some of them were very substantial, being cakes of *sycee*-silver,* of good size. The bridegroom is obliged to take a bumper with all his friends, and no doubt feels very merry before the

* Lumps of uncoined silver used by the Chinese as money.— *Ed.*

day is over. Ought we not to be thankful that we are so much further advanced in civilization? Though, I dare say, never having known better, the China-woman is just as well contented with her situation as we are with ours, and indeed I am sometimes inclined to believe that she is to be envied when compared with a woman of fashion, who is tormented with envy, malice, and all uncharitableness.

Everybody has gone, and here I am still writing and waiting for Caroline. If I don't give her a scolding for letting "Tom" stay so late! It is more than "five minutes past eleven," the usual hour with you, you know, when I made inquiries in old times. The clock has begun to strike little ones, and it is time he was gone. If I were as mischievous as I used to be, I should walk in and disturb their *tête-à-tête*, but I believe I am a little more compassionate than of yore.

February 22. — C. has promised to be married in three weeks from this time. Short work of it! I think my mind will not be regulated till she is *nuptified*, so I shall be glad when it is over, and I tell her I will do my best to get her out of the house. This morning I went to work and cut out a satin dress for her. I consider myself No. 1 at the trade.

23*d*. — Uncle came in early this morning, he is looking much better. Went out to walk with him after dinner, it is delightful to have some one to walk with and talk to that belongs to me. He says that in going to Canton they picked up part of the crew of a China boat very near perishing, five were drowned. I can hardly account for the indifference we feel regarding these creatures; it must be that we have no sympathy with them, they appear to me to be a connecting link between man and beast, certainly not equal to civilized man. You see different grades and links in all the rest of Nature's works, is it not reasonable to suppose that there are higher and lower orders of men? These certainly do not possess the sensibility of other nations, and, when we hear of such accidents, our imaginations never picture happy families bereaved and destroyed, for, knowing their brutal customs, we cannot think that such distress exists.

February 24.—After dinner read Aunt and Uncle two of Mr. Buckminster's excellent sermons, sermons which make you wish to be better, exalt your feelings, and incite you to make good resolutions, to reflect upon your errors and desire to amend them. A lovely afternoon; we three went to walk, and had a delightful time, the weather was warm and clear, and we sat upon the rocks and mused. Met young H. R. walking, a victim of consumption, a perfect picture of it; the brightness of the eye, the hectic cheek, the attenuated form, all bespeak this melancholy disease. I came home, reflected awhile on the vanity of this world's possessions, ate my dinner, and then Latimer and Clifton came in, and L. and I had a little "spat," and then forgave each other. Caroline would say that my steps from the sublime to the ridiculous and the grave to the gay are very sudden, but so it is, our lives are made up of it, inconsistencies and caprice are found in every human breast, I believe. Well, I think I have moralized enough for to-night. To-morrow is your birthday, my dear sis, methinks your twenty-fifth year. May God bless you, and give you many happy returns of the day! We are growing old, my dear, I should think it was almost time for you to be married. I have thrown aside my once cherished theories of long engagements, and think it best they should be as short as possible. Don't ask me why, for I am sure I cannot say!

February 26. — Busy all day helping Caroline. Am astonished to find how very capable I am! It is a long time since I have made such a speech, I think I have been rather going upon the modest lately. A gentleman, who professes to be a great observer of human nature, wrote me a letter the other day, telling me what he thought of me. One thing was, he thought me too modest, that is, too diffident of expressing my own opinion. In an instant a look of my dear father's came to my mind, that accompanied an anecdote of a friend of his, who said that "a certain degree of modest assurance was necessary to show a lady to advantage." I remember father used to think I possessed a good share of it. I wonder what he would say now. I think the lady perfectly right, and am sure nothing makes a person appear so well as a little self-confidence, but it should not border upon self-conceit.

Well, to go back to my capability, this is in the dressmaking line. I think nothing of cutting out a satin or lace dress and making it up. This is a dreadful place to get married in, no shops to go to, and you must pick up such things as you can, "asking no questions for conscience' sake." You would laugh to hear us tell the *comprador* to send and catch a tailor, and then to see a great long-tailed fellow trot in, impregnated with tobacco-smoke, to take your work, which after much trouble you get stuck together, often in a manner that would little suit our particular ideas at home, but to get it done at all is the thing. If they have an exact *muster* (pattern), they sometimes do pretty well, but the grievances are many, and one has to bear and forbear. Captain J. dined with us, and College has been here all the evening, and now he and Caroline are in the drawing-room. Happy? Yes, but will it last, can such happiness endure? A little while ago I had almost the same feelings (only we never met after the engagement); I thought I had found one on whom I could lean, I thought — but there, it is vain, let it pass, it was but a dream. It makes me tremble, though, and yet I am sure that C. can never change.

March 1.— H. and L. called this morning to congratulate Caroline. It seems to me a very odd custom to congratulate a lady upon such an occasion. One would suppose that she had accomplished some great enterprise, or that she had been endeavoring to win the gentleman's affections (and you know a lady is never supposed to do any such thing), and had at last accomplished her designs. She may be offered their kind wishes, but in my opinion the gentleman is the only one to be congratulated. I forget whether it is a common thing with us.

March 5.— This morning heard of the "Boston's" arrival from England. Does not bring much news, except that of the death of Sir Walter Scott,* who has done so much for the amusement of the world and the improvement of the taste of the age. How different the style of our novels since his time! I think he certainly has not lived in vain.

7th.— This morning busy as usual of late, cutting out work. A note from College says a company of Italian singers has just landed here, four gentlemen and two ladies. It seems they have been driven from South America, and came here on their way to Calcutta, but they propose to stay here a few months. It will be delightful to hear some good music, and I hope they will give concerts. Read the "History of France" by Crowe, one of Lardner's collection. It is extremely well written, and very interesting I have just got to the reign of Louis XIII., or rather of Richelieu, for Louis was a mere cypher. R. was a tyrant, but with such talents that you cannot help respecting him, and trying to attribute to necessity many of his ungodly acts.

March 9.—"Another six days' work is done!" Yes, and another week gone, never to return. The

---

* Died Sept. 21, 1832.

weather is perfectly calm and foggy, I have not been out of the house for a week. Uncle has been trying all day to get away, but the weather is so bad and the water so calm that it is useless to start in a European boat, and the Chinese demur at taking foreigners in their "fast boats," partly for the chance of extortion, I suppose. An ugly, wicked-looking creature came here this afternoon, and had the audacity to ask forty dollars to take Uncle up to Whampoa. A creature that anywhere else I am sure one would be afraid to trust himself with, and to think of paying that sum to be put into a miserable little hole where you cannot stand up, with fifteen or twenty of these ugly creatures, who resemble more our ideas of evil spirits than anything else I can compare them to!

March 11.—Cut out a gown for myself. Thick fog again this morning, this visitation is really very distressing, and everything so damp and nasty, as the English say. You would be astonished to hear how common this word is; it is applied to everything, both people and things. I think they cannot laugh at the Americans for odd expressions. Dined at Mrs. D.'s, everything very elegant. A gentleman asked me to-night if the sacraments were ever administered in America. Only think what a question! One would suppose they thought the Americans perfect heathens to hear the questions they ask. We are all endeavoring to have the marriage ceremony performed in the evening. It is so awkward in such a place as this to have it before twelve o'clock. The D.'s are going to see Mr. W. (the clergyman) to find out his reasons for declining. Had a letter from Mr. Russell, written the evening he called on you. Says you all seemed as happy as possible. How happy I am to hear it! Am afraid our poor country is in a bad way, from all accounts. I think I shall weep if Jackson is re-elected.

March 14. — Mr. P. called this morning, and invited us to come to the Company's to-night, as the Italian singers were to be there for the first time. We declined going to dinner, but went about nine, and heard some very good music, though they were suffering from colds. The Italian music requires some little time to get accustomed to, but before they had finished the evening I began to feel its power.

15*th.* — Making preparations for the wedding, I have been writing cards all day. I shall send you a *muster* to show you what the English custom is. If it comes in season, I think you had better adopt it. I think it very pretty. And I have been writing notes to all the people in the place to come and breakfast at twelve on Monday morning to meet the bridal party. We sent about sixty-five invitations. Something of a party, but the Company's steward will arrange it.

18*th.* — This morning soon after breakfast I dressed the bride in white satin, with a lace handkerchief over her neck, and veil on her head. I dressed myself in white muslin,* and at eleven

---

* This reminds one of "The Critic": "Enter Tilburina in white satin; enter Confidante in white muslin." — *Ed.*

our party, consisting of the bride and groom, Aunt
and Uncle L., six groomsmen and Miss Pereira and
myself as bridesmaids, proceeded to the church, or
chapel, where the ceremony was read in the most
solemn and impressive manner by Mr. Wimberley.
There is much in the English service that I should
think better omitted, but, however, we got through
very well, and returned to our house, where the
tables were all elegantly laid for about seventy
people. They were all introduced to Mrs. College
as they came in, as at our evening wedding-parties
at home. The Governor thought to make himself
of consequence, and kept us waiting an hour, so that
we sat down to breakfast about one. Mr. Latimer
sent a band of music to play as we returned from
church and during the repast. Everything went off
very well. The Italian singers volunteered to
sing, and they were a great acquisition. The party
broke up about four, and the bride and bridegroom
went to their house about six. We had the bridesmaid and the groomsmen to dinner at seven, with
several other gentlemen. Altogether the day was
passed in a very satisfactory manner. I thought at
the time that you, my dear sis, might possibly be
going through the same ceremony; if so, may God
bless you, and make you as happy in your choice as
I think Caroline is. There is no mistake about
College, nor do I think there is in George. Therefore, I resign my two sisters with the greatest cheerfulness.

Now, my dear, as I am coming to the end of my

fifth book, it is time to give you a few parting words. So, my dear, make all due allowances for the errors that may be found here. "What is writ, is writ,—would it were worthier." Farewell.

BOOK VI.

MACAO, MARCH 19 TO AUG. 22, 1833.

FOR the sake of variety I will have no prelude, but endeavor to think where I left off in my other book, as I must look back some days. I closed with the wedding - day, that memorable day! A day which witnessed the union of two people who two years ago did not know of each other's existence. How strange! Meeting in the uttermost parts of the earth, and linking their interests for life, and perhaps longer. What a change in their manner of living! How delightful to find one on whom you can bestow all your affection with a certainty of its being reciprocated! That their horizon may be always as cloudless as at the present moment is my earnest prayer.

March 19. — Was very busy all the morning, arranging my room and putting things to rights (for everything was disarranged for yesterday's entertainment), so that I have had no time to feel the loss of my "better half." Everybody thinks it necessary to call upon us after the party, and I thought I should never get out of the house.

March 20. — Had a note from the bride this morning, asking me to come and see her. I went about one, and found her looking blooming, with everything comfortable and elegant about her.

21st.— The bridal party dined with Mrs. College at seven. Had a very pleasant evening. The bride does the honors handsomely for a beginner.

23d.— Uncle went back yesterday. We shall feel gloomy enough, now he has gone. Our house seems so still and quiet, and we can get no walks, the weather is so bad. Busied ourselves this morning cutting out work for the tailor. After dinner finished the "History of France" by Crowe, beautifully written and very entertaining. His remarks appear to me excellent, and his ideas of Napoleon just. What a series of crimes and wickednesses one reads of in history, what contrasts in character! One cannot help wishing, when reading of a man with great talents, that they were hereditary, though the men of the greatest talents seem to do the most mischief. You seldom meet with a great and good man, the two seem almost incompatible. I am exceedingly fond of reading history, and yet it always disgusts me with human nature.

March 27.— The "pea-soup," as Chinnery calls the fog, has cleared up, and we have had no rain to-day, though it is not clear; the sun is very sparing of its cheering beams at this season. Read aloud to Aunty the "Life of Frederic the Great," by Lord Dover. He was certainly an able general, and Napoleon says the only one of modern days for whom he had any respect. Voltaire says he was greater than Charles XII., for he was a statesman as well as a hero.

28th.— To my book, to my book, to tell my dis-

tresses. It is the receptacle, the depot, of what?—
shall I say miseries? I daresay you will think,
and perhaps rightly, that they are all imaginary.
Spent the day reading, visiting Caroline, and
sketching at Mr. Chinnery's. When it was time to
dress for the Company's dinner (in honor of the
bride), I tried very hard to make the boy understand that I wanted some flowers to adorn *mi cabeza*
(my head), but all my bad English could not accomplish it. He said, "No could catch, in Canton
could catch." I said, "*Masque*," and told him he
was a very stupid boy, which was all the satisfaction
I had. Soon after, however, I was supplied by a
friend, made myself very beautiful, and at seven
went to the party, from which I have just returned,
having had as pleasant a time as is possible here.
I laughed and talked a great deal, heard some music,
and was apparently the gayest of the gay, but, alas!
it was only skin-deep, for the moment I got home
I could have had a good cry, and indeed I could not
restrain my tears. I did feel so lonely to be the
only spinster in the room. It is no doubt very foolish to feel thus, but I cannot help it. I wish I
could stay at home, then I am contented, but to be
dragged to places night after night is too much. I
think I am a little bilious, therefore I'll say no
more. I daresay you'll laugh at me, but I cannot
speak my feelings to any one, and so you get them.
You will say, if this is the sum of my grief, it is
imaginary, and perhaps you will agree with an
author I was reading the other day, that "there is

nothing like real evils to banish imaginary ones, for which matrimony is a sovereign cure." A very true observation, I dare say. It is not that I wish to be married that makes me feel so, the many that I can have I do not want, there is no one here whose friendship I covet, that is the worst of it. Now, my dear, I feel better, and you, no doubt, will call me a foolish girl, and that is all I shall get. Never mind, I am at a good distance, and hope ere this reaches you I may be thinking of packing up to remove from here, I care not much where.

31st.—I seem to have been in a very dismal mood when I closed my book; the weather is my excuse, for, in spite of Dr. Johnson, such a spell of nasty, dirty, drizzling weather is enough to make one gloomy. But to-day is lovely, like our delightful spring mornings, the very air reminds me of home. My spirits revived at the sight of the sun, and I feel quite myself again. The house is opened to dry up the damp and mould, and a regular "Saturday cleaning" is going on. I have had quite a feast of letters per "Bela." I suppose before this, my dear, that you are Mrs. Archer. Would that I could have been there on that occasion, but it is useless to regret; I think you were wise to defer it no longer. Before you receive this, you will be an old married woman, and, having had no experience in that line, I can give no advice. I doubt not that you will have all the happiness possible with so dear a friend, and I feel happy in the thought that you are thus united. All you say about the children is very gratifying, and read with great interest. After I had read my letters, we went to C.'s, and with her and some others to Chinnery's, to see Mr. College's picture. It is a most interesting thing, a group of five figures,—but first for the likeness, which, I am sorry to say, is not so striking as in many of Chinnery's pictures, the face is in profile, which is, perhaps, the reason. The figure, a full length, is perfect. One hand is resting on the forehead of a China-woman whom he has restored to sight from total blindness. He has lifted her spectacles and is turning to Afun, his Chinese servant, and telling him to explain to the woman how she is to proceed in future. Afun's likeness is excellent. The son of the woman is on his knees before College, presenting a *chop* (or letter of thanks, always written on red paper) for his kindness. The fifth figure is a poor old man sitting on the floor in a corner, with his eyes bandaged, waiting for attention. It is a most interesting and touching picture. I hope to have the pleasure of bringing an engraving of it home with me. Mr. College has cured an immense number of Chinese afflicted with diseases of the eyes. Some have thought that something in the rice they live on causes the trouble, but College thinks it is because they pay no attention to these complaints in the beginning, or often use medicines not at all suited to the disease. It is not uncommon to meet four or five blind people together in the street, and the number of deformed people is quite shocking. I never saw anything to equal the distortion of limbs one often meets here. As I came out of Chinnery's to-day, I saw one cripple, a perfect picture of suffering, misery, and despair. I could not help asking myself what feeling or prin-ciple he could have within that could induce him to bear such loads of misery. It could not be the fear of death, for the most intelligent Chinese have no idea of a future state,* and it appears to me that this poor wretch could never have looked beyond the present, and it seems impossible that it could be the love of life.

April 2.—This morning called on Caroline, and then went to that amusing man, Chinnery, and stayed till after two sketching. There is a good deal to be gathered from his conversation, and some of his similes are most amusing. He has been a great observer of human nature, for which he has had every opportunity, his profession having brought him in contact with people of high and low degree. He has been in Calcutta for twenty years, and has seen a great variety of characters, as you may sup-pose, in that changing place. He has excellent sense, and plumes himself upon being, "though not handsome, excessively genteel"; his personal ap-pearance, I think, however, is rather against him, for he is what I call fascinatingly ugly, and what with a habit he has of distorting his features in a most un-Christian manner, and with taking snuff, smok-ing, and snorting, I think, were he not so agreeable,

*This observation was made without reflection. Many Chinese believe in the transmigration of souls.— *Marginal note by writer.*

he would be intolerable. But, to give him his due, he is really polite, and speaks well of every one. Being one of his especial favorites, I must say something for him; to use his own expression, he "buckles" to me. We were asking him if Afun (in Mr. College's picture) could keep still enough to be painted. "Ma'am," he said, "the Rock of Gibraltar is calves'-foot jelly to him."

[Mr. Chinnery was a great epicure, and my mother told us that, having once asked a gentleman at his own table how he should help him, the gentleman replied carelessly, "Oh, I don't care, Mr. Chinnery: help me as you would help yourself." Whereupon the artist laid down his knife and fork, and looked at him in dismay. "Good Lord, sir!" he ejaculated. "I wouldn't do that for my own father!" — *Ed.*]

April 9. — Spent part of the morning translating English into French. About twelve, Caroline came in with Chinnery. He is going to take her picture, a full length, for Papa College, and he wishes to have her on our couch, with screen, fireplace, etc., for background. Then we went to his room, to see Aunt L.'s likeness, which is excellent. I am to have my phiz painted, great presumption on my part, I think, but it was the request of Uncle and Aunt, and the thought of the pleasure it would give you all that induced me. I sat for an hour, looking at one of the ugliest men in existence, but he makes himself so agreeable that you quite forget how ugly he is. He requested me to have the mouth open, a thing which I abominate in a picture, but he says it will never do to have it shut, as I generally keep it a little open.

> "O wad some power the giftie gie us
> To see oursels as others see us!"

Now I am sure I was not aware that I had this habit,—it is the ugly formation of it. Well, there I sat, with my head screwed and twisted in a strange manner, till after he had finished the first sketch, and then I looked at it. Oh, ye powers, what a thing! and yet I think it must be like me, because I saw mother's look about the eyes, also Cousin Forster's whom I was always said to resemble, but such a fright! I have laughed fifty-one times since, to think of it. The head appears about ready to take leave of the neck, the mouth is open as though I were snoring; there is a little something yclept nose, and a place where eyes should be. I suppose I must wait with patience for a few more sittings, but I think it will rather lower my vanity, though on the subject of personal appearance I never had much.

After dinner read the "History of Greece," and then Aunty and I walked the veranda. Talked of going home, the feelings we shall probably have, the changes that have taken place, etc., till we got quite melancholy, she at the retrospection, I with impatience to be there. We were comparing our blessings and troubles,—hers, I see, have been all positive, mine mostly negative. She has certainly tasted, and deeply, too, of affliction, but then through all she has had her husband, and while he lives she can bear anything, I verily believe. She is an extraordinary woman, and indeed I never knew any one who possessed so much fortitude; if all the world were like her, there would be much more happiness in it. Now I pass along as with the current,—I have never as yet had either positive happiness or positive misery. I have thousands of vexations and annoyances, but they are not to be mentioned in comparison with her afflictions. For my part, I think happiness is very equally divided throughout the world; we are all suited to the circumstances in which we are placed, either by nature or by habit, which is second nature.

April 15.—A glorious morning this, the air so delightful, it smells like home! You may think this a foolish notion, but you have no idea what a trifle brings home and its delights before us. Byron has something like this in "Childe Harold," when he writes, "It may be a sound, a tone of music, a flower, the wind," that strikes the electric chain that binds us,

> " And how and why we know not, nor can trace
> Home to its cloud this lightning of the mind."

Say what you will of Byron, he could write poetry. Follow his " Childe Harold" through Italy, go with him to the Coliseum, his description is beautiful, and so is his apostrophe to Time. His description of St. Peter's is perfect, not a word too much or too little. When reading his poetry, you wish almost that nothing of his character had ever been known.

However, I have sadly digressed from my subject; and, if I can find my way back, I will tell you in plain prose what I did with myself yesterday. Every moment I had before eleven, I was studying French, then I went to Chinnery's, and looked at the man till two, when I found myself in better humor with my portrait, which will, I think, be an excellent likeness, and a little paint will make it better-looking than I am, I fear. You can make allowances for the paint. Chinnery said some good things, and we passed the morning very pleasantly. He compares aristocracy to laudanum and salts, which taken moderately have a very good effect, but take too much of either, and you know the consequences, exceedingly dangerous, and extremely disagreeable. After dinner I went to Caroline's, and College lent me an English and French dictionary, so now I am made. Worked all the evening, and now it is near twelve, which is my bedtime.

April 26.— Went to the opera this evening. Our box holds seven, or rather it consists of seven chairs placed in a row, which we dignify by the name of box. Aunt L., Caroline and myself, Mr. College, Mr. Chinnery, and two other gentlemen made up the party. The opera was called "The Father and Daughter." It is one of Mrs. Opie's tales dramatized and translated into Italian, with Italian music. The heroine was Mme. Scheroni, Ernesto, her seducer, was Mme. Caravaglia, who took the part of a man, both good singers, but Mme. S. the better of the two, and she appeared to more advantage, being in better health. They all did very well, and we were very much entertained. The music was very good, much better than we had anticipated. The opera was over about eleven, when we went to Mrs. D.'s, and had a *petit souper*, which relished very well.

April 28.—Caroline dined with us, her *sposo* being at the Company's, and after dinner we all sallied forth to enjoy the pure air of heaven, which is delightful at this season. We seated ourselves on the rocks at Casilha's Bay, and a lovelier view was never beheld by mortal eye. It is a place where we can sit and reflect without wishing for company, for

> "There is a rapture on the lonely shore,
> There is society where none intrudes,"

but we were not alone, for on Sunday evenings the *noñes* (idlers) all turn out, and such a display of figures you never saw, they are really very amusing. They generally walk in groups of ten or twenty, and smoke as they go, and it is quite dreadful to get in the rear of one of these groups with the wind ahead; for you are in danger of being suffocated with smoke and fumes of garlic. As I passed along, I noticed some Chinamen about, "chin-chining their fathers," as they term it. I walked up to the grave to see what they had prepared. They had an immense quantity of gilded papers, which they were about to burn, and I counted fifteen different messes of "chow-chow" (food), which they place on the graves with the idea, I believe, that their ancestors or their spirits come forth and eat it, and find they are still remembered. At this season all the graves have pieces of red and white paper put upon the top of the mound, with two pieces of fresh turf on them to keep them down. There is something written upon these papers, which, of course, I cannot read.

May 4.— Expected to have gone to Chinnery's this morning, but he could not wait upon me. The opera is postponed till next Tuesday night on account of the sickness of the opera-tors. So, you see, we make plans for a day, but they are all defeated without our having the least power to prevent it. What passive creatures we are! Walked on the terrace in the evening, longing for Uncle's arrival, and had the felicity of seeing the dear soul just coming on shore in a Tanka boat. He is looking well, and I hope will stay with us for some time. Uncle brings us dreadful news from America *via* the Sandwich Islands. That is, the re-election of Jackson, and the declaration of independence of the South Carolinians. Well, it is "truly awful," I think, that the people should choose such a man. It is a disgrace to the country, and I shall be prepared to hear anything. The dissolution of the Union will follow, I daresay, and next thing Jackson will be declared king, emperor, or something of the kind, and about the time we are ready to come home there will be civil war, and all sorts of evils may be anticipated. [What a furious little Cassandra! — *Ed.*] Well, I shall no longer stand up for our government, when such a man as Jackson can fill the highest station, by consent of the people, too.

May 7. — Uncle sat for his picture to-day. Spent the morning with Caroline. We pinned up turbans to wear to the opera to-night. They were pronounced elegant,* and were made of Benares muslin scarfs. Caroline's was blue and silver, mine white and silver. They are such as the higher class natives of Bengal wear. The same opera was performed to a full house, and the singing was very good, but I do not much like the play. Mr. Wimberley has risen two or three pegs in my estimation by declining to go to the opera, though he had tickets given him for the season. It seems that he can make some sacrifices for his profession, which I fear would not have been the case with my friend V.

May 8. — Dined with Caroline. A number of gentlemen were there, and our turbans were spoken of. I find mine was not generally thought becoming, indeed, they begged me not to wear it again. The fact is, the house was not lighted enough to display its beauties. Besides, it was a turban that belonged to an ancient spinster. So you see how we are deceived! I went to the opera perfectly satisfied with myself, and not having a doubt but that I should be "the observed of all observers,"

That was by partial eyes; you will observe what follows regarding them.— Marginal note by writer.

that, perhaps, I was, but not "the admired of all admirers." Well, I don't care much. I generally have the credit of dressing with taste. The American ladies are said to be the best dressed of the place, because we are always neat; the clothes of many of the ladies, the gentlemen say, look as if they were thrown on with a pitchfork.

May 10.—Went to Chinnery's this morning to have my own face painted.* Sat with all the patience I could muster from eleven till three, in hopes it would be the last sitting, but there is one more to come. The room is so hot that it is almost insupportable, not a breath of air from out-of-doors is allowed to enter, but I have the one satisfaction that the picture must give you pleasure, for the likeness is said by every one to be perfect. They say I must have run against the canvas and left an impression there, so the thought of the pleasure with which you will see it consoles me for all the exertion I make in this hot weather. I was quite exhausted before I left, however, but some dinner and a rest on the couch made me feel better. Had a walk with C. to one of our old haunts. We turned our thoughts towards the past, and painted some fancy pictures for the future, and talked of the present, a time we are too much disposed to undervalue. There is no comfort in writing to you at night now, my dear, the mosquitoes are so troublesome that I am glad to put myself under the curtains for a little repose. I must confess that insig-

* See frontispiece.—*Ed.*

nificant as they are, they ruffle my temper and discompose my nerves, and it is the more annoying their boasting so loudly of their triumphs. I would not grudge them a living from my person, if they would take it quietly and go off, but that does not seem to be their aim, and much as I often feel inclined to write at night when I am still, and everything else, too, I am obliged to acknowledge myself conquered, and retire from the field. So, my dear, you do not know what brilliant ideas you may lose, and what fine sentiments; the collection of a day, which may all evaporate before the next morning.

May 13.——This morning about two we were awakened by the guns, drums, and bells all proclaiming in their different languages Fire! A very rare occurrence here. Indeed, I hardly remember an instance of it, so that I did not think of fire, but, hearing a great noise, concluded it must be some feast-day, which is certainly not a rarity, so I turned over, and went to sleep again. It seems it was a salt-merchant's establishment in the bazaar. In consequence, the price of salt has risen twenty *cash* on the *catty*,* so you see they make the public pay for the damage. After breakfast I went to my own room, where I stayed till three o'clock undisturbed, turning English into French. You may think I spend a great deal of time learning languages, and so I do, for, independently of the pleasure and benefit of knowing the language, it is an advantage to have some fixed occupation.

May 15.—— Went to Chinnery's this morning for

* *Cash*, a small coin worth about ½ cent; *catty*, about 1½ lbs. avoirdupois.— *Ed*,

my last sitting. The likeness is said to be perfect, but I think it is a very ugly face. It has not raised my vanity in the least. I sat there till nearly three, when I was quite exhausted, and very glad to leave the "studio." Spent the evening with Caroline, and read a tragedy called "Fazio," one played by Miss Kemble lately in New York. It is very good, and she is said to have acted the character of Bianca perfectly. Came home feeling very *triste*, why I cannot say. I do suffer more from low spirits than I ever did before. What a light-hearted thing I used to be! Now I hardly find anything to make me feel really merry. I laugh, of course, but I have lost the feelings I once had. 'Tis retrospection, I think; the past year has been, I can truly say, the most melancholy that I ever passed, at least I have had more positive feelings of both kinds, pleasure and pain,— but would that it had never been ! "*O monde, O monde!*" as Napoleon used to exclaim. I sometimes feel quite sick of it, and I will bid you good-night, or I shall become sentimental, and that is out of fashion.

May 18.— My twenty-fourth birthday. How shocking! Well, it cannot be helped, can it? I see I am looking much older than I did. Went to Chinnery's with Uncle, as he was to have his last sitting. Drew a little, but I do not take the same interest in the amusement as I did last year, the change of masters makes a great difference, I find. At seven Bradford came, and we went to the opera. It was called "The Italians in Algiers" (*Gl' Ital-*

iani in Algieri); the dresses were rich, and most of the characters well supported. It was very amusing. You would laugh at our stage, which is ten feet high, sixteen wide, and twenty deep! The tallest man, Pizzoni, nearly touches the ceiling, but the music is the thing, and we laugh at the rest. It was over about eleven. Thus has ended my birthday!

May 30.— Latimer and Green arrived last night very unexpectedly. They came down for the opera. The first thing I heard from L. was about the turbans C. and I once wore there. I tell you this to give you an idea of the trifling things these people talk about. I told him I did not wish to hear anything about it. It makes me feel cross to think they make such a fuss about nothing. Went to the opera at eight. The house was very full. "All the beauty and fashion" of Macao were there. We were, however, very much scandalized at seeing a certain lady enter (with whom no decent woman would associate, and no gentleman would have sent there), covered with diamonds, head, neck, and ears, and looking as impudent as possible, with her servant behind her. When I come home, I can a tale unfold concerning this, which would "harrow up your soul," but I cannot disgrace my book with it. Now to the singing. Scheroni as Almenaïde was quite enchanting, and the dresses one and all were splendid; but what appears to me almost a miracle is the compass S. screws herself into to come on to the stage, and then to sing laced in this manner, is shocking to think of. Caravaglia in the character of Tancredi did very well, but, poor thing, she is quite *passée* and not fit to sing. I begin to admire the Italian music very much. It is quite an acquired taste.

May 31. — At three we went to dine with Mr. P. A party of twelve, no ladies but ourselves and Caroline. After dinner we jumped into a boat, which was waiting for us in front of the house, and went to the Lappon to see (or hear) a sounding rock, which, from its peculiar situation or the metals in it, sounds like a church bell. Indeed, there are a number of them, and they are very curious. The walk was delightful. The scenery on that side is quite perfect, much prettier than in Macao. All the way, at one side, ran a clear stream called the Inha. It is about two feet wide most of the way, but in places broadens into a lake, where the washing is done for the English and Portuguese of Macao. The rocks are the scrubbing-boards, and you may judge what work they make of the clothes.

June 7. — We hear by to-day's letters and papers of war in Europe, the taking of the citadel of Antwerp, etc. Ten thousand French reported killed. I was exceedingly pleased with the President's proclamation regarding Carolina, and think with him that they (the Carolinians) ought to be whipped if they do not behave. I do not give the old gentleman the credit of writing this spirited and elegant production, but that he has had the good sense to subscribe to such sentiments has raised him some degrees in my estimation. I do not feel very anxious now about the division, as I think the Carolinians will certainly yield. There seem to be terrible times in Europe, too, rebellion here and rebellion there, and all owing to this independence, a spirit which is placed in every human breast. I got Rossini's "Memoirs" from the library, and amused myself with them till it was time to go to hear one of his best operas, "*Il Barbiere de Seviglia.*" It is a capital play, and some of the music is very beautiful; but on the whole I prefer the music of "Tancredi," that has made a lasting impression upon me. Mr. Inglis was very entertaining, as usual, and gave us some anecdotes of Rossini, whom he saw daily at Naples. He says he was the most indolent person in the world, as well as reckless and extravagant. He said, too, that after the opera in Naples the Italians would assemble at the house of one of the principal patronesses for a *petit souper*, and as they came in, one after another would go to the piano and play parts of the opera they had just heard, till among them the whole was often given from memory. They trusted to that altogether, as there was no printed music in Italy. Oh, the Italians certainly have the soul for music! If I were anything but an American, I would choose to be an Italian, with an English education after I was twelve years old. I admire their nature, their enthusiasm, their strength and warmth of feeling, and their love of music, which I think must be innate. Read an article to-day in a magazine about a new-fashioned bed for invalids called the "Hydrostatic Bed," made upon water, an odd idea! But I should think it must be very comfortable. People certainly stretch their imaginations now to invent comforts, but I doubt if fewer people die nowadays than in old times, when they had not so many.

June 16. — Slept till eight o'clock this morning, quite abominable. Asked Josepha why she let me sleep so long. She said she went to mass at five, and did not get home in time. She thought, as it was Sunday, Miss H. would not want to study. You may think her getting up at five to go to church is an instance of piety, but I think far otherwise. Much as she goes to church and many prayers as she says, there is no more religion in her than there is in a bamboo. As to virtue among these people, there is no such thing. I asked her the other night what she did when we were out late. She said she read prayers. I said, "For two or three hours?" She said sometimes she did not get time to read any for several days, and then she had to make up for it. I said, "Do you like to read them, Josepha?" She said, "Must, liky or no liky!" She gave me to understand that it was not at all agreeable, but that she was accountable to the padre for a certain number, which she must either read or take the consequences! Oh, it is a vile system! Mr. W. came down in the "Sylph." I do not know whether he will honor us with a call. He dined with Caroline. I read the "Life of Washington" all the afternoon and evening. Had to read some pages over a number of times before I could take in the sense, — *savez-vous pourquoi?* Oh, dear!

June 18. — Another blowing, miserable day. I read awhile, then went to Caroline's, as she had something to say to me. It was a message from Mr. W. He does not intend to call. So be it! Came home at two, and felt *triste* enough, did nothing all the afternoon. Had the blues in good earnest. However, before night I made some good resolutions, and intend to act upon them. I began this evening, took up my book, and by dint of exertion became interested in it, and went to bed satisfied that for once I had conquered my feelings. For there is a satisfaction in conquering yourself, to feel that you have some power over your own mind, if not over that of other people.

June 22. — Went to the opera this evening, where Rossini's opera of "Edouard and Christine" was performed. The music was very fine, but the company does not excel in the *serio*. With comedy everything is in keeping, but tragedy does not answer. My friend was there, but did not speak to me. I am more and more convinced that all in regard to that affair is as it should be. My feelings were very much hurt this evening, as I may tell you in a letter, but I am afraid of this book. It seems as though I were doomed to all the annoyances possible, little things that one must bear quietly and submissively without any credit for it, but which are ten times worse than some great event, which, if conducted with dignity, wins you some applause. Mrs. Opie says in one of her books that it is easy to perform a great action now and then, when the eyes of the world are upon you, but that it is the little, petty every-day occurrences which try you, and those about you. I went to bed in a very unhappy humor to-night, only wishing I could have an opportunity to give the gentleman a piece of my mind with my own lips. I would not spare him.

June 23. — After dinner took the chair and went to our hill, and ensconced myself where I could see every one, but not be discovered. The soft wind blew upon me, and in spite of my sadness I was enchanted with the beauties around me, — the setting sun, the green forest just behind me, the ocean beyond, literally beaming with sunny smiles. I had been there about half an hour when a gang of Chinese men and boys came up and surrounded me, so that I ran half-way down the hill, but was determined they should not disturb me farther. They saw I was alarmed, and followed me, but I took no further notice of them, and they soon went off. I knew there was no danger, as there were people about on the other hills, but I didn't know but they might give my ear-rings a twitch, which would not have been agreeable. However, a Chinaman is a great deal more civil than I fear the same class of my own countrymen would be. I am sure, had these men been English or American, I should not have dared to sit there. Well, in moving from the top of the hill, I was discovered by Mr. W., who came

to my rescue, and made a very humble apology for
his conduct of last night. I was perfectly astonished at my own apparent coolness, while he was
choking and stuttering; but it is wonderful what
pride will do, and for those few moments you would
have thought me perfectly indifferent. Well, I
was satisfied with myself, and came home feeling
much better. As I have given you the whole history in a letter, I will say no more.

June 24. —A dreadful day, hot as possible. I got
tired of reading about two, and went to Caroline's.
She had been making some gingerbread, and, not
having any butter, the servant brought her some
mutton tallow, which she put in! The Chinese
think anything in the way of grease will do. For
their own cooking, they use lamp oil. C. told me
that my friend W. had been to her in the morning,
and told her with how much coldness I had received
his apology. He seemed quite piqued. Well, I
am glad he could not see inside, as the Chinese say,
he might have been too much flattered. Went to
the opera in the evening. Enjoyed the music very
much, and quite forgot the heat. I saw Mr. W.
there, but he did not speak to me. It reminded me
of the song, "We met, 'twas in a crowd." He left
soon after with S. for Canton, — perhaps the last
time I shall ever see him. Well, God bless him!
All is as it should be, I am convinced, and could I
but forget, I should be glad; but "Time, the comforter and only healer when the heart has bled,"
must be my friend.

June 28. — A melting day again. This morning Caroline sent me Mrs. Trollope's "Refugee in America," a novel just arrived here. It is a very interesting story, and pleasantly written, that is, the style is amusing. I daresay she touches upon many of the real foibles of our countrymen, but I think she caricatures all she touches. She certainly uses a great deal of language that I never heard, but I do not know what they may do in Rochester. I should like to know who this Mrs. Trollope may be. I do not believe it is a lady.

June 30. — A letter from Uncle this morning says that Father writes that one of the boys will come out in the autumn. I sent to the Library, and got Priestley's Memoirs and Sermons, and read them throughout the day, and enjoyed the book much. I find that every day I am the more convinced that I am a thorough Unitarian, and, having in a manner my own ideas upon the subject, I am delighted when I find them supported by wiser and greater people. I rejoice now that I have been placed in a situation which has compelled me to form my own opinions by my own judgment, and I earnestly hope that the love of such a religion will grow with my years and strengthen with my strength, for I am very sure that it is the only consolation in adversity, and the securest refuge in times of disappointment and trouble.

July 3. — This morning after breakfast, having had a little molasses given me, I undertook to make some candy; a delightful employment for a hot day, but upon my word I felt no hotter for the fire, indeed I have not been so comfortable for some time. I had a little furnace put on the terrace outside my room, and there I sat and stirred, reflecting on the many candy frolics I have had at home, and the work we used to make for the servant, *alias* "help." In spite of my reflections and my attention, my candy all of a sudden burned, because the fire was too hot,— a very good reason, surely. So I sang out to Achow that he must take it down, and bring me another kettle (or whatever name it might be dignified with), and some more molasses, and I would begin with the remains of the coals, and be sure not to burn it this time. Sundry and divers regrets, which were of no avail, so I laughed it off, and was soon under way again, thinking, as I had less fire, I might take it more comfortably. So with my bamboo in one hand stirring with all my might, and my book in the other, and a fine breeze upon my back, I began to think I should make candy often. Suddenly I looked at it ; the fire was defunct, and my 'lasses had stopped boiling. "Thinks I to myself," this won't do, so I sang out to Achow that the fire was defunct, and the molasses would not *walky*. So up he came, the cooly with some coals, and the boy with some fire, for it takes three to do anything here, and you would have laughed to see me sitting there in the midst of them with my bamboo and my book, and their operations were very amusing, too. Finally, all was in order again, and I succeeded *à merveille*. The candy was delicious, and the only trouble was that once in.

the dishes, we could not get it out again, for they had not been well buttered. After much trouble I succeeded in getting some out for Mr. Wimberley and Mr. Davis, which they thought very nice, and sent me some facetious notes in return. To Caroline I sent a dish just as it was, and told her she would probably have to eat it dish and all, for I despaired of ever getting it out. She sent me word that her ayah was tilting at it like any knight in romance, not to unhorse, but to undish it, and she thought there was some prospect of her succeeding. But, alas! the worst remains to be told. In the evening I wanted some of my candy, and lo and behold! it had returned to that from which it came, and I saw nothing but a dish of molasses. It reminded me very much of the old woman's soap which comes and goes, but I fear this goes, not to come again. Well, I hope you will be edified,— it has at least filled a page in my journal. After dinner I had a letter from Uncle, praising me for my spirit on a certain occasion about which I have written you. He tells me it is Abbot * who is coming out, and now I shall be all impatience till he comes. I think from Uncle's letters we shall be condemned to stay here another year. The thought is intolerable, but we cannot be positive yet. I try to cheer up, for I am actually tired of melancholy, but how can one be merry without a single circumstance to cheer them?

July 12.— Letter from Uncle this morning. Says they are inundated in Canton, and cannot

---

* Her oldest brother, A. A. Low, father of the present president of Columbia College.— *Ed.*

leave their houses except in boats. It is dreadfully hot there, and I fear after this it will be unhealthy. I wrote Mr. Chinnery a flourishing note this morning, and gave him a little "soft soap" (for flattery is a thing, he says, "he cuts mutton-chops out of"), and returned his sketch-book, hinting that I should like another. Whether the "soft soap" had a good effect, or what other motive he may have had, I cannot say, but in about half an hour he came himself, with another book. We had given orders "no could see," so asked him to tea.

July 14.—Read two excellent sermons written by Thatcher. He is certainly a superior writer. After dinner read Zimmermann on "Solitude." I fully agree with him as to the virtues of retirement, but, for my own part, really to *enjoy* solitude I would have one kindred spirit, as the poet says, to whom to say, "How sweet is solitude!" When we wish to commune with ourselves, to examine our weaknesses, and rebuild those parts which have not a good foundation, then we must be alone. But it is not in solitude or retirement that our strength is to be tried, we must go into the midst of temptation for that, we must be tried in actual service before we can be pronounced strong. But, as none of us are all evil, therefore none are fit for endless misery. Every one has duties to perform in society, and these are not to be omitted for your own selfish gratification, every one has a sphere to fill, and, however small it may be, it is still to be filled and well filled. Oh, dear! how easy it is to sit down and say what one should do, to create your own little world, and fill it with beings of your own fancy, to be troubled by none of the cares or annoyances which constantly assail you in real life, and in fact to live in an ideal world of your own. Living as I do here in Macao, if I went to bed every night feeling that each moment of the day had been well employed, I should say, I have had no temptation to do otherwise. Now this is what I call negative virtue, and merits very little praise.

July 17.—This morning received some newspapers; do not see any news of importance, except that peace is restored in America by the modification of the tariff. So I hope they have done with nullification, and that our President will presume no more upon vetoes.

Mr. Stevens, the missionary in Canton, called today, and for the life of me I could not think who "Mr. Stevens" was, and what to say to him I knew not. However, I asked him to sit down, and I told him it was a hot day, which fact he seemed to have been fully aware of, having walked through the streets. I told him it had been raining very violently, which he also seemed to know. Finding that he would not contradict me, and knew so well all I told him (thinking, I suppose, that I of course knew his whole history, whereas I had not the slightest idea of the animal), and finding that he would not enlarge upon any of my safe observations, I said I would call Mrs. L., who fortunately remembered his name, so I left her to entertain him. He

is a rosy-cheeked, bright-eyed fellow, but something
of a Goth I think, nevertheless Aunty asked him to
tea.

July 18.—Went out to Casilha's Bay in my
chair. Rainy weather; there is no such thing as
a walk, had a good shower while I was out. Sat at
the Bay some time with Mrs. M., and chatted upon
different subjects. She had her little pet boy with
her, whom she considers a paragon of perfection.
All I can say for him is that he is the most disagreeable child I ever saw. I do not think it right
for mothers to select one of their children as a special favorite. My lady went home, and I sat musing
still, and had a short chat with Sir George R., who
came up, waiting upon his son on horseback, a little
boy of six or seven. I do not know what papas at
home would think to have to trot after children in
such a manner. Every day we meet Sir George
running by the side of the pony which carries one
of his children; three times in an afternoon he trots
out to Casilha's, and back again. I think, if he
knew the value of life, he would hardly be willing
to spend so much of it in tending babies, but every
one to their fancy, as the old woman said (when
she kissed the cow).

Titles do not always bring sense, nor *cents*, either,
as, for example, in this case. Saw a boat come in
from Canton this evening, and thought I should
get my letters, but *comme à l'ordinaire* I was disappointed. I despair of hearing from home again, but
I smiled and said, "My all was not laid there," was

not that heroic? I walked the terrace, and asked myself if it was not a great weakness to feel disappointed at such trifles; but when I reflected that it was but the result of natural affection, and that all my happiness came from that quarter, I concluded that it was not a trifle, that it was right and proper that I should grieve, and that it was not weakness. So you see how ready I am to excuse myself, and in this instance I think I am justified, do not you, my beauty? Uncle says brother Abbot was to leave the 20th of March, so that I shall soon see him, I trust, and he will be able to answer all the questions I should wish to ask. Now I shall be so impatient! The Empress of China is dead (or rather the mother of the Emperor), and all the people will have to mourn for a hundred days; the men are not allowed to shave for that space of time, so we shall have beautiful-looking servants.

July 22.—Uncle came home about five o'clock this morning. Brought me a long letter from my friend in Canton, humbly apologizing for all that has passed, expressing his regret, and lamenting the dreary prospect before him, deprived of all hope, etc. Having lost the powerful motive that has hitherto actuated him, he dares not hope that any of his good resolutions may be kept,—a whole sheet full of this, but I daresay "it is all in my eye," as the boys say. I feel my heart grows harder every day, my dear, and I am perfectly astonished when I think how differently I view all that has passed from what I did a few months since, and wonder what has produced the change. Why, in this instance, it is reflection, and a thorough conviction that all is best as it is. Circumstances I have no power to change, therefore it behooves me to suit myself to them. There, my dear, is not that philosophical, does it not meet with your highest approbation? This happy frame of mind which I happen to be in is owing to a perfect state of bodily health, which certainly has a great influence upon the moral — or mental — condition. How long it will last I will not pretend to say, but it shall be my aim to keep it, for I am tired of moping. It seems foolish to take out this book every morning to write you such uninteresting accounts of my days, but in the hope of coming to something better I go on through thick and thin, as I do when reading a dry book, fearing that I may lose something. So I go on from day to day, hoping to find out for what I was created, it seems impossible it can be only to pass my days in such a manner. I suppose there must be such beings in the world, if only to fill up the chinks, but I do wish, if I am only to fill up a chink, that I had had a quiet and contented spirit, and not so much ambition, put into me. Well, since such is the case, and Dame Fortune will treat me as she pleases, I will e'en amuse myself as much as possible, and "study to be quiet," as Saint Paul tells us. Every one is anxious for ships now, husbands expecting wives, brothers sisters; and sisters brothers and other friends. This is the return season, as all who went home two years ago must come back now. Moreover, all the English are anxious about the renewal of the charter.

August 6. — To-night the rain held up for a while, and Uncle and I went to the opera. We were very much pleased with the music, but, when it was time to go home, we looked out in despair. It was raining in torrents, nothing to be seen but water, and the chairs appeared to be swimming. The coolies with their enormous hats, wading up to their knees, and with lanterns in their hands, presented a curious picture. This was the scene below. Above, the heavens appeared to be one sheet of flame, for the lightning was incessant. What to do we did not know, — it seems the house has sunk, and all the drains were closed up, so that the water was all around it as far as we could see. It reminded me of the descriptions of Venice, and I took the chairs for gondolas. At last, as we despaired of the rain's ceasing, the gentlemen thought they would try to bring the chairs up the steps and back us down. I must confess I rather trembled at the prospect, knowing the steps were so wet and slippery. However, I presently heard "Miss L.'s chair stops the way," and I sallied forth with two gentlemen, I forget who, to meet my fate, whatever it might be, with all the courage of a heroine, in the midst of thunder, lightning, rain, and darkness, and the roaring of the Chinamen, which exceeded the thunder, for they all holloa together, and thereby hear nothing. I presently found myself shut up in my box, and going down the steps backwards, rather an awkward predicament, but I knew I must make the best of it, and kept perfectly still. When I got into the streets, I got along pretty well, till I found my lanterns had gone out, and I was left at the mercy of three Chinese coolies in the midst of the dark streets. However, they lighted the lanterns again, and I arrived at home safely, after much tribulation, my face the color of scarlet, and my head aching violently.

August 7.—This afternoon started for the Peña, the Campo was too wet. On the way we were stopped by a group of gentlemen to inquire after my health, after last night's frolic. In the group was a *ci-devant* admirer of mine who had the politeness (when he discovered who it was) to turn his back to me without speaking. This is the one who last year about this time vowed he would be my friend forever, if he could be no more. So this is the friendship of rejected lovers! Well, there is one comfort, I wish neither for his love nor his friendship, they are not worth the keeping. I was exceedingly amused at his folly, for he gave everybody reason to suppose what had happened. Came home and talked to Uncle about the Chinese, their cruelty, their recklessness of life, their belief concerning a future state, etc. It is almost impossible to know what they do believe, there is such a great variety of sects. What makes me think that some of them believe in transmigration was reading some letters to College, in which they said that, although they could not pay him for his services in this world, yet they would serve him as a *horse* in another, with many other expressions of the same kind. I recollect hearing a Hong merchant say that, if he should live again as a man, he would be a Chinaman, but, if a woman, he would be an Englishwoman. The other day I asked Achow where that Empress would go, that died recently. He said "to a good place." I asked, if she had been a bad woman, would she go to a good place? He said, "No, more good, more better." They are very superstitious about the place in which they bury their dead. Amwa, a merchant in Canton, whose mother died two years ago, has just found a satisfactory place to bury her in, having kept her above ground all that time, and it seems he was not very successful after all, for the late inundation came up within two feet of her grave, so that he was in great trouble, and obliged to have her taken up again. They endeavor to get the driest place possible, and have samples of the earth brought to them, that they may judge of it. The rich about Macao bury their dead on the tops of the highest hills, and put around the graves an immense deal of stonework. Caroline and I concluded the evening with one of our old-fashioned frolics. I don't know when I have laughed so much.

August 11.— Another week gone, and what is there to show it has been? To look back upon the past three or four months, they seem to me a perfect blank, or like a voyage at sea, nothing that I can remember with any particular pleasure, or a moment that I could wish to recall. It seems as though every feeling but hunger and the desire to sleep were extinct, and I almost fear they are, for I have almost done hoping that I shall be capable of feeling either pleasure or pain again, for it appears to me that it is only by the constant exercise of the feelings that they can be kept alive, they must die without nourishment. Did not go to church this morning, but took up a book which led me to reflect a great deal upon original sin, but I am too lazy now to give you the result of my reflections.

August 17. — We intended to have made some calls this morning, but, alas! we were made to feel our dependence. We called for chair-bearers, but they were not forthcoming, "no could catch." You might fancy from such an expression that they were wild beasts or birds, but no, poor creatures, they are far from that, but under bodily fear of every petty mandarin who has the honor of wearing a button. It seems the mandarins have come short in meeting their expenses, and so they have put an extra "squeeze" upon the poor bearers, and, until that is paid they forbid their carrying the chairs, and their poor backs would suffer sadly did they disobey the order. We cannot help pitying the poor wretches who are subject to such tyranny, but also feel annoyed that we are so dependent upon them, for we lost not only our calls in the morning, but our opera in the evening. Amused myself with the Memoirs of the Duchesse d'Abrantès, she is so perfectly French in her feelings and style of writing that I laugh heartily at times. It is truly a woman's book, that is, she is so minute, dwells a great deal upon "pretty white hands," "pearly teeth," "curling hair," and "white foreheads." There is a great deal of nonsense in the book, but upon the whole it gives you a good idea of the state of society at the time. It is more a history of private life than of public events.

August 20.—That good-for-nothing personage, the *Sotow*, has not yet recalled his order respecting the chair-bearers, but not choosing "to trust our charms to the perilous keeping of Caffre-men's arms," we made ourselves independent, and with the aid of Mr. G. got to the opera very comfortably on foot. It was a fine evening, but the pavements of the streets are horrible, they remind me often of "Old Paved Street" in Salem, in days of yore, but perhaps worse. The whole width of the street is very little wider than the sidewalk there, and paved in the same way. We had some fine music, and I enjoyed the opera much. Messrs. H. and G. walked home with us. How you would stare to see the exhibitions that we see in the streets! They are literally lined with sleeping Chinese and Caffres. They make "the cold flinty rock" their pillow, and lie there at the mercy of cockroaches and mosquitoes, though I much doubt whether the latter could make any impression upon their well-tanned hides.

August 22.—As usual, I spent the whole day at my books. Aunt L. was not well to-day, and so *bon gré, mal gré*, I must stay at home, for the idea of a spinster walking out alone is an enormity we never could be supposed guilty of. There is no gentleman here that I can call upon, and, even if there were, it would be another crime for me to go out unattended by a chaperon. Oh, hard is the lot of spinsters in Macao! Aunty and I fully agree upon these points, and I cannot enumerate the thousand little ways in which we are compelled to surrender our own wills to those of other people. I verily think, if I were condemned to live here for ten years, I should go crazy! After dinner I had the pleasure of receiving letters from home. They were satisfactory, inasmuch as they assured me of your health, for which I thank God most sincerely, but they refer to old letters, and you do not at all seem to feel that it is a long time since I heard from you. From October to May is a great space. However, I shall wait patiently till I can see Abbot. You tell me you are married with as much indifference as though you told me you had dined. I should be most happy to know when A. sailed, but that I cannot find out. Our boys all seem to be separating, to seek their fortunes here, there, and everywhere. Now, my dear, I have come to the end of another book. I tremble for some of the last, as I know I have expressed my sentiments often, and perhaps not fully enough to be understood. I have regretted this sometimes, as I think they may lead my dear father to suppose that my morals are more corrupt than they really are. Not that I should mind your all knowing every sentiment of my heart if I could but talk and explain, but in writing one often gives a different sense for want of explanation. I hope you will all make due allowances, and believe I mean well, whatever I may chance to write.

BOOK VII.

August 24–29. — Are you not tired, my dear, of my importunity? For such it may be called, I think, when it comes to the seventh volume, and, now that all the delightful cares of matrimony are coming thick upon you, I sadly fear I shall not receive such patient attention as heretofore. It has been a burning hot day; about two o'clock the breeze strengthened, and there was every prospect of a visitation from one of the Typhoon family; by seven very little doubt about it, as Achow says, "It's Typhoon *he own*," that is, himself. We were watching the destruction of our comforts, which were vanishing like chaff before the wind. One after another of our mats flew off, and the tiles came tumbling from the roof, and destroyed our grotto, that monument of our industry. The unsparing hands of the coolies pulled down my pretty vines to save the pots from destruction. The severity of the gale was over before ten o'clock, and I hope it was not so bad as that of last year. But I feel so anxious about Abbot that I cannot be easy, he has been out now five months, and it is quite time he was here. Went to bed, but not to sleep, for the house seemed like a perfect Babel; the wind blew a tremendous gale from the south-east, and although the windows were bolted and lashed and fastened in every possible way, it seemed as though they could not stand the force of the wind. Now this morning it continues, and the house is as dark as Erebus. I have got my Venetians tilted a little, so that I can just see to write. The Chinese say it will be worse to-morrow. The house rocks now like a cradle.

30*th*.—This morning found us still in bed at half-past nine. Having had no sleep the night before, and the house being dark as midnight, we did not awake. The wind is still blowing furiously, and it is raining in torrents. Aunt L. and my little bird and I sit all day long in one corner of the room at the only window from which we can get any light, our only interruption being the coolie coming with his tub and cloth to save us from drowning, for windows in China are not made to keep out rain, and every now and then we find ourselves in a pond of water. But the coolie discovers our situation by its dripping through (to his quarters below), and comes to our relief. I can easily fancy a person in prison becoming attached to a spider after a time. I am sure I should feel quite melancholy without my bird. He seems to get very pensive now and then, but then again he says, like his mistress, "What is the use of sighing?" and cheers us with a merry song. To think, my dear sis, of your sister living without a care but that of feeding a bird, she who spent her young days as one of the most diligent of her sex! Well, I look back to those days with pleasure, and would willingly have as much to do now.

September 9.—This morning, while we were at breakfast, who should come in but Uncle, looking like death. Poor soul! I never saw a person so altered in so short a time, but I daresay Macao air will soon restore him. He had landed a long way out, having got very impatient in the boat, and had walked so far that he was quite faint when he came in, but before night he looked better. College came to see him, and I hope will soon cure him. Canton is now in a terrible state; the river has risen so high that it has completely deluged whole villages above the city, the houses have fallen in, many thousands of Chinamen have been killed, and the rice is ruined. They cannot move out of their Hongs in Canton except in boats; Uncle says the water was up to their doors.

September 11.—We were all just comfortably in bed to-night, when I heard the outer door open, and soon after a knock at my own door, and in a second I was in my brother's arms. How rejoiced I was I leave you to imagine. The thought that after all my anxiety he had arrived safely, and the strange feeling of seeing one of my brothers here, and the excitement altogether, quite drove sleep from my eyes. He brought me oceans of letters, but I left them till morning.

12*th.*—Got up early, and ordered a bath for Abbot, and the barber, which was very necessary, for his head and face were enveloped in a mass of hair of four months' growth, and you could scarcely discern his features. He is as brown as a mulatto, and has grown a little taller, otherwise I see no change. He is astonished at Uncle's appearance, but thinks that, with the exception of having lost my color, I have not altered at all. I have never passed so happy a day in China, with such genuine home feelings. If Uncle were only well! I have at last found out that you were married just four days before Caroline. Rather singular that we should both have been engaged in wedding preparations in such different parts of the world! I have talked to A. all day, and now feel acquainted with you all; you will not be such strangers to me when I come home. Dr. College says that Uncle requires great care, and that it will not do for him to go back to Canton for at least six weeks. I am astonished to hear Abbot say he does not like reading. I thought he was fond of it, but I find business is his ruling passion, and he is already impatient to get to Canton and begin operations. Received your wedding-cake this morning, my dear, it is super-excellent, I never tasted better.

September 23.— Abbot left us for Canton at ten o'clock this morning, and it is hard to have him go, for I may not see him again for five or six years, but he was quite impatient to be employed, and I could keep him no longer. Uncle went out in a chair to-day for the first time, he is much better.

26*th*.—We spent the evening in talking about going home. Only think, to leave here in January!

I have hardly dared to believe the hints I have heard to that effect before, but now I think it is Uncle's intention, if possible. Oh! how delighted I shall be, and I feel almost sure the long sea voyage will restore Uncle's health!

October 5. — College told Uncle to-day that he could not leave this place too soon, that the northerly winds that are coming are too bracing, and that he thinks the voyage home *may* restore him. I wish he could leave at once, but there would be a disadvantage in that, because we should get to the coast in a bad month. We feel very anxious, as the north winds that have begun blowing make him very uncomfortable. Oh, how I long to be among you, it seems as though I could hardly wait! Had a letter from A. this morning, and wrote him one in return. We keep up a pretty steady fire. I admire his stability of character, and prudence. I think he bids fair to make a sterling man.

October 9. — College told Aunt L. this morning that she could not get her husband off too soon, that he never would be any better here, so we may get off in a month. Busy all the morning cutting out work, but the thought of the end in view softened all my labors, and I would willingly wear the skin off my fingers, were it necessary, for the sake of leaving this place. Uncle expresses great astonishment at my industry, and hopes it will continue. I only want a motive to exertion, and no one is more active. Am sadly afraid I shall not be able to fill up this book before we go, for want of ideas, as they are all concentrated at the present time on linen and a sea voyage. So, my dear, you must not expect much. Finished Uncle's flannel jackets at ten o'clock this evening, and glad I am, for I am quite tired of the sight of them. We could not give them to the tailors, for they smoke everything they take, and, unless the things are to be washed, it is very unpleasant.

October 19.— Dined at Caroline's, with Captain and Mrs. H. She is a very pleasant woman. She struck us rather singularly, as she had her hair dressed in the new style,* as plain as possible, parted on the forehead, and put up plain or braided on the top of the head in a round lump, and two little "spit curls," as Mrs. Trollope says, at the side. She has a small face, and, after the eye became accustomed to this style, it did not look so badly, but it would be very trying to most faces. Uncle seems very feeble to-day, owing to having leeches on last night.

24*th.*— Uncle sent up this afternoon to have our passages taken by the "Waterloo," sailing the middle of November. He is obliged to give up the hope of going to Canton again, which is a great disappointment to him, but everything must yield to illness.

October 28.—This morning went to work at packing directly after breakfast, and was on my feet till three. Am happy to inform you that I have found the use of both my feet and my hands, and display

* The style still prevalent was masses of large puffs on each side of the face and very large, high combs.—*Ed.*

much less reluctance in packing now than when I last thought of spending four months on the water. We have enough to do, I assure you, packing things to send home, things for the voyage, and things to make ready for auction and for England, besides attending to Uncle and writing for him.

31st. — The last day of October. This time last year I was at Lintin, how everything has changed since then! Went to dine with Caroline, she had Dr. Bennett there, a famous phrenologist, who is travelling about the world. He is exceedingly agreeable, and we had considerable conversation upon different subjects. He says he is well acquainted with L. E. L. (Miss Landon), the poetess, and told her character very correctly. He says she is a most agreeable person when she pleases, but is sometimes quite the reverse. She has great talents, but is dreadfully satirical, and exceedingly fond of flattery. Dr. Bennett is acquainted with all the literary people of note in England, and gave me a little sketch of the characters of many whose works I am acquainted with, Mrs. Hemans, Mrs. Norton, Miss Jewsbury (lately married), Mr. Bulwer, etc. He spoke of Dr. Spurzheim, who died in America, and of his great talents. Says he was most eloquent as a lecturer, but not so great a practical phrenologist as many others.

November 2.—A dreadfully hot, oppressive day, thermometer standing about 84°. A. sent me a pair of Chinawoman's shoes, which I shall bring or send home for your first girl. They will fit her when she is about a week old. It seems incredible that they can wear such things, but I have seen them as small upon the Campo. After dinner wrote letters for Uncle, and began the work of destruction in my own room by tearing up two large baskets full of them, which made me sad, but it is impossible to keep them all. I have not yet torn up one-third, and not one of my really valuable ones.

November 9.— Busy this morning preparing a bonnet for sea. Mr. C. and Captain R. called, and I talked till my throat was sore. These Yankees do make such unconscionable morning visits that they quite wear one's patience out. I had exhausted all my stock of small talk, and was indebted to the boy's setting the table at last, which saved me from being "hard up," as the sailors say. Abbot has come down from Canton, with Uncle James Low. He looks pale, and thinner than when he went up, but he is very well, and it is only the effect of living in dark Hongs where they never see the sun. They quite put us ladies to the blush, they look so much more delicate. [To "look delicate" was the height of a young lady's ambition, at this period.— *Ed.*]

12*th.*— This morning we sallied forth "to see the world, and falter out Adieu." Saying adieu in this place is not like saying it in most others; it is true that people do not care much about each other, and do not pretend to, and in saying good-bye there is more envy than anything else in the feelings of those who stay, so they all congratulate you, and hope their turn will come next. Still, say what you will, it is not pleasant to leave the most indifferent with the thought that it is the last time we may ever meet.

November 16.— I am nearly all packed up, and think to-morrow my book must be. I hope my next will be more full of incidents, and therefore more interesting. I shall have no time to write any more letters till I get on board our "Castle." Think, my dear, of a ship of thirteen hundred tons! You never saw such a one. The accommodations are fine, and I think of it with pleasure. Captain Roundy arrived after dinner. It is very odd, he has been with us at all our embarkations, and has now come to see us safe off. He is one of our best friends, I think, and so few deserve the name that they are worth keeping who are such. Mr. Chinnery called this afternoon to bid us good-bye. Spent the evening with Caroline. Felt very *triste*, and I am sure they all thought me very stupid. To-morrow we shall be packing up, and on Tuesday we shall probably go on board, there to remain till we reach St. Helena, which will find us much nearer home than we are now. The one prime object is to restore Uncle's health; for that, as well as for everything else, we must rely solely on the One Being who orders all things. My daily prayer is that we may all live to meet once more in our own land, where we can dwell with those whom we call our own. I am tired of living among strangers, as

I have often told you before, and I sigh to be again at home.

Thus finishes my life in China. It is useless to make reflections upon it, suffice it to say that it has been like everything else, variable. Clouds will rise wherever we are, and the sun will shine, and I can say has very often shone upon me in China. Therefore with gratitude for all the peace and quiet I have enjoyed, and hoping the troubles will serve for my good, I close my book, and trust myself to Him

> " Who has spread out the skies
> And measured the depths of the sea."

BOOK VIII.   PART I.

ON BOARD HON. E. I. C. SHIP "WATERLOO,"
NOV. 19, 1833–JAN. 13, 1834.

"Once more upon the waters, yet once more."

Nov. 19, 1833.—Left Macao this morning at nine o'clock, with brother A. and various friends to see us off, and after a little squeeze by the mandarins, and satisfying the boat-girls, we made sail, and left Macao I trust forever. Four years' residence there cools one's love of it, and I for one give up all the pleasures and comforts it does possess without a sigh.   I shall often think of it, and with much pleasure; time, like the grave, will bury many of the thousand annoyances I had there, and I trust it was not all time spent in vain.   But to proceed with our voyage.   Our "Lorcha" made sail with a fair wind, cool and delightful, and we were alongside our "Castle," which sat like a rock in the water, at eleven o'clock.   Our party was all cheerful, none of us was at all seasick, we were whipped on board, our friends saw us safe in our cabins in the midst of tons of baggage, and had only time to say a few words, as the boatmen hurried them off, and our ship was soon under way.   Well, we have to make the best of these things, and with a few tears, and a wave of my handkerchief as they passed our stern, I lost sight of them all in a few minutes. God bless them! We were soon obliged to give orders about our cabins, everything must be "cleeted" and "lashed," to keep them from "fetching away," and the most must be made of the room. Fortunately, we remained pretty well till about dark, as the ship was steady, and the sea very smooth, but the wind increased, and we were very glad to seek our couches. Poor Uncle, sick as he was, was the only one not quite helpless, and, instead of our nursing him, he was obliged to turn nurse himself.

November 20. — I awoke this morning, but with no desire to move, speak, or look at anything; I was sure I was alive, but I cared very little whether I remained so, or whether any one else did. I defy any one, even the most brilliant colorist, to depict the horrors of seasickness. *O tempora, O mores!* I shall never forget this day!

November 22. — To-day, finding ourselves much better, we dressed, and went to the "cuddy" table to dinner. Methinks I hear you query, "What, or where, is the cuddy?" Well, I can only tell you that in land phraseology it is the dining-room, a room that goes the whole width of the ship (with the exception of a small cabin off at one end), in front of our rooms. We met at table here the captain, the first and second officers, the purser, the doctor, two other passengers, and a little sick boy, named Johnny. We were introduced to those we were not already acquainted with, and relished our dinner very well, felt marvellously refreshed and comforted. Poor Uncle is not well enough to come out, and is obliged to dine alone. After dinner we went upon the poop and had tea, a clear sky above us, and about eight thousand yards of canvas to waft us along, assisted by a good breeze. I enjoyed the perfect order of the ship, everything goes on with so little noise that it is really surprising when you consider there are one hundred and fifty men on board. Have read a little to-day, for the first time, and begin to feel like myself.

November 30. — The cool breeze lasted till about ten this morning, when it died away, and now it is as hot as possible; it is difficult to breathe, the air is so close. When I got up and looked to see what I could see, I discovered the long low coast of Sumatra on one side, stretching a long distance without any inequality of surface as far as the eye could reach. The island of Banca on the other side presents hills and valleys, which is far more agreeable to the eye. There was also a brig in sight, which we soon left astern, and a Chinese junk, which looked quite natural. We were obliged to anchor about six, as the wind was quite gone, and we were drifting on to the Sumatra shore. I could see with the glass that this coast is completely covered with wood, not a habitation is to be seen, indeed it is nothing but a marsh, and the trees come actually into the water. A hot night, went below and thought I should certainly not sleep, but I threw myself down and slept soundly till seven o'clock, and they *fiddled*, weighed anchor, and made sail, and I knew nothing of it.

December 2. — By the help of squalls and a favorable tide, we managed to get out of the Straits about two. Passed the shoals safely, but had several narrow escapes. Had a most uncomfortable night, for in addition to the heat we had a quantity of mosquitoes, which we took in at Banca, as souvenirs, I suppose, of that delightful place. They were buzzing about all night.

December 4. — When I got out of bed this morning, it was blowing a little gale, with a great deal of rain and very heavy thunder and lightning. However, we are steering our course and getting on, and anything is better than a calm. After dinner I thought I heard the ship's bell tolling, and, opening our door to see what it was, I saw everybody assembled at the gangway, about to consign one of our men to a watery grave. We were not aware that he had died, but it seems he had been sick ever since he left England, and died this morning about six. The captain read the burial service over the body, and then it was consigned to the deep, and all went on as before. Such an event to a thoughtful mind calls forth solemn reflections, but it has much less effect here than on one of our small ships, for among so many one is not missed. There is something awful in the sound of the last splash, though.

December 5. — Went on deck this morning to look at a ship which was approaching us. She proved to be an American, but we were braced sharp on the wind, and could not go near her. I wish you would make my compliments to General Jackson, and request him to order our ships to learn to *talk*. The English ships all have "Marryat's signals,"* which enable them to converse on any subject (even metaphysics), but our ships have not arrived at that pitch of perfection. This was a large ship, but she had no bunting, and was dumb.

December 6. — Got under weigh this morning (after being at anchor all night), with a strong head wind. A fine morning, and we had a pleasant run to Anjer, where we anchored at twelve o'clock. The scenery about here is very beautiful, the land very high, and covered with verdure. Along the coast grow cocoanuts and plantains, and it is such a contrast to all that we have seen in China that it is quite enchanting to our eyes. The purser went on shore as soon as we arrived, carried our letters, and procured all the good things he could find, but brought us no news. Plenty of *proas* lying alongside, bringing fruits of different kinds, monkeys, birds, shells, etc. The Malays disfigure themselves, to our eyes, by chewing betel-nut, which makes their teeth quite black, but they do not consider themselves presentable until their teeth are black, and filed off besides. What different ideas different nations have of beauty, as well as everything else! Everything looks just as it did when we were here before, but then our feelings were different, and all was novel. The captain and most of the

---

* A system of signals invented by Captain Marryat, the famous novelist. Born 1792; died 1848.— *Ed.*

others went on shore after dinner, and wished me to go with them, but Aunt L. could not leave Uncle, and I did not like to go without her, and besides they were going to sail, which I dislike very much. The captain is disappointed at not getting any more passengers, but they were not forthcoming. The town looks very pretty from the ship, and after dark the fishermen make fires all along the shore to attract the fish, which has a very pretty effect.

December 7. — Had a fine run out of the Straits of Sunda to-day. Passed very near the Island of Cockatoo, which is the prettiest spot I have seen for some time. It was completely covered with woods and quite green; one high peak, with lower hills around it, was beautiful. Before night we had a strong breeze, and were very sure that we were once more at sea, and shall probably have to undergo another siege of seasickness. How many times have I wished with the sailor that, "if Britannia ruled the waves, she'd rule them straighter"!

December 10. — Still going on well, though by squalls. It blows ten furies, and then dies away. Uncle does not seem so much better as I thought he would in this cooler weather. His symptoms are no better, and I feel quite discouraged at times. I heard the ship's bell tolling again this morning, and another body was consigned to the deep. We have sixteen now on the sick list. I am almost tired of walking at an angle of forty-five degrees, and fetching up in a corner, but I will not complain, for we have been highly favored in regard to weather.

December 14. — A fine breeze still, and we have made a good week's work of it. We were very fortunate in taking the trades so soon after leaving Anjer, which we did not expect to do at this season. We have run over one thousand three hundred miles this week, and have three thousand and some hundreds yet to run before reaching the Cape, which, if we average two hundred miles a day, we can do in three weeks. Uncle has asked the captain to-day to leave us at the Cape, as the climate and accommodations will be much better there than at St. Helena. The captain has been wanting an excuse to stop there, and thinks this will do, but has not yet decided. The doctor thinks it would be much the best thing. Uncle proposed that I should leave them at the Cape, and either go to St. Helena, to wait for Uncle James, or go on to England, but I should be unwilling to leave him in his present state, although I would jump at the proposal, could I see him in a fair way to recover.

December 17. — A rainy day, and quite calm, going only two knots part of the time, a state of weather very disagreeable in itself, but in these latitudes made doubly so by often being the precursor of a gale. So you see, my dear, we run from one danger to another, we have left the rocks and shoals behind us for the present, and we are now in these tempestuous seas, nearly in the latitude of the Isles of France and Bourbon, where they have tremendous hurricanes. This reminds me of the affecting story of "Paul and Virginia," which deeply interested us both in our childish days. These hurricanes are very sudden; a year or two since, the "Duneira" an English ship, had her three masts snapped off in five minutes; they sometimes last an hour, and not a cloud to be seen. The captain told us to-day that he had made up his mind to leave us at the Cape, so we shall have the chance (if we live to arrive) of trying that climate for Uncle. He is very feeble to-day. I do not mention him daily, but you may judge how many of our thoughts are given to his condition. I am happy to inform you, my dear, that I got a new idea at dinner to-day, which I am glad to impart to you, and which I think surpasses anything a spinster ever dreamed of, and that is, that *sugar* is extracted from old clothes! Query: how many old coats and shirts would it take to sweeten a cup of coffee? After this, I shall not be surprised at anything. I must confess I could not restrain an incredulous laugh, but the asserter of this marvellous fact says it is veritable.

December 27.— Fair morning and good breeze, but pitching in a most inhuman manner. Have been reading Boswell's "Tour in the Hebrides with Dr. Johnson," and find it very interesting, but I cannot understand how a man of Boswell's abilities could have been such a shadow to Johnson; it appears to have been a complete infatuation on his part. I think, begging his pardon, that the doctor must have been a disagreeable companion. I find that Johnson complained of his exile of a month or two in those islands, and begged Boswell to return, that he might "commence existence again"; it is a waste of life, he said. Do you know, I begin to think I was justified in complaining of my residence in Macao? I wonder what the old doctor would have said, had he been shut up there for four or five years? He says a ship is as bad as a jail, with the fear of being drowned in addition.

December 30. — A splendid run of two hundred and fifty-four miles since noon yesterday, with which the captain professes himself satisfied. Went on deck after having read an hour in what seems to me a very silly book, "Contarini Fleming." I fancied it ought to be good, because it was written by the author of "Vivian Grey." Talked and walked awhile with the captain. We were very much amused by the sailors, who were manufacturing a donkey. We saw this thing walking round the capstan, and it afforded us a good laugh. Two men composed it, with something thrown over them, and swabs, old shoes, and a variety of other things seemed to make up the animal. It had two panniers by its sides, and was ridden by a monkey. The poor thing seemed to have less amusement than any one, as it was tied on, and its hands were tied behind it. Speaking of monkeys, the sailors have fifty or sixty on board, and it is very amusing to see them frisking about. They never come aft.

Jan. 1, 1834. — "Pleasant, with light airs," *à la* Log-book. I therefore, with like pleasure and calmness, wish you all, my dear friends, a happy New Year, and hope that next time I may do it *in propria persona.* My thoughts have often wandered to you to-day, my dear sister, and I have wondered whether married ladies sit for company to-day, or whether it is only for spinsters. The captain says he expects to land us at the Cape in a week. Oh, dear! I don't want to go among strangers again, but it must be done! Went on deck after dinner, a glorious evening. It is not dark now till eight o'clock, and light again at four, so our nights are very short.

January 4. — I was awakened this morning by the pelting of books, which came into my couch by dozens from a book-shelf over my head. Thanks to my good condition I had no bones broken. A violent gale began about four this morning, and continued to blow with great violence till twelve, when it gradually diminished. I will not pretend to say that I saw much of the sublime outside, but I can vouch for the ridiculous inside. Had I not been violently sick, I might have enjoyed the sport, but I defy any one to be amused with anything in such a situation. I did manage to look out of my windows, and the sea was one sheet of foam, and our great ship seemed trembling for its safety. The wind was dead ahead, and we only had three storm-sails set, all the usual sails were furled. The sky was perfectly clear, and the air pure and dry, with the thermometer between 68° and 70° all day.

January 7. — A dead calm. Seven weeks to-day since we embarked; we thought to have been at the

Cape to-day, but there is a chance, if this weather holds, that we may be here a week longer. Some of our officers have been nine weeks getting round the Cape. Our luck seems to have blown away in the gale. The black cats are petted, but all to no effect. Our captain pretends to have great faith in these creatures, but he is far too sensible a man to put faith in such superstitions. However, they (the black cats) are always treated with great respect, while the poor tortoise-shell cat is sadly abused, if she goes farther aft than the mainmast.

January 11. — A nearly fair wind. The captain thinks, if the wind holds, that we shall see the Cape of Good Hope to-morrow morning. I cannot realize as yet that we are going on shore again; while we have nothing in sight but sea and sky it seems impossible. Went on deck after dinner, and found Cape Agulhas nearly abreast of us; it is low land, and takes its name from its resemblance to an eagle.

January 12. — A fine day, with a fresh, fair breeze. Looked out after breakfast, and found we had the Cape of "Good Hope" nearly abeam. Attended prayers on deck, being Sunday, then went to look at the chart. We are sailing past rapidly. Table Mountain was covered, as the captain says, "with a cloth," which looked light and airy, but is said to be the sure sign of a south-east gale. This mountain is 3,582 feet high; I wonder if I shall ever attempt its summit. Our abode will be at the foot of it. The land all along here is black and barren; not a trace of a shrub or anything green have we seen as yet; not much to be wondered at perhaps, when we think of the scorching suns and the bleak winds that are continually playing over it. The purser will go on shore to-night, and get some accommodations for us, and we shall land to-morrow morning. I almost dread it for Uncle, he is so weak, but we must trust to Providence; we do what we think for the best, and I hope he will benefit by it. After I wrote the above, and we came nearer the shore, there was enough to delight the eye. We anchored about four o'clock. The health boat came off, told us of the annihilation of the E. I. Company's charter as a trading body, of the abolition of slavery in the West Indies, and various other matters, but nothing of America. Query: Where is the English government to get £20,000,000 sterling for the emancipation of her slaves? Well, never mind that. It will be proper, before I proceed, to say what I think of Cape Town as seen in the distance. It has a most singular appearance, the land is so curiously formed. Table Mountain is directly back of the town, and well deserves its name. Its top is so flat that it actually looks as though it had been planed off, its sides, apparently, are rugged and barren. There is a very curious peak near it called the "Cloof" I believe. The town itself looks pretty, and more like civilization than anything I have seen for a long time. Table Bay is not deep, and is a shelter for ships only in the south-east monsoon, or trade-winds. A most lovely evening. Took my last walk on the "Water-loo" with the captain and Mr. C. Never shall I forget her, though, every one has been so kind and attentive that I shall **hold them all** in grateful remembrance.

PART II.

CAPE TOWN, JAN. 13 TO MAY 5, 1834.

January 13. — This morning the air feels sharp and cool, and reminds me of our delightful May mornings in America; it brought the color into my cheeks at once, and it actually seemed as though I was breathing my own native air. We breakfasted at half-past seven, and had ourselves and our baggage put into the boats. Uncle had a couch arranged so he could be put on shore very comfortably. We were landed at the jetty about nine, and a coachman walked up to us, and said the carriage was ready. A novel sound to us, for we have not seen a carriage for nearly five years. Nevertheless, we jumped into it, and drove to our boarding-house. Everything looks strange, of course, but, though I do not feel at home yet, I feel as though I was nearer to it. I shall never be able to tell you of all the strange things I have seen, but here I am, on Afric's shores, and by degrees you will know how and where we live. To describe my feelings would be impossible, they were so mixed; you may imagine them if you can.

We drove to our boarding-house then, and were introduced to a very pretty and genteel young lady, whose name I learned was Crugwagen. Her mother, who is a widow with two daughters, keeps the establishment. The daughters speak English, and have the charge of things. They had a breakfast ready for us which we could not resist. Oh! the delicious bread and butter, the tempting apricots, figs, and grapes! We are just in time for fruit of all kinds. Soon after breakfast we had the pleasure of seeing a Highland regiment pass, and hearing the most delightful band; it seemed as though all our senses were to be regaled at once. I was in a maze, I assure you; I sat at the window all day long, gazing out. Every one seemed so busy, and there were so many people moving about. What astonished us most was to see ladies so plentiful, and walking about so briskly in the middle of the day. Our officers were in and out all the morning, but at two went on board, after having bid us adieu. Had a delightful dinner, and such an appetite! After dinner, as the carriage was at our disposal for the day, and Uncle felt too tired to go out, the two young ladies and I had a delightful drive. We went to Green Point, and saw the "Waterloo," some way out and with all her sails set. God bless them all! Stopped on our way home and got some splendid flowers, mignonette, heliotrope, and a thousand others that I have no names for. The weather is delightful; the people here call it warm, but we do not. I noticed, while driving, a hill covered with geranium growing wild. We passed some lovely little cottages with grape-vines growing over them, forming such a pretty contrast with the white houses. The houses all have flat roofs, and at first had a very odd appearance, but I begin to like it.

January 14.— Dr. Murray called this morning to see Uncle. Says he must go directly into the country where he will have finer air, and that he is to have no medicine, but to eat everything good, in fact to live on the fat of the land, which is rich enough, I assure you. I do hope Dr. Murray will cure Uncle, I really have hope again, he is a most skilful physician. After dinner I went to walk with Miss F. in the Company's Gardens, a most delightful shady walk, very extensive, and with two rows of oaks on each side. It is laid out in large squares, and turfed, and seems to be the resort of ladies and gentlemen and children.

January 16.— Am still amused looking out of the windows, and watching the variety of faces, African, Hottentot, and Caffres, all ugly enough in their way. The ladies all look alike, that is their dresses. We find ourselves quite *outré*, but I do not care much. Miss Crugwagen and I dressed and went shopping this morning, a thing I have not done for five years. I made poor work at it, for I did not understand their money at all. Rix-dollars and schellings are new to me. We went to Mr. Vallet's Museum, and saw a great collection of stuffed animals, birds, and snakes, natives of this country, and a great variety of insects and butterflies from Rio, but among all the birds I saw none to equal Mr. Beale's bird of Paradise. The new governor, Sir Benjamin D'Urban, his lady and suite, landed this morning, and there has been such a running to and fro by the slaves to get a peep at him; they all fancy they are to be liberated at once. Poor creatures, they will never be so comfortable and well off as they are now, in my opinion! In this family they are treated more like children than servants, I never saw anything to exceed the kindness.

January 17. — A south-west wind blowing, which is considered very bad for invalids. Poor Uncle soon felt the ill effect of it. The clouds of sand were so thick that we could not see across the street. We were obliged to close every window, and even then the sand came in. The south-east winds, they say, are much worse. I have often heard of them. Every place, as well as everybody, must have its "something."

19*th.* — Sunday, and a rainy morning. Went to the English service, which is held at eleven, the church is just opposite our house. Heard a pretty good sermon, and was delighted with the organ. I heard one of the familiar tunes we used to sing. I cannot tell you how pleased and yet how sad I felt. The English, I am astonished to find, have been in-debted to the Dutch for the use of their church for the last twenty years, and have just begun to build one. Sunday is very strictly observed here, the town was as still as Salem on Sunday, at Macao the day was just like any other.

January 21. — I wish you could take a peep at our breakfast table, we have seven different kinds of fruit upon it, and the most delicious ones of all, green and purple grapes, fresh figs, pears, apricots, peaches, green gages, and damson plums, and sometimes mulberries, then, besides, we have the most delicious bread and butter, etc., so you may judge that I eat a good breakfast. I expect before long to be a "dicker fatty," as the Dutch say. I have such sport with this language! I hear it constantly spoken here, but I doubt if I ever speak it; I have tried to pronounce many words, but they are so guttural I cannot. The above and one other word make the chief of my Dutch vocabulary at present. This morning being very fine, Aunt L. went into the country to Kirstenbosch, to see the house where we intend going as soon as the doctor thinks best. I stayed at home to take care of Uncle, who certainly seems much better. Spent the evening upon the "stoop," amusing myself with Dutch words.

January 29. — Finished packing this morning, and made ready to leave our kind friends, and go again among strangers, however I am not long in making myself at home anywhere now. I shall never forget the kindness of this family. We bade them good-bye about half-past three, and, accompanied by Dr. Murray, had a most delightful ride through one of the most charming countries I ever saw. Nature seems to have done her best to bring all things to perfection, and to have concentrated them all here. The tall pines and magnificent oaks that line the roads are larger than those in our own forests, the "silver tree" grows in great abundance and looks very beautiful, and there is a great variety of heaths in full flower to delight the eye, and "any quantity" of blackberries might have delighted the taste, could we have stopped to get them. We arrived at Kirstenbosch about half-past four; it is a most delightful little thatched cottage situated on the side of the mountain, and, being high up, we have a fine view of the country around us. We were kindly received by our host, hostess, and daughter, a very genteel and respectable family, who all speak English. The air is very different here from that in town, cool and bracing, and I do hope it may be beneficial to Uncle. He bore the ride well, and is quite comfortable after it. We are upon the other side of the mountain now, and not exposed to the south-easters, nor so much scorched by the sun. There is a vast difference in the two, I assure you. Dr. Murray left us after having seen us safely landed, and we surveyed the premises. My room would look quite English, were it not for the floor of Dutch tiles. It opens on to the "stoop," in front of which the roses are blooming in great abundance. I took a short walk with Miss Eksteen to one of the most romantic little spots I ever saw. We went through their gardens to a fountain, where there is a fine spring of water. They have planted a seat under the shade of a weeping-willow, from which there is a most lovely view in the distance, and no sound was heard but that of the turtle-dove in the forest behind us. We passed through the vineyard where grapes of every kind are growing, and came back to the cottage with a splendid collection of flowers. Nature is certainly most bountiful to this part of Africa. We passed a very pleasant evening in company with this interesting family, which consists of Mr. and Mrs. Eksteen, a noble-looking couple, and three nice daughters and one son under sixteen. They have an English tutor, who lives in the family, and made one of our group this evening. The young ladies gave us a little music, and then we retired.

January 30. — A cloudy morning, but cool and comfortable. I feel once more as though I had my liberty, which is a very happy feeling, so I ranged through the orchard and picked blackberries, which are large and nice, and admired everything I saw, and then came in to my books. Mr. Eksteen killed a hyena last night near the house. To support my assertion a few pages back, that every place has its "sussin," as the old woman said, I must tell you what this has, millions of fleas, as large (Aunt L. says) as *coach-horses*. Now no doubt this is exaggerated, but I assure you they have power enough, whatever their size may be, to make me exceedingly uncomfortable, and to disturb my repose. Uncle says he should have no amusement if it were not for them, but I must confess I am too much fretted by them to be pleased.

After dinner I went to walk with Mr. E. and all the children, I cannot say where, but I know that we brought home some beautiful flowers, some pears, and some lemons. Although it is said to be not yet the season for flowers, you cannot take a step without finding them. The flowering heaths were very fine, there are seven hundred different kinds about here. Dr. Murray told me his wife had painted over a hundred varieties.

February 1. — Oh, such a lovely morning! I was up at six, the birds were singing, but all besides was still and quiet as possible. How much pleasanter than the town, where there is nothing heard but the rattling of carts and carriages, and the noise of the Dutchmen's whips! By the by, these said whips are worthy of note. Coming from the country over mountains and sandy plains, with loads of wine, they are obliged to have an immense team, I have often seen ten yoke of enormous oxen. A boy runs ahead, and guides the first pair with a rope, while the driver sits upon the wagon far aft, and wields this immense whip, which reaches to the foremost oxen. You can judge of its length; I should think it required much strength of arm even to hold it, and I am told it requires a great knack to use it.

2d. — A beautiful Sunday morning, and, as we had no temple to worship in, I thought it best to go to the woods, where none but pure and holy feelings can be excited, so Miss E. and myself first went to the orchard, and admired the ripening fruits, and then got our bonnets and books, and went to *la belle fontaine*, where we spent two hours very pleasantly.

We had the lemon, the citron, and the loquat to shade us from the sun and to shed their fragrance upon the breeze. The birds were making music in the branches, and everything was so still around us that one could not but adore the Author and Disposer of all.

After dinner we took a very pleasant walk "over the hills and far away," and came back loaded with flowers, among them a white rose, which smelt of home; I have not seen one before since I left America. There are many things here that recall that blest place to my mind. Dr. Bailey has been to-day, and finds Uncle much better. He puts great faith in a Caffre medicine Uncle is taking now, made of herbs from the Caffre country. It would seem to me little short of a miracle if he were restored. Dr. Bailey says the heat has been intolerable in town for the last few days, while we have been delightfully cool and comfortable here.

February 4.— The wind this morning is burning hot, as though it had blown over fire, and answers to all the descriptions we have had of the simoon of the desert. My face felt quite scorched passing along the stoop to breakfast. Uncle has been very ill to-day, much weaker. We were obliged to keep quite close to-day and shut all the glass to keep the air out. Dr. Murray was out after dinner. He says the heat is intense in town, 96° this morning in the house, and 90° at night; this beats China, but it is very uncommon.

February 8.— After dinner to-day, Mrs. E., the young ladies and myself walked to Newlands, formerly the residence of Lord Charles Somerset, while Governor here. Mr. Crugwagen, the present owner, told me that Lord Charles spent £70,000 upon it, and that he bought it for £3,000. The grounds are very extensive. After walking through immense avenues of fine trees, we ascended a hill, which is flattened, and excavated to a depth of some twenty feet, forming a basin, at the bottom of which is a fine spring of water, constantly running summer and winter, and supplying two mills. There is a broad gravelled walk around this basin, where seats and tables are placed for loungers and picnic parties; on each side rows of tall trees arch over the walk and the fountain. It is a most romantic place. On our way to the house we regaled ourselves with grapes and peaches, and, after having gathered a handsome bouquet, Mr. E. drove us home. I was talking with Mr. Jones (the tutor) after dinner about the missionaries. He says the Moravians and the Wesleyan Methodists are the most numerous.

February 11. — After dinner Miss E., myself, and Mr. Jones mounted horses, and went a long way up the mountain, had a fine view of the country around us, and the sea in the distance. I had no idea it was so near. Heard the noise of the baboons, which are numerous on the mountain, and sometimes come down into the orchard. After letting our horses breathe a little, we turned their heads, and took a good canter nearly down to Newlands. You would have laughed to have seen our party and our equipment, and the boys would certainly have hooted after us, had it been anywhere but in the *bush*. We neither of us had habits, Miss E. put a skirt of her mother's over her pink dress, and I had a black silk. Little Jesse was mounted with

Mr. Jones. Had a very pleasant ride, and a pretty decent jolting, but still meditate another excursion to-morrow.

February 12.— About half-past three we mounted our steeds, and commenced our ride to "Bergvlyt," the residence of Mr. John Eksteen. We arrived about five, and I must say it was anything but pleasure to me. In the first place, my horse was lazy, and if perchance by whipping I urged him into a canter, it was almost at the expense of my poor bones, for I had not yet recovered from yesterday's frolic. To add to my miseries, the breeze was strong, and the pins came out of my dress, and I had great difficulty in keeping it in decent order. Then my bonnet kept blowing off, and what with my lazy horse, my sore bones, my whip, the reins, my bonnet, and my dress, I had more than I could manage. I could have cried almost, with vexation. Whether Mr. Jones saw my knees or not, I do not know, but he was kind enough to keep in front a little. Before we got to our destination, my comb had contrived to make its escape, and my hair was hanging over my back, so you may judge how I looked, but I cannot tell you the agony I was suffering. Miss E. had an easier horse and an easier saddle, and was enjoying herself comparatively, though her hair plagued her some. We arrived at last, and, having arranged our hair and our dresses a little, took a walk in the garden with the young ladies. It was as romantic a spot as I ever saw. We sat there some time, and then prepared for our return, which I dreaded, my bones were so stiff. I gave my horse to Mr. Jones, and took his, hoping it might be easier. It was not quite so lazy, but cantered harder. There was not so much wind going home, and, saving the pain I endured, it was pleasant. I certainly never was so tired before. We made out to get home soon after seven, and never was I more happy to find a resting place, nothing would induce me to suffer so much again. I tell Mrs. E. that she is related to everybody in Africa, for between Kirstenbosch and Cape Town, and for many miles round in every direction, there is no one but Cloetes and Eksteens. On every birthday all the families meet at one place, and for three days and nights they keep up a regular frolic, dancing and feasting, and I am told that it is the bounden duty of all the old (that is, married) men to get tipsy, and the young ones are thought more agreeable if a little funny. They are jolly people enough and very social in their habits; a kind-hearted people, the Dutch, but I think I should not like them tipsy!

February 16.—Sunday morning, and a beautiful day. Read two sermons to Uncle. Miss E. asked her father to take us to drive after dinner, as it is too dusty to walk. He consented, and we went to the famous "Constantia," where all the celebrated Constantia wine is made. I had an idea it was a village, but it seems it is the residence of Mr. Jacob Cloete, Mrs. E.'s brother. It is a most delightful place, with a fine house, and a beautiful.

view from the stoop of the country round, and of Table Bay in the distance. Mrs. Cloete has a large family, and an interesting grown-up daughter. I am astonished to find what polished and elegant manners all the young ladies here have. You would suppose they had been brought up in a great deal of society. This place was built many years ago by one of the old Dutch Governors, and named for his wife. The wine made here, which is so famous, is very rich. I was told that of the real Constantia there are only one hundred and fifty gallons a year made. They leave the grapes on the vines till they are so ripe that they begin to look shrivelled like raisins, and there is very little juice to express. It is consequently very sweet and rich. But, if the seed of this grape is sown elsewhere, the flavor of the wine is quite different. There is no doubt that an immense deal of spurious wine is exported, and that much of the common sweet Cape wine is drunk for Constantia. They say to witness the making of the wine is enough to sicken you, and from all accounts I should think it would be as good as a temperance society. The little sweaty, dirty negroes are sent into the tubs to express the juice with their feet; it cannot be done by machinery, which would break the stones. After they have got the juice out, the skins are pressed, to give the wine a color. There are four different kinds of Constantia wine, the white and the red Muscadel, the Frontignac, made of a light-colored grape, and the Pontac, which is the most expensive and the most rare. There are

now several other places built near Mr. Cloete's, to
which they have given the name of "Constantia,"
but this is the real one.   These people all live very
genteelly, very differently from our country people,
and more like the descriptions I have had of Virginia planters, as they have a great many slaves who
do all the work of the farm.

February 24.—Oh, if you could conceive how I
am tormented at night with these abominable fleas,
they are so thick, and they bite like the *deuce!*   We
sometimes pick off fourteen before going to bed,
and still manage to have some remain.   I have no
peace night or day for them, so you see there is
always something to disturb one's quiet.   This
morning I found our hostess was to have company,
and a little after nine four ladies were seen approaching the house.   Ye powers! said I, are they
coming to spend the day?   I soon found they were
"located" in the drawing-room, so I kept close to
my own and Uncle's room, for I could not think of
spending a whole day with them, and was very busy
with my books till dinner-time.   I sallied forth
once to find out how they were employed, and found
them all at work, some knitting and some sewing,
looking as cosey and social as possible.   Had they
not all been strangers, I think I should have enjoyed being with them.   The Dutch are more like
the Americans than the English, in their habits and
feelings; there is none of the formality and stiffness
that you find in John Bull wherever he is.   I never
saw more domestic happiness, more quiet and con-

tentment, than in this family through all its branches. — Dr. Murray was out after dinner, and finds Uncle better. If he only remains so for a few days, I shall feel quite encouraged. What do you think the farmer's call to his bullocks is? Mr. E. had to send for them this morning, and as he spied them through the glass coming very lazily along the road, he got out an enormous whip, five or six yards long, and snapped it three or four times. Each snap reverberated through the mountains, making a great noise, and the bullocks were immediately seen to quicken their pace, although they were a mile away. I do enjoy this country life whenever Uncle is well enough to enjoy anything. A most lovely night; I was out on the stoop till very late, and everything was so quiet and still that it seemed as though all thoughts and feelings should be as calm and tranquil. It seemed to be a holy stillness, as though it were wrong for any but holy thoughts to arise, and I could cry almost that I cannot still each anxious feeling and desire, and be as calm and celestial as everything in nature seems to be.

February 27. — Uncle being so much better, I accepted an invitation to drive to Wynberg with our family. Wynberg is a thriving little village, with a neat little church and some delightful residences. We stopped at Mr. Maquier's, and saw his two daughters in the bloom of youth and loveliness, with their hearts unsoured, and as cheerful as their ignorance of ills and wickedness can make them. You will, I dare say, think I make some queer observations, but you know, my dear, I am a novice to the world at large. I have been living for so long among people of our age and people well versed in the ways of the world, that I am quite enchanted to be among those of all ages and sizes, and especially when they laugh at nothing, as I used in my *young* days.* One cannot help giving a sigh for days gone by, and saying with Byron,—

> " There's not a charm this world can give
> Like that it takes away
> When the early glow of youth declines
> In feeling's dull decay."

But a truce to romance; I thought I had done being sentimental. The Duke of Sussex arrived yesterday from China. For the last three days the wind has been blowing tremendously in Cape Town, while here we could sit with a lighted candle upon the stoop, and hear the wind roaring upon the other side of the mountain. Dr. Bailey said he could not get his horse to face it yesterday, the dust and sand were quite smothering. Some of the ships were driven out of the bay, and nine were trying without success to get in. These south-easters, as they are called, are confined chiefly to Cape Town, a few miles back in the country they are not felt. In some exposed situations the gravel-stones actually drill holes through the glass of the windows. I am busy much of the time now writing for Uncle. I am his private secretary, and am glad to find myself of some consequence.

*The lamentation of a " spinster" aged twenty-four! —*Ed.*

March 12.—A beautiful day, and after dinner Mr. E. drove us to Wynberg, from there to Stellenberg, and home by a road I have never been on before. We passed through Schoenberg, where Sir John Herschel, the son of the great astronomer, is residing.* He has an immense telescope here, not so large as his father's, but one by which he has discovered volcanoes in the moon. He pursues his studies of the worlds above, and, I suppose, will tell us, one of these days, what the inhabitants in those unknown spheres are like,—and Heaven only knows what else! I am afraid we shall be obliged to winter at the Cape. I almost despair of ever reaching my native land again, it seems as though the fates opposed me. It will be a very long while before Uncle can regain his strength; he is dreadfully weak, though all his symptoms are better.

March 15.— Uncle was very anxious to have me go to town to-day, and notwithstanding a strong south-easter was blowing, as I could hear from the stoop, we started after breakfast, Mr. and Mrs. Eksteen, Joanna and Jesse with me, and arrived safely. The houses were all shut up, and very few people were to be seen in town, the dust was rolling in clouds along the streets. I attempted to do a little shopping, but could not force myself along. However, I did all my odd jobs indoors, and, as that was the principal object of my visit, I left the out-of-door for a future time. I had a *triste* enough day

* At *Feldhausen*. He arrived at the Cape Jan. 15, 1834, in order to explore the southern heavens, and remained there for four busy years. He was created a baronet by the Queen at her coronation. Born in 1792, he lived until 1871, and was buried in Westminster Abbey, close to the grave of Sir Isaac Newton.—*Ed.*

of it. Saw Dr. Murray, who told me that he has no doubt now that Uncle's lungs are diseased. That being the case, we can have little hope of his recovery. He feels himself growing weaker instead of stronger, and told Aunt L. this morning that he should never be any better.

. . . .

March 30.—A dreadful chasm since I wrote last, on the 15th, in which time I have witnessed one of the most solemn scenes possible, the sick and dying bed of my dear Uncle (my father in feeling), and I pray that it may make a lasting impression upon me, that I may never forget it, and I pray also that my end may be calm, peaceful, and happy like his. . . . On Saturday, the 22d, he appeared much weaker, and soon after eleven P.M. he breathed his last, quite easily,—the spark of life went out like a dying lamp. . . . My dear Aunt has truly been a ministering angel to him; I never saw her equal for devotion, for firmness and fortitude, for tenderness, kindness, and deep, enduring affection. . . . Although strangers in a strange land, we have been thrown among the best and kindest of people, who have done everything for us. The remains of my dear Uncle were consigned to the grave on Monday, the 24th. He was the first to be buried in the new Episcopal cemetery at Cape Town, which was lately consecrated by the bishop on his way to Calcutta.

We remained at Kirstenbosch till Thursday, the 26th, and then we thought it best to change the scene and go to town, where we might be making preparations for leaving, for now all our duties are performed, and there is nothing more to keep us here. The spirit of our dear friend is, I trust, happy in heaven, and all has been done for the poor body that we are permitted to do. . . .

April 1. — We begin now to be very anxious about our ship. We hear the "Buckinghamshire" is not coming, and we shall probably be obliged to go in some nasty India ship, full of cockroaches, centipedes, and scorpions, to say nothing of hosts of passengers. For two lone females it will be unpleasant enough, but endure it we must, before we can reach our journey's end. Once there, it appears to me I never can be induced to leave home again! Mrs. Crugwagen has her house full now; there are four ladies and a gentleman here, and seven children of the most noisy kind, they, however, go on in a few days. Two ships are going on, but all full.

April 3. — The "Madras" sailed to-day, and our house is quiet again. How little you know in America of the miseries of the rest of the world! India, I believe, is full of such. I could fill volumes with stories of unhappy marriages, of dreadful separations of parents and children, indeed of domestic misery in all its darkest colors. Ambition, envy, jealousy, and all the bad passions, are fully displayed there. Dr. Murray made me a long call this morning, Aunt did not see him. He is a kind creature, and gave me something for my face; for the last month I have been dreadfully afflicted with pain in it, a sort of rheumatic pain.

April 7. — Two ships arrived to-day, but are quite full of passengers, and cockroaches, and no room for us, so we must wait awhile longer; there are plenty more coming. We had an addition of ten to our family to-night, from the "Madras." It is melancholy to see these India ships bringing in, every day almost, the widows and the fatherless. This ship had in it ten ladies, and of the ten seven are widows. We have three at this house, and one poor lady is mourning for her husband and three children, her all. She goes home childless and alone. As we dine in our own rooms, I have no opportunity to observe how their afflictions are supported. I can only witness the sorrow of my dear Aunt, who bears hers with the most Christian resignation, though at times it seems as though her heart would break. I long to get her away from here, she has nothing to do, and nothing to take up her time and thoughts.

April 13. — A beautiful Sunday morning. Ayok came to me at noon, and told me he had been to *chin-chin* at his master's grave. He asked me if it was not our custom to do so. I told him no. He said with great feeling that he thought it a very good custom, and they (the Chinese) do it twice a year. I was pleased with his attention and apparent good feeling. Indeed, I have never met a Chinaman who has manifested such good feeling as he has ever since he has been with us, and at Kirstenbosch particularly. We have become quite attached to him, he has been so faithful. If he only continues so, we must consider ourselves very fortunate.

19th. — Mrs. Murray sent me the first volume of "Men and Manners in America," by the author of "Cyril Thornton." * I like it pretty well, but it displays the Englishman throughout, that conceited feeling which is in all of them, and that disposition to sneer at everything American, and I do not at all like his observations upon New Englanders generally, and particularly upon Unitarians. Many of his remarks are no doubt very correct, particularly upon manners, as far as I can judge, but, as regards morals, I should think not. I wish Americans would improve in their manner of eating, they are, I know, *piggish* in that particular, and especially so in public houses and steamboats. I should think they would profit by the observations of all travellers and foreigners. The fact is, there is not enough attention to *les bienséances* of life in America, they are too much given to money-getting, and not enough to *les politesses*, and, more than all, they have inherited much of the conceit of their mother-country, which, with their ignorance of things in other parts of the world, makes them appear very ridiculous to enlightened travellers. [Could Captain Hamilton himself have been much more severe? — *Ed.*] They have much to learn. I only wish they would be more modest, and not boast so much of their government and their institutions, and let their visitors admire or not as they please. The doctor came to inquire for me this morning, and, finding my face still obstinate, examined my teeth, thinks the pain may come from them. Told me to

* Captain Hamilton.

take a walk, and gave me something new, which I tried, and for the first time in six weeks I slept all night without pain.

April 23.—The "Royal George" was signalled last night, and Mr. Thompson writes me that there is one cabin vacant, which we are now thinking about. The captain is exorbitant in his demands. I have agreed to go off to her, to see what the accommodations are.

April 25.—This morning at nine Mr. T. and Captain Embleton called, as agreed, for me to go off to the ship. I tried very hard to get Miss Crugwagen to go with me, but she had a bad cold and could not, and Aunt L. did not feel like it, so there was nothing to be done but to go by myself, not very pleasant, but I started off and said nothing. We were three-quarters of an hour beating off; a fine breeze, but dead ahead. Found the captain a pleasing person, and the ship very neat, but very small compared to the "Waterloo." However, I smelt no cockroaches, and think the accommodations are as good as we can expect; there is but one small cabin for us though, and we shall be well squeezed. There are many passengers, mostly French, so we may learn to speak it. Stopped about a quarter of an hour, and then made sail for the shore. My reflections were melancholy enough, as you may imagine. Only the hope that I may see you all once more cheers me, but the recollections of our last landing, and the changes since, were almost too much for me. I was glad Aunt L. did not go.

I reported favorably upon the ship to her, and she has made up her mind to take it. I am sorry to say she does not sail till a week from to-morrow. Dr. Murray came in to see me just before night. He wishes me to have a tooth out, which, he thinks, may be the cause of all my pain. I suppose it had better be done before I go to sea. This afternoon I saw the hearse pass to attend the funeral of a gentleman who died here the other night. It was dressed with plumes, and the top was covered with black ostrich feathers, as well as the horses' heads. Eight or ten men walked behind, dressed in black, with feathers and black bands. I must confess that it made no impression of solemnity upon me, mere pomp and show, and nothing to arouse one's feelings like the tolling of the bell, which they omit here. None but gentlemen ever follows the body to the grave. This poor man had no relatives here, I believe, but had come in search of health, leaving his wife very ill in the Neilgherry Hills in India. Thus families are separated in this part of the world.

April 30. — Persuaded Aunty to go down to breakfast; it is better that she should meet some one before she goes on board, then she *must*, for we have only one small cabin. We were neither of us sorry we went below afterwards, for we met some very pleasant and delightful people, particularly Colonel Craigie and Mrs. Craigie. Her appearance was to me exceedingly interesting, her countenance of rather a Grecian cast, I should say, with regular features, and she wears her hair *à la grecque*, which adds to the effect. Her manners are elegant and easy, affable and pleasant. From the first I was prepossessed in her favor. The colonel appears a gentlemanlike man, and I think must be a sensible one, from his having chosen such a wife. Methinks I hear you say, "You are very hasty in your conclusions." So it would seem, for, though I write them afterwards, they were all made in my mind at the breakfast table. I said to myself, If that eye does not speak purity of mind, I will never trust again to appearances. After dinner we went to visit dear Uncle's grave, a melancholy thing enough. It is a quiet spot, looking upon the sea, toward Green Point; there is an iron railing five feet high all round it. We are going to have cypress and myrtle planted all about it. How one longs to know, when standing by the grave of a near and dear friend, where and how the spirit is existing! We returned, and spent the evening with Mrs. Craigie, who has not disappointed my first impressions, on the contrary, my opinion of her increases with my knowledge of her character and of her mind, which is highly cultivated. I have discovered that she is a near relative of the Duke of Marlborough.

May 2. — The place is crowded with strangers, and the nobility have been in an uproar to-day on account of the arrival of the Commander-in-chief from India. We had one of the party from the ship here, the Hon. Mrs. Churchill, a relation of Mrs. Craigie's, a handsome woman, but not so pleasing.

Dr. Murray came in to-day, and would not let me escape, but took out the tormenting tooth, and I behaved very well. We spent the evening most delightfully in conversation with Mrs. Craigie, the most interesting woman and the most profitable companion I have met for many a day; I believe she is a true Christian, though perhaps a little wanting in Christian charity. She is a thorough Trinitarian, and I could not entirely agree with her, but I gained something, for I brought out many of her high-toned and noble feelings, and, though I had neither convinced nor been convinced, I was pleased with my evening. To me it appears that a creed is of very little importance, not so to my friend. Would that I were more like her! She is an ornament to the religion she professes; so cheerful, so kind, so affectionate, so humble, so devout, and, I may add, so energetic and indefatigable in the performance of her duties. She regrets, as we do, that we are not to be together longer.

PART III.

HOMEWARD BOUND (MAY 5–JULY 12, 1834).

May 5. — Got up early this morning, and packed up our last trunks, and prepared for our departure. At half-past ten Mr. Thompson called for us, and we bid adieu to our kind hostess and her family with much sorrow; we have experienced great kindness from them. We parted with real regret, too, from Mrs. Craigie, for, though our intercourse has been short, it has been exceedingly pleasant. The colonel and Mr. Thompson waited upon us to the boat, and we retraced the steps which three months before we had taken under such different circumstances.

There was a busy scene enough at the landing-place. Eight ships had arrived the day before, and one or two this morning, all full of passengers, who were landing with their baggage as fast as possible, while others were going, and we among the number. I could not help thinking what different histories they might all give, and then I thought how few of them were probably here from inclination! Well, leaving their inclinations to themselves, or any one else, we went on board the "Royal George," where there was as much confusion as upon the jetty, the passengers were coming in rapid succession, with quantities of baggage and the like, so that the deck was hardly to be seen, and, "thinks I to myself," all this is for the comfort of these poor bodies of ours. Well, we proceeded to our cabin, which looked as though it could contain little besides those bodies, but we set Ayok to looking into the berths and drawers, and we found, to our great horror, that it contained many other bodies in the form of cockroaches. Then there was the smell, and a thousand other little miseries, all of which are ready to salute one on first entering a ship, and to all of which we become accustomed after a certain time, but, until that time arrives, they are hard to be endured. After a while we learn to move in a smaller space, and our cabins begin to grow larger, but I must not be prosy. We had dinner about five, very nicely cooked, and I did justice to it, thinking it best to improve the time, as I shall get none to-morrow. We had about twenty at table, mostly French, so that I understood very little of what was going on. We went to bed as early as possible, and "tired nature's sweet restorer" did not refuse to come to our relief. There was a heavy sea, and we were pitching badly all night.

May 16.— Light winds most of the time so far, and all our calculations on a short passage to St. Helena disappointed. A little more wind to-day, but before night we were braced sharp up, with every prospect of a head wind. We are still a long way from the island, and we begin to get rather impatient. The thought of being penned up in this place for months and months is dreadful, and poor

Aunty is most unpleasantly situated. There is no peace nor quiet for her, and the constant noise in the cuddy is most discordant to her feelings. Our cabin is more noisy than the others, as it adjoins the cuddy, and these noisy French people keep up such a chattering from morning till night that there is no such thing as reading in peace. After breakfast many of them remain at the table and play piquet, backgammon, écarté, chess, and all sorts of games, and keep it up pretty well most of the forenoon. At four we all assemble for dinner, where we are wedged in so tight that it is difficult to eat, and such eaters as our friends are I never saw before. After dinner Aunty and I generally take a constitutional walk together, and we walk till we are quite tired rather than join the others, by whom we find it difficult to make ourselves understood. At seven we have tea, and as soon as that is over the different games begin again; the old and the young, the grandmamma of seventy and the child of seven, all deeply interested. We do not join in, I sometimes look on, but generally return to the deck.

May 17.— We are very little farther than we were yesterday. Time passes swiftly enough, but I wish we were making more progress. I am at present very much interested in Cobbett's "French Grammar," it is more simple, and makes the idiom of the language more easily understood, than any I have seen. I am also reading Spurzheim on "Phrenology," and begin to look at people's heads very scientifically. To-day completes my twenty-fourth year, and what account can I give of it?

Was on deck all the evening, a most lovely night, and we were cheered with the sound of a fair wind, but, alas! so little of it that I fear we shall not reach St. Helena to-morrow night, as we might very easily with a little breeze, we were only about one hundred and fifty miles from it at noon. We shall probably spend one day 'there, which will give us time to visit Longwood, and the tomb of Napoleon, which we must do, as we shall never have another chance.

May 19.— Wind still light, but about sunset the captain called me to see the Island which he had just made out, and none but the eyes of a mariner would have supposed it to be anything but a small cloud. We all hailed it with joy, and anticipate the pleasure of being near it to-morrow. Spent the evening in conversing with Mme. N., a lady of seventy years, and this is her sixth voyage. What would grandmother say to that? She has seen great changes in her day. She is nobly related in France, has lived in great style, and has had a first-rate education. She is elegant in her manners, full of life, and very active. She was in the same convent with Josephine at the time she was separated from her first husband, the Vicomte de Beauharnais, and just before he was guillotined. She says that Josephine was beloved by all, and gives the same idea of her character and manners that we get from books generally.

May 20.— When we awoke, we found we were very near the Island, and the anchor was dropped about eight o'clock. There is no bay here, but good anchorage under the lee of the land. I know not how to give you an idea of this place as it looks from the ship, but I will do my best. At first it looks like a huge rock, rising perpendicularly out of the sea. After a while you discover a few houses and some trees at the entrance of a ravine between two mountains, which appear to have dissolved partnership from time unknown, and retired from each other in mutual disgust or by mutual consent. Since which time the town has grown up between them, and is inhabited by most of the people on the Island. On the summits of these mountains and on other high places are fortifications. The vast ocean is all around, and we wonder in vain what could have produced this enormous excrescence in the midst of it. Two ships are anchored near us, the "Duke of Argyle," which had as long a passage as we had, and a French ship, from the Isle de Bourbon. After breakfasting, and having gone through the customary visits from health boats, etc. (and having put on our best bibs and tuckers), we were whipped into the boat, in company with some dozen of the passengers, and in a few moments were again on *terra firma*, which is always pleasant, be it what land it may, but how delightful it will be when we again set foot upon our native land! There are very good steps, and everything convenient for landing, but such a queer place I never saw. Our eyes had not deceived us, we were actually walking on the quay, with the rock rising perpendicularly for a thousand feet or more, and in some places jutting over our heads, and not a trace of vegetation to be seen upon it. Some miserable little houses were built at the foot; the sides and roofs of some being formed by the rock itself, and making one tremble lest some convulsion of nature should bury them all. We marched on a little further, and the next thing that struck our eyes was a ladder, also nearly perpendicular, reaching from the foot of the mountain to the fortifications on top. The idea of going up made one dizzy. I have been told it is three thousand feet long* (it certainly *looks* two thousand), it was built by the East India Company, and cost $200,000. A little further on we entered a gate, which locks in the "city" at night, passed through a very clean street, the principal one, saw some pretty-looking houses and one pretty girl, and arrived at the hotel of Mr. Solomon, a Jew, a very neat and commodious house, and well furnished. Made inquiries at once for American papers and letters, but no papers of late date were to be had, and the only letter for us had been sent to the Cape! Very gratifying; well, one must pocket one's disappointment, and see others reading theirs with patience.

The captain immediately ordered carriages to take us to the tomb of Napoleon, as we had no time to lose, and our *voitures* were soon at the door. I hardly know what to call them, I should say they

---

* It is really about six hundred.—*Ed.*

most resembled double buggies, with four very low wheels, which brought us very near the ground; the driver sat upon the horse, and led it part of the way. There were no tops to the carriages, so we were exposed to the sun, which was not very agreeable. Our course was up a zigzag path cut into the side of the mountain, the valley far below us, the hills towering above, a low wall guarded the edge of the precipice. Being above the valley, we had a fine view of the town, which runs up some distance above the mountains, till it finally tapers off and is no more. It is not a quarter of a mile wide, the streets very narrow, but clean-looking, the houses mostly small, and built of mud and stone. We saw some pretty gardens, and a variety of beautiful green trees, the banana and other tropical fruits. The scenery is grand, the ravines and precipices are magnificent. I was enchanted with the scenery, and, as we ascended, felt much nearer heaven, for somehow or other it always seems to exalt the feelings to be towering so high. When we had nearly gained the summit we were obliged to get out of our carriages, and descend a little way to visit the tomb. Our companions were all violent Bonapartists, and looked sad and solemn as we approached. The tomb is situated on the side of the mountain, in a most quiet and delightful spot. There is not a letter upon the stone to tell who or what lies there, owing to the foolish jealousy of the English government. The tomb is enclosed by a neat iron railing, a sort of lily grows at the two upper corners, and the four sticks are remaining which supported the forget-me-not planted by Mme. Bertrand after Napoleon's decease, but which has since died. Within the outer enclosure are two large willow-trees, which waved over the grave, but they are nearly dead, a few green leaves upon the branches alone show that they once had life. The present Governor Dallas has planted some cypress-trees, which are doing well. It is a most enchanting spot, but far too quiet for the spirit of such a man as rests here, as Byron says:

"Quiet to quick spirits is a hell."

Finding a visitors' book at the entrance, I took it up, and how quickly it recalled one of the favorite sayings of Napoleon himself, "There's but one step from the sublime to the ridiculous," for one glance at this receptacle for names and remarks was quite enough to excite one's risibles! Here were huddled together eulogy and invective, sentiment of all kinds from friend and from foe, poetry and prose, good and bad, of the literate and the illiterate, of all nations, tongues, and countries. One bit I was particularly struck with, but unfortunately I can only remember part of it, enough, however, to give you some idea of its merit. It began, "Here lies *Bony part*, he rests in *peas*," with much more of the same sort written in a very bad hand. I wrote merely the names of our party, and we returned to our carriages and proceeded to Longwood, but there is hardly a trace left of what it was while Napoleon lived there, it has been converted into stables, etc., and is in a most shocking state of filth and dilapidation. It is a pity, I think, that they did not let it fall into honorable decay, but his bedroom is now turned into a stable, the sitting-room where he died is a room for machinery and in a wretched state, and his flower-garden is a pig-sty. Pity, pity, I think. They showed us the grounds, etc., but there was no trace of anything belonging to him. We saw the rooms of Las Casas and Montholon, and passed the house of General Bertrand. I was amused to see our French friends carrying away large pieces from the wall and the floor of the room where Napoleon died, and saying how happy they should make their friends in France and at the Mauritius by dividing the spoil. We saw the new house built by Napoleon, containing fifty-two rooms, but, as the Governor is residing there at present, we could not go through it. We returned by the same road, and were almost suffocated with dust and the heat of the sun. Our first demand was for a bath, and we were exceedingly refreshed and comforted by it. Then we sallied forth into the streets, bought a spool or two of cotton, and inquired the prices of some things; all and everything here is awfully dear. After we returned, the American consul called upon us with his two daughters, one a Mrs. B. of Salem, who gave us some news of the place, as she had come from there lately. We dined at five o'clock, and had a good dinner, which cost fifteen shillings sterling apiece. We should have said nothing about that, for it was a very nice dinner, soup and fish, of course, turkey, goose, fowls, partridges, pies, pastry, etc.; figs, delicious plantains, pears, guavas, native fruits and imported dried fruits. But, when we were asked seven shillings sterling for each bath, we exclaimed in perfect astonishment, and I said, "Never say any more about Chinese impositions, Europeans excel them!" But there was no disputing it, and we found everything was charged accordingly, so we were not sorry to find that our stay at St. Helena was limited to one day. There may be reasons for all this, and it is true that the bath-rooms were very nice, and well fitted up, and I suppose they do not get customers very often, but I cannot forget the price of their hot water! At eight o'clock we walked down to the quay, a most beautiful night, and went on board again, quite tired enough with our day's exertion to go straight to bed.

May 25, Latitude S. 9° 18'. — Five years yesterday since we bid adieu to home and friends, and took the last lingering look at our dear native land! The weather is getting very hot as we come to the top of the world, but we are chasing the sun yet, and shall have it still hotter when we get further north. We find the cockroaches begin to feel the effects of the heat, and come out abundantly. Attended prayers on deck this morning, and then returned to our cabins, and I read aloud one of Dr. Wardlaw's sermons on "The Divinity of Jesus Christ." In reading these different views of the same subject, I get puzzled, my dear sister, the texts brought forward and shown in different lights confute without convincing me, and I am left, though in the same faith essentially, yet puzzled regarding the meaning of many parts of the Bible. I sometimes think I will never read another book upon creeds, but then I should feel that I was sinning against my own conscience, because I think we should read all sides of a question before we make up our minds. I pray most sincerely that my understanding may be enlightened, but, alas! there are many things hard to be understood in the Scriptures, and to me particularly the eighth and ninth chapters of Romans.

May 28. — Still fine weather, and we are all well, and, with the exception of minor evils, get on amiably and cheerfully. We begin to have some communication with our fellow-passengers, as we find they are ready to converse with us without laughing at our blunders, and assist us with pleasure in our endeavors to learn their language, while we readily return the favor. The cuddy is a regular school-room after breakfast, and might well be called a *bedlam.* This is the public resort, as it is cooler than any other place. We generally spend the evenings on deck, and our quiet is very much disturbed by the nocturnal rambles of the cockroaches, which sometimes take the liberty of promenading over our heads and necks. To-day finished Spurzheim on Phrenology.

May 31. — Last evening about six o'clock a delightful seven-knot breeze sprang up, which wafted us most splendidly across the line, and we are now once more in the North Atlantic. I awoke this morning with the sun, and saw him rise from his watery bed in great splendor. I fancied the sky looked more homish than usual,—how much fancy can do! The breeze continued this morning, but grew rather light through the day. I suppose the winds will be very light and variable now. The weather is very hot, and the cockroaches swarm. In the lower cabins they say they have them by the five hundred thousand! They are a great nuisance, in fact I cannot relish anything for them. They get in our drawers, they eat our apples, and in fact there is no peace for them.

June 7, Lat. 7°, 36'.— Have made but little more than twenty miles a day for the last four or five days. Just before I was dressed, I heard the sound of the trumpet,—"Ship ahoy! and where are you bound?" Looked out of the scuttle, and saw an English brig abreast of us; we sent a boat to her, and got three newspapers and some nice potatoes. She was twenty-four days from the Scilly Islands, and thirty-two from Liverpool. I assure you it was no small pleasure, although we did not get much news, and not one word from America. She was bound to Rio Janeiro. I am sorry to find that our ship is rather a slow sailor; she is not in good trim, and has a list to port which retards her progress, however they mean to "fix" her to-morrow, as the Yankees would say. A smacking breeze to-day, and we are pitching about merrily. But, go as rapidly as she will, it seems slow to me, for my wishes go and come back again,— everything is accomplished in my imagination very often.

Sunday, June 8.— I intended, when I rose this morning, to spend the day in a most Christian-like manner, and arranged in my mind my books and my employments, but so little can we control events, and so much are we the creatures of circumstances, that not for one little day can we pretend to say what we will or will not do. Until eleven o'clock I read as I intended, and then went out to prayers, which were cut short by the sight of a ship on our lee bow, outward bound. What was our joy when we discovered she was an American! We bore down upon her, and though the captain was rather unwilling to take in his studding-sails to speak to us, when he found we were resolute he slackened sail, and in a few minutes we were alongside the "Italy," Captain Ritchie, from New York, bound to China. We sent a boat to see if he had any news or letters. I assure you I was made quite happy by hearing you were well, as far as he knew, and he had had a note from father a few days before he left, which was about the 9th of May. A most happy *rencontre!* He sent us a lot of papers and a few stores as a mark of attention to his country-women. So our day was spent in reading news-papers. I saw Uncle James's arrival, but not much else in the papers except politics, which I regret to find are in such a state. Our old general seems to be wishing to play Napoleon, or dictator, and I should fancy from the papers we have that it won't go! Oh, dear, I hope we shall not find civil war when we get home! He is certainly carrying things with a high hand. We were busy all day reading the news, and thus all my plans of the morning were deranged, but I could not help excusing myself for this innovation, as I had heard nothing of consequence from my home for many months. We drank some Philadelphia cider at dinner, which was very nice.

June 15.—Since my last date, my dear sister, nothing has occurred worthy of note. We have jogged along to latitude 22°, and in my opinion if our ship was good for anything, we ought with the fine breezes we have had, to have been much further, but perhaps it is my impatience. You may think that with so many passengers I might find something interesting to relate, but to tell you the truth I can say but little in their favor. Their rapidity of utterance debars me from taking any part in the general conversation, and in my private chats I never venture to express my sentiments. The manners of the party are not very elegant, and judging from the very frequent utterance of *Mon Dieu!* I should not say much for their reverence of One whose name is so irreverently spoken, but on this subject I dare not judge.

June 19.—We have made precious little since yesterday, and shall make still less to-day. We now find ourselves in what is called the Sargosso

Sea, or the grassy sea, on account of a grass or sea-weed that is seen in great quantities in these latitudes. We are surrounded with it. The weather is very hot now, there is so little wind, and faces begin to lengthen at the prospect of a long voyage. All our calculations are upset as to arriving the last of June. We sigh in spirit, I assure you, and complain that the weather is too fine. Though in my heart I feel that it is all right, I cannot help wishing the "right" were otherwise. Patience is having her perfect work with me. The sea is like glass, and we invoke the clouds in vain for wind; they come and go, but heed not our wishes. I fairly got the blues to-night, and was glad to go to bed, and forget myself in sleep.

June 26. — We have now a good, strong, and steady wind, which will carry us in a short time beyond the Western Isles. We begin to feel a great change in the temperature, and it is so cold in the evenings that we have the cuddy full, some reading, and some playing. All look serene and contented because we are getting on. All we want is plenty of exercise to make us feel delightfully, for I really recognize my native air in these breezes, though I do not know how you will account for it when I say they are from the south-east; never mind, they are just like it, at any rate. To-day we are in the latitude of New York, even that is pleasant to me.

July 1. — Overtook the brig "Penelope" of Glasgow from Trinidad to-day; spoke her, and soon left her behind, so we do sail faster than some things.

A most lovely evening, and every prospect of being in before many days, say five or six, and all our passengers seem happy at the idea of setting foot on shore again. We have had a dozen ships about us to-day, and have been quite amused by beating several of them. It is very cheerful after a monotonous voyage of six weeks.

July 4, and the fifty-eighth anniversary, I believe, of our Independence. Fine weather yet, though the breeze is falling off a little. "The peace and prosperity of our country," with a pretty little speech from Captain Embleton, was proposed as a toast, and drunk in good fellowship by all, after dinner.

July 7. — A thick, foggy morning; but nevertheless a pilot-boat came alongside from the Scilly Islands, and told us we were but twenty-seven miles from them. About four it cleared up, and at the cry of "Land ahead!" we left the dinner table as soon as possible, and soon discovered the coast of England, the "Land's End." Much to our joy, the fog had entirely disappeared, and we had a fine breeze, which cheered us up at once. We had the "Duke of Argyle" ahead, that left St. Helena the day we did. By means of Marryat's signals people can hold long conversations at the distance of five miles or more; they are quite delightful, but not generally in use with our countrymen. I suppose the bunting costs too much for "Jonathan," but it is very stupid to meet a deaf-and-dumb ship nowadays. When I went on deck, I heard a great noise, and, looking half-way up the "ratlins," there were two jacks busy in tying the legs of one of the passengers to them. I found it was the first time he had been aloft, and they immediately took advantage of his novel situation by practising the permitted joke upon him sanctioned by old custom, to the great amusement of the party on the poop, who witnessed his struggles for liberty without trying to assist him. Made the Lizards before dark.

July 8. — Wind quite fair to-day, and we are running along finely. Had the coast of Devonshire on our lee, and about ten o'clock three of our impatient gentlemen passengers left the ship in the pilot-boat and made for shore, thinking to land at Dartmouth. It looks good to see land again, though at a distance, and I would gladly go ashore, too. After leaving these passengers, we were obliged to change our course, and with a fine, fair wind, and the most beautiful weather possible, we steered for Havre, where we are to land our French passengers. Had the island of Alderney in sight about seven. There is now daylight in the sky till eleven.

July 9. — Was awakened this morning at three o'clock by the captain rousing his French passengers, and I got up at four to see them off. We then had the coast of France in sight, and the pilot-boat all in readiness. The immense quantity of baggage delayed them a long time, as there were twenty people in all to leave. They did not get away till half-past six, when we bid them adieu and were saluted in French style by a kiss on each cheek. I was amused yesterday to see young ladies and all offer their cheeks with the most perfect *nonchalance* to a French gentleman who left. It is true he was a married man, and elderly; I do not know whether it would have been the same with a young man, but, however, custom sanctions everything. At eight we lost sight of the boat and our friends, probably forever. Our head was again turned towards England, and we made Beachy Head Light at nine, a very brilliant revolving light.

July 10.—Captain E. called us early this morning, as we were nearly abreast of Dover. Dressed and went on deck, to see "the chalky cliffs" I have so often heard of. We were then about a mile and a half away. (Took our pilot last night off Dungeness.) Soon afterwards we passed Deal, with which I was also much pleased. Indeed, my dear sister, I fear I shall not have receptacles enough in my brain for all the fine things I shall be called upon to admire. I shall be obliged to intrust them to my memory instead of my book, for it will take too much time and paper to note them all, and my memory is not a faithful friend; I give many things to its charge, and, when I demand them, they are either lost or so snugly stowed away that they are not to be found at the proper time and place. My head, I think, resembles chaos, I would somebody would put it in order! But, in a word, the scenery here is beautiful, would you could look at it, too! for when I enjoy a thing, I always want those I love with me. There are plenty of boats, ships, brigs, and all sorts of vessels flying about, no doubt for

our express amusement! As we got abreast of
Dover this morning, the "Steam boat" (*sic*) had
just started for Calais. It is really beautiful to see
it, it truly goes "like a thing of life." Ayok was
highly delighted, and said, "They say, suppose have
got foul wind can walky"; I replied, "Yes, suppose no got wind at all, can walky," which seemed
to heighten his pleasure and surprise. At noon we
turned the corner, and are now steering west. The
wind is no longer fair, and we are beating up the
river. Have been making preparations for landing.
We were boarded this morning by a boatman with
yesterday's papers; he said, "Sir, the Vig ministry
is dissolved, and the Queen has gone to Germany."
These boatmen all call for rum, temperance socie-
ties do not flourish here, I fancy. A head wind
and tide obliged us to anchor for the night, as we
were among shoals and quicksands. A lovely evening, and a boat came off to us, bringing cherries and
all sorts of tempting things from shore. It is six
years since I have eaten cherries, and I assure you
we did not grudge the fourpence a pound.

July 11.—Obliged to remain quiet till ten this
morning. Wind still ahead, and very little of it,
but we have had plenty to do, in arranging our luggage and preparing to land to-morrow. We have
Essex on one side and Kent on the other, a most
beautiful country, where all looks peaceful and
happy, but one cannot always judge from appearances. Certainly, I have seen no appearance of star-
vation in any of the boatmen, every one looked well,

and worthy of the title of "John Bull." A splendid steamer passed us just now, full of passengers,
and a band on board playing merrily. She was running easily against wind and tide, while we are
tacking and toiling, and shall soon be obliged to
anchor again. It calls forth a eulogy upon steam,
I assure you. Anchored at four o'clock. Lovely
weather, a beautiful moon in the evening, and time
enough for silent meditation, for everything was
quiet except now and then when a schooner or
smaller boat would pass us, with some one playing
the flute or exercising his vocal powers. I was
walking by myself on the poop till nearly ten,
when I went to bed. Oh that I were a poetess! for,
rather than express my feelings in bad prose, you
will lose all my musings, my dear, which would no
doubt have been highly edifying, as well as amusing; but, alas! alas! Nature, as I have often said,
was certainly going upon an economical plan, both
physically and mentally, when I was created.

July 12.—We made sail about ten, and got under
way, with hundreds of other vessels of all descriptions and sizes, of all nations and from all nations.
Such a busy scene I never saw before. We were in
the narrow part of the river, and the land was very
near us, so that we had a delightful view of the most
charming country that ever was seen, most highly
cultivated, and as I had always imagined it, beautiful without being grand, hilly in some parts, but
nothing approaching a mountain, or even a good-
sized hill. But the beautiful lawns, the thick-set

hedges, occasionally a venerable-looking church "with its spire pointing to heaven,"—indeed, my dear sister, go to Irving's "Sketch Book" to find, beautifully expressed, what I would fain give you some idea of; suffice it that I was much pleased to find all my fancies embodied before me. We were in a perfect Babel till about two o'clock, nothing but tacking ship, etc., till we arrived at Gravesend, where the confusion was made still worse by the landing of our live stock; the pigs were rebellious, and the geese ditto. Then all our steerage passengers went, and soon after a steamer took us in tow, and we went on smoothly, in defiance of the wind. About five we arrived at Blackwall, and our trunks were looked into on board, but passed without trouble, and we congratulated ourselves; but when about going ashore there, and in full view of all the houses, another "Philistine" boarded us, demanded our keys, and overhauled the trunks again. My blood boiled, but we were obliged to submit and bear it patiently, but I never felt so much annoyed. We got off very easily, however, and landed in a few moments. We called for a coach, to proceed to Captain Embleton's house, and were put into an "omnibus," after some fighting between the coachmen as to who should have us. Captain E. was obliged to collar one man, who was running off with my dressing-box. I thought upon the whole we were in a sad place! In a few moments we were kindly received by Mrs. Embleton. They live away from the city, in Canton Place, East India Road.

It was pleasant, and yet painful, to see the happy meeting between friends when there was none to welcome us, but our turn will come, and we are accustomed to strangers now. We had a fine treat of strawberries, gooseberries, and cherries to-night, and went to bed quite tired after the excitement of the day.

PART IV.

ENGLAND, JULY 13–AUG. 2, 1834.

Sunday, July 13. — Very like a Sunday at home, no mails, no penny-post, so that we could not communicate with any one. Did not go to church, but spent the morning writing to you. At noon Mrs. E.'s mother and sisters from the country called on us. I was delighted with them. They invited us to go to their country-house next Sunday, which I hope we shall be able to do, they appear to be just the kind of people I like. After dinner Mr. Ibar, our old friend from China, and Mr. Iglesia called to see us. I was most happy to see the former, I assure you. He told us much news, of marrying and giving in marriage. My *friend* V. is married, and gone back to China. We spent the evening very pleasantly with our friends.

July 14. — This morning took a "fly," and started for the city, the busy, bustling city, the noise of which almost stunned me, and the many fine things nearly dazzled me. We passed the great St. Paul's, and Heaven knows what else, carriages innumerable, and such quantities of those detestable "omnibuses"; I can't abide them. We drove first to the "Adelphi," and engaged lodgings at Wright's Hotel, No. 2, Adams Street, where my dear uncle wished us to go, and where he put up

before. It is a nice house, with a respectable land-
lady. Having engaged to come to-morrow, we then
drove to the Pantheon, a new bazaar just opened.
To attempt to give you an idea of it would be great
presumption, there was a little of everything under
heaven in the building. On our way home we
passed the celebrated "Newgate," a dismal-looking
place enough, one would think it would be a warn-
ing to all evil-disposed persons. At dinner had a
note from Mr. Bates, and had the pleasure of hearing that all our letters had been sent to the Cape!
So it goes, you see,— I could have cried, but
thought it best to laugh!

July 15.— Went to the West India docks with
Captain E. this morning, and after tiffin to our
new lodgings, where we arrived about two, arranged
our affairs, and then did not know what to do with
ourselves. Not a book had I, the tables, chairs,
etc., could afford no amusement, and I was tired of
seeking a familiar face among the myriads that were
momentarily passing. In short, we felt as desolate
as possible, and at last determined to sally forth.
We sauntered through the Strand, passed Charing
Cross, and found our way to St. James's Park. We
should have enjoyed this much, but we took Ayok
with us, which made us so conspicuous that we were
glad to return. The Park is a most delightful
place, and again I sigh for the painter's or poet's
art to bring to you some of these fine things
wherein art and nature are so beautifully combined.
The weather, too, is perfect, and it is not dark till

after nine. We returned home to dine, and soon after sallied forth to a book-seller's, for we had nothing at all to read, and, having walked as far as Waterloo Bridge, returned to those dear companions (our books), which cheer us in every situation, and are, indeed, the only antidote to the blues. A gentleman from Boston was announced soon after our return, and who should it be but Mr. O., the gentleman who fell in love with Jane S. in the coach, and followed her to Salem. How singular that we should meet again here! He advises us to go to Liverpool to embark.

July 16. — Did some shopping this morning, and then walked to Somerset House, where we saw a vast collection of paintings, and were very much delighted. The house is immense. There was one room filled with statuary, that looked very old and extremely dirty. I could not prevent a blush when I entered the room, for it seemed indelicate, and hardly fit for a lady. However, I thought it would hardly do to be so unfashionably delicate, so I walked through with apparently great *nonchalance*, but I was very glad to make my exit. I am a novice at these things as yet; indeed, I would not be quite dead to such feelings, but I saw some ladies sitting down and enjoying it. I must confess I directed my attention to the models of buildings, with a sly look at the figures, but even this was nothing to some of the public exhibitions. [Such being the proper state of mind of an "elegant female" in those days, it is not so surprising that

Mrs. Trollope, visiting the Pennsylvania Academy of Fine Arts a very few years earlier, found a screen placed inside the door of the "Antique Statue Gallery," (to prevent any incautious glance being shocked by the specimens of sculpture within), and an old woman posted at the door, who told her to make haste and go in while nobody was looking, as most of the ladies liked to go into that room when no gentlemen were watching them. — *Ed.*]

July 17. — A very hot day, but Captain and Mrs. E. called, and wished us to go to the Zoölogical Gardens. It was so hot there that we could not really enjoy it, but we went from there to the Coliseum, passing through a gallery lighted with lamps as we entered, that was so delightfully cool that for the moment I felt I could pass my life there. We entered a statue gallery next, with a mellow light thrown in we knew not how, but through tapestry which covered the semicircular apartment in a most fanciful and elegant manner. All around in arches were little marble tables and delightful crimson-covered spring-seats, where we immediately seated ourselves, and partook of ices and cakes, and felt much refreshed. Then we examined the statues and busts. Some of them were beautiful, and there were very few that the most modest would blush at. We then went into a little octagonal room about ten feet in diameter, and were wound up to the top of the building,* where we saw a panorama of London that was quite perfect. It looked so like nature

* This must have been about the first of all " lifts." — *Ed.*

that I thought I might be deceived with regard to my standing-ground. Ayok was quite "stabbergasted," to use a vulgar but most expressive word. After this, we went through the conservatory, filled with plants of all countries, beautiful grottoes, *jets d'eau*, etc., indeed, it was so enchanting that we said, What cannot man's devices accomplish? Many more things we saw, and drove home at last quite tired enough. All the gaiety and fashion of London were out as we drove through Regent Street, a most magnificent street.

July 19. — A rainy day. About two we started in a one-horse "fly" for Mr. Daniell's studio in Bedford Square, where we saw the pictures of Mr. and Mrs. College, and were very much pleased, it seemed like bringing them before us. Ayok burst into quite an hysterical laugh when he saw his father's face in Mr. College's picture. The pictures were unfortunately all too late for the Exhibition. Chinnery's paintings are much liked here. Poor Ayok excites so much attention that I believe he will be very willing to doff his Chinese costume. Being rainy to-day, he had on his great umbrella hat, and cut a curious figure, to be sure, to those who are not in the habit of seeing them. We dined with the Embletons, and about six took a carriage and went to "Woodhouse," Eastham, Essex, the house of Mrs. E.'s mother, where we were invited to stay as long as we could. After an hour's drive, we arrived at one of the sweetest little places, with a fine large house, handsomely furnished, and quite enveloped in trees and shrubbery, with delightful smooth lawns, but it rained so hard we could not enjoy them much. However, there were attractions inside which prevented our sighing for those without. Mrs. M., a very fine-looking and extremely kind personage, welcomed us as though we were old friends, making us quite at home at once. There were two unmarried daughters, both very pleasing, and four sons, all at home to spend Sunday, so that with Mr. and Mrs. E. and ourselves we had quite a table full. There was the respectable-looking footman, with his breeches so tight and so white, who seems to be a necessary appendage to such a place, and every comfort and many luxuries in the house. We took tea, and then adjourned to the drawing-room, and the young ladies played and sang most of the evening, and showed us their paintings. Miss Sylvia, the eldest, had made a chess-board, inlaid the black squares and painted flowers from nature upon them, and transferred a little picture to each of the white squares. There was a splendid wreath of flowers round the edge, and altogether it would have done any one credit. At ten we had a little supper, and then prayers, and retired for the night.

July 20, *Sunday.* — Still rainy; however we drove and the gentlemen walked to the little village church, built in the year 1100. It has lately been repaired, and looked in good order, though very ancient, as you may judge by the date. There were several ancient monuments of noble families, and some rude statuary. We had a very good sermon from the vicar of the parish, and came home quite pleased. It cleared up at noon, and we took a walk round the grounds, had a pull in a little boat on the fishpond, got some fine fruit in the gardens, and seated ourselves in the summer-house and had an interesting chat with the young ladies. Had some sacred music after dinner, and passed the evening very pleasantly.

July 22.— This morning we had all our baggage examined, and at twelve took a carriage and drove to St. Katherine's Docks to look at the "Montreal," and were very much pleased with her accommodations. Finding it will be an immense deal of trouble and expense to transport ourselves and luggage to Liverpool, we at last decided to take a cabin on this ship, for the first of August. Once decided, we felt relieved of a heavy load, for we had had great anxiety about it. The ship has splendid accommodations, and having no cockroaches we shall feel quite happy. From the Docks we drove to St. Paul's. We spent a long time there looking at the monuments, and went as far as the whispering gallery. Everything looked smutty, dirty, and ancient. They are just now erecting a monument to Bishop Heber. We then went to the Soho Bazaar to make some purchases, and, on returning to our lodgings, found a number of cards that had been left for us. Heard to-night that Mrs. College has a son, but is not very well.

July 24.— Went to the House of Lords and Westminster Abbey. Let me refer you to Irving's "Sketch Book," and his reflections in this place; be assured, my dear sister, it is impossible to enter it without moralizing on the mutability of all things, it would take volumes to tell you the thoughts that rush upon one in such an ancient and venerable building. In one little chapel there are wax figures of Elizabeth, William and Mary, Queen Anne and many others, all robed in the fashion of their day. They were all quite dusty and defaced by time. Queen Elizabeth struck my eye the moment I got up the narrow staircase, an ugly-looking, rattish sort of face, but very like her pictures, and seeming to express her character perfectly. Some one had seen fit to clean her face, leaving a circle of dust on the forehead and round the features, which certainly does not add to her beauty. Next to her stands Nelson, most lifelike I should think, judging from his pictures. Over him were the words he used when he went to battle, "Victory or Westminster Abbey." He had both.

We wandered about a long time, and then drove to Hyde Park. The first thing that meets your eye on entering is an immense statue of the Duke of Wellington in bronze,* quite naked, erected by the ladies. If it had been an equestrian statue, I think it would have been more to the purpose, and have done greater credit to the delicacy and good taste of said females. This is a most lovely Park, where one can see all the gaiety and fashion walking,

---

* The statue of Achilles, erected in compliment to the Duke.— *Ed.*

driving, sauntering, flirting, reading, musing, etc. We passed Kensington Gardens, where we could see the different groups among the trees, and the children sailing their boats upon the Serpentine.

July 27. — Went to church this morning with Mrs. Embleton. They have a fine organ, and I find it is the custom for the charity children of the parish to sing and make the responses, but they make too much noise, and, until you become accustomed to it, it disturbs you very much. It was a very pretty sight to see them all dressed alike, and ranged round the galleries; the little girls with black or blue dresses, and white bonnets and mits, looked as neat as possible; the boys in brown linen frocks, looked neat and behaved well. There were about six hundred in all. When we went in, there were about six couples at the altar being married. I thought from that and the number of publishments that there is not much regard paid to either Malthus's or Chalmers's "Political Economy." We heard a very good sermon from the vicar of the parish, a venerable old gentleman of eighty. In the evening I attended the Limehouse Church, and heard a most solemn and eloquent sermon, and singing by the children again. Their dress was a little different, as they wore neat white caps instead of bonnets. Behind the altars of both these churches were handsome painted windows, with a figure of our Saviour pointing to heaven; very well done, but savoring very much of Popery. (!) The evening hymn closed the service, which was very solemn and gratifying.

July 29. — At home all day, "tooing" about and preparing for our departure; one more voyage, and we are done for the present I hope, for it requires all one's energy to be moving about in this way. N.B. — Never travel for pleasure without a gentleman at your command, for there is no pleasure in it. In our case, it is our misfortune, and sad it is, — however, I do not complain, we have too much to be thankful for.

31*st.* — This morning took a carriage to pay our parting calls. Went first to the Jerusalem Coffeehouse, and delivered some letters to the far-famed Mr. Hardy's care, then to the watchmaker's. Were much surprised to find our coachman could not read even a sign. Who would have thought we should have found such an instance in London? I was quite astonished! Made our calls, and then went to the Pantechnicon, a magnificent bazaar. Then we paid another visit to Westminster Abbey, where we left the guide and walked round by ourselves, and saw much more than before.

August 1. — Got up early, and packed up our duds to send on board with Ayok; they started at ten, and to-morrow we are to go to Portsmouth, to join the ship there, and that is all for the present, my dear. I think I shall not edify you with any more of my long stories, my next will be *viva voce*, I hope. Adieu.

In reading "Outre-mer," I found the following observations, so applicable to my own feelings that I could not resist copying them : —

"These, fair dames and courteous gentlemen, are some of the scenes and musings of my pilgrimage, when I journeyed away from my kith and kin, into the land of 'Outre-mer.' And yet amid these scenes and musings, amid all the novelties of the Old World, and the quick succession of images that were continually calling my thoughts away, there were always fond regrets and longings after the land of my birth, lurking in the secret corners of my heart. . . . Truly, the love of home is interwoven with all that is pure and deep and lasting in earthly affection. Let us wander where we may, the heart looks back with longing to the paternal roof. . . . And now farewell. The storm is over, and through the parting clouds the radiant sunshine breaks upon my path."

THE VOYAGE HOME.

AUG. 2–SEPT. 21, 1834.

[A supplementary diary, written in pencil, relates the journey from London to Portsmouth, and the voyage to New York; and, as the conditions of travel were so different then, a few extracts may be found interesting. The diary was not kept regularly, owing to the hardships and the monotony of the voyage. — *Ed.*]

Aug. 2, 1834. — Left London for Portsmouth in a very nice coach, holding four persons inside, and loaded outside with all sorts of *etceteras*. We had two very pleasant ladies with us, who were on their way to the Isle of Wight to rusticate for a time during the hot weather. The steamboats are constantly plying between there and Portsmouth, and are generally full. We travelled through the most delightful country imaginable, and passed through the town of Guildford, the only large town on our way. The scenery beyond Guildford was very beautiful; there was everything to make a perfect landscape, a romantic old ruin, a castle in the distance, a highly cultivated country everywhere, and in short I was delighted, and wanted to bring it all to America. I am charmed with England, but do not be jealous, I am ready to leave it, for the heart is constant still. We left our lodgings at nine in the morning, and arrived at the Fountain Hotel, Portsmouth, about six in the evening, without having left the coach. We changed horses seven or eight times with the greatest despatch, and were never detained many minutes for the noble horses were all harnessed and waiting for us; splendid animals, I think we do not have such in America. It was very hot and dusty, and our wheels were troublesome; on account of the friction we are obliged to quench one. The roads were very fine, and I do not wonder that Englishmen complain of ours when they make comparisons.

When we got to the hotel, and found ourselves all alone, we began to be very miserable, feeling tired and solitary and beginning to wonder what we came for. However, we had some tea, and went to bed, and rose refreshed the next morning.

August 3rd was Sunday, and we passed the day quietly and rather satisfactorily, the first quiet Sabbath for many months, but an inn is a disagreeable place at any time.

August 4.— At home all the morning, reading. I was finishing the Life of Legh Richmond, a good and valuable man, pity there were not more such! After dinner we sallied forth and surveyed the place, it is strongly fortified, I should say. It is surrounded by embankments or bastions (or both, for I am quite out in these descriptions), with a moat below, running all round the city.* A gravelled walk, shaded by trees on the embankment, is very

* The moats and embankments were destroyed as unwholesome a few years ago.— *Ed.*

pleasant, and on the side next the sea makes a cool and delightful evening walk. The beautiful Isle of Wight is in full view, and pleasure yachts and other vessels in abundance. There is nothing particularly novel or lion-like in this place except the docks and a block manufactory, which is very famous; but, as we had no one to wait upon us, of course we did not see them. We were quite satisfied with Portsmouth by the time we got back, and sorry not to see our ship in sight, but head winds prevail.

August 5. — Got up very leisurely this morning, but before long heard the summons, our captain was below, and said we must be ready to go on board at ten. Ate our breakfast, and met him at the cutter, with many of our fellow-passengers. Were soon on board the ship, and had all the confusion attendant on such occasions. However, we have become so accustomed to this that we take it very coolly, and quite astonish the inexperienced ones. We got all our things to rights, and I fully expected the usual feelings, but, wonderful to relate, I felt quite well, went on deck, read papers, walked, and felt as though I were on land. We have fifteen ladies on board, and shall have confusion worse confounded no doubt, but everything seems nice and comfortable, and there are no cockroaches.

August 6. — Head wind this morning and a rough sea, but I keep well, though all around me are ill; indeed, I never was in such a scene before, but I shall not be very particular in describing it, though it would be most amusing. Some are very, very ill,

and suffer much, others doubtful, and all envious of
me and two other young ladies who went on board
at London. The wind continued ahead, and a most
uncomfortable sea is pitching in from the westward,
which makes it exceedingly disagreeable. No prospect of getting out of the Channel to-night. Our
cabin, and indeed the whole ship, is a perfect hos-
pital. The first thing we heard this morning was
that a man in the steerage had cut his throat and
thrown himself overboard in the night, judge of our
feelings if you can! The weather is dark, rainy,
and dismal, and altogether we are surrounded by an
odd mixture of the comic and the tragic. Some of
the ladies are not charmed to-night with the sea!
We do not get on at all. In the evening a young
lady was taken very ill, fainted, and remained in-
sensible for a number of hours. We felt seriously
the need of a physician, and think it very wrong for
these ships to be without one. It was difficult,
even with the most powerful remedies, to keep Miss
M. alive; I was up with her all night. Fortunately, Aunt and I are both well enough to attend
upon her, for she has no friend on board. We felt
miserable enough, I assure you, for it was an awful
responsibility. A blister relieved her, and the next
day we had a change of wind and weather for a
while, and our faces and hearts were brightened. I
never was in such a scene before, and hope in mercy
we shall have a short passage.

August 9.—Tolerably pleasant day, and the invalids begin to turn out, an odd mixture enough; it

might with propriety be called a menagerie. To see the people perched about in their respective berths reminded me of the Zoölogical Gardens. I have certainly not laughed so much for the last year as since we have been on board. I shall tell you many anecodotes if we ever meet, but at present I see no prospect of it.

August 11.— A little breeze this morning, which I believe took us a few miles beyond Scilly. By night it strengthened to a small gale, so that we could carry but very little sail, and a monstrous and frightful sea was pitching us about tremendously. Although it was very awful, yet we could not help laughing, and I defy any one to help it, at the scenes we had to-night. Many of the party wisely kept their berths.

August 12.— Wind increased, but I went on deck, and even walked. The sport commenced about tea-time. It was almost impossible to keep our seats, the lurches of the ship were dreadful; one overthrew all the crockery; over went pitchers, plates, cups and saucers, and it was with great difficulty that we saved ourselves. The Rev. Mr. S., who was sitting on the lee side, was deluged with milk; he looked so perfectly ridiculous with the milk dripping from eyes, nose, and mouth, and his coat and all completely covered with it, that, though we trembled at our danger, we could not resist laughing. Another lurch, and over went another pitcher of milk upon a lady who was lying on the floor faint; it restored her, however, so it was no matter.

Altogether it was such a mixed scene that we knew not whether to laugh or cry, but the night was dreadful, some of us dared not undress. Miss M. and I *clamped* each other in one corner of the cabin, and there were various groups in different places, but very little sleep.

August 14. — Calm again, but the motion not much better. We have been all this time (nine days) doing four days' work. We are now only 14½° west. Horrible! Was amused to-night by one of our passengers telling me that neither he nor his wife had ever seen the sea before, and could not imagine that they should not see fields and trees on our way! They are missionaries.

August 28. — Since my last date we have had very little besides head winds and calms, principally calms. Have now been out twenty-three days, and we have had only thirty hours of fair wind in the whole time. We are quite discouraged, and what with the combination of disagreeables, and the anxiety about getting home or not getting home, I am quite unfitted for anything. I certainly never read so little on board ship before. The weather is very pleasant, but we are not yet half-way, and, although we have been going at the rate of eight and ten knots for the last three days, we have not made more than one degree (about sixty-nine miles).

August 31, *Sunday.* — Had a very excellent sermon from Mr. B. in the cabin to-day. We have had a delightful ten-knot fair wind since noon, which has cheered us all, and we begin to make calculations about going on shore. But I am too used to this fickle element to be very sanguine. We were all very much frightened to-night at tea-time by an alarm of fire, one of the worst of dangers aboard ship, but it was a trifle, and soon over.

September 1. — Our fair wind lasted till this morning, when we had a most magnificent squall. We were all in the round-house, admiring the scene. The glass fell very much in the course of the day, and after dinner we had another squall, which ended in a severe gale. I never experienced anything like it before; every bit of sail was taken in but the foresail, and the noise of the whistling wind was tremendous. We were all alarmed in the night, we shipped such seas, and many of us did not venture to go to bed. The gale broke about midnight, but the sea was worse afterwards, and the next morning, September 2, we were *worser*, and felt as though we had been beaten. The adventures of the night were marvellous and amusing, and I, for one, felt very grateful that we had been preserved.

September 7. — Another week gone, and we have not made much more in the whole of it than we did last Sunday. We get on only about half a degree a day. We are now on the Banks of Newfoundland, and had a specimen to-night of the fogs which are so celebrated in that region, together with a calm, which does not conduce at all to our mirth. It seems as though we never should reach the desired haven, hope deferred truly makes the heart sick. We have such a strange medley of passengers on

board that we shall not have much regret in parting.
I never heard the king's English so maltreated
before. The H is totally dismissed where it is
generally required, and called into office where it is
not necessary. They talk of "'orrible 'ot," lead-
ing ladies to the "h'altar," and "h'anchoring."
One says when he gets to New York he'll have "a
pat of parter" (pot of porter,— this is Hampshire
dialect.)

September 8.— Morning calm, fair wind about
ten, which increased before noon to a violent gale.
We went on deck about half-past ten to look at our
ship flying through a smooth sea at the rate of fourteen knots. The sight was grand, but a cloud in
the north-west, from which proceeded vivid lightning, added much to the brilliancy of the scene, but
predicted a head wind. We had one of the most
awful nights I ever experienced, and were up till
nearly five, the wind blowing tremendously and a
frightful sea. We felt our dependence on an Al-
mighty power at such a time, and have great reason
to be thankful that we were preserved. The captain says we were in great danger, as the wind
nearly amounted to a hurricane.

September 10.— Still very uncomfortable, and
pitching in an awful manner, and, what is worse,
the wind is again ahead. We do have bad luck.
We have made only one good day's work in the last
week, every inch of water is fought for. We had a
little push across the Banks yesterday, but are now
drifting back again, I believe. My patience is al-

most exhausted,— and wardrobe, too; as is the case generally, I am afraid.

September 11.— Head wind. We are now in longitude 57°, only three days' run from home with a good wind, but, alas! alas! the fates are against us! Oh, dear! Finished a little piece of work yesterday, and therefore indulged myself to-day, by lying in my berth and reading.

Calms and head winds till the morning of the 18th, when we were rejoiced to feel a fair breeze, but we rejoiced with trembling, for they are always fleeting. We feel anxious enough to get in, for nearly all our passengers are at swords' points. I do not think there was ever such a *mélange* of people before. Being charmed with our fair wind this morning, September 18, we were all on deck, and by way of variety went to visit the steerage, and inquire for their health and condition. Poor creatures! we complain, but we ought not, when we consider how comfortable we are in comparison. There are a hundred and twenty people there, huddled together, getting short of provisions, and quite comfortless.

September 19.— Fair wind, which continued all day and night, but we hardly dare mention it, though we all have our private opinions, as well as public, and I for one was anticipating the pleasure of crossing Brooklyn Ferry to-morrow night at six o'clock, which we might easily have done had the wind lasted, but, alas! we appear to be doomed to be tried to the extreme, and the wind gradually died away, leaving us becalmed.

September 20. — Oh, dear! I am almost sick with anxiety and hope deferred. The time since we heard from you seems so dreadfully long that the dread of what I may hear takes away the pleasure of arriving, and, though I am wishing the voyage over, yet I tremble too, when I hear we are going on well. It is a strange feeling, and one not easily described. Went on deck after dinner, and found we were becalmed in a thick fog. Pleasant prospect! All our speculations as to arriving to-morrow at an end. So, you see, our hopes vary with the wind, and to prove it, before we left the deck the wind increased, and we fully expected to be in sight of land by daylight. We went to tea, the haze had vanished, the moon was just rising clear and beautiful from her watery bed, and my poor little heart was going pit-a-pat at the idea of once more meeting my dear mother, father, and all hands. About 10 P.M., as I was playing chess, the report from deck was that we were just ninety miles from Sandy Hook, and the wind was dying away. The next sound, when we were retiring to our cabins, was "Haul in the studding-sails, and brace the yards." That was the end of the ups and downs of this day. Say you, my dear, that there is no variety in the life of a sailor? I sat up till after twelve, but no change came for the better. The night was perfect, save and except that we were two points off our course.

21*st.* — I think you will begin to look anxiously for us now, for we are a week or two over our time.

The first questions this morning were, "Any land in sight? and how's the wind?" The responses were anything but agreeable, — no land, wind ahead, and the ship but just moving, can't possibly get in to-day. Got up, and breakfasted in the ladies' cabin, and then stoned some raisins for a plum-pudding, with some of the other ladies. Next time, I hope it will be for Thanksgiving at home. It reminded me of old times. A most lovely morning it would have been to have gone up the Bay, so bright and clear! The wind is light and ahead, I have no work to do, I cannot read, and the day has seemed as long as six when employed. I sit and muse, and cannot fancy at all how I shall find you, but I endeavor to keep myself quiet, trusting to that Being who has been so merciful to us in all the perils by which we have been surrounded, and not doubting that whatever he sees fit to do will be for our good, and feeling, too, that sufficient unto the day is the evil thereof. I cannot explain how I feel, it is a sort of all-overness, and yet it appears to me that I am going to a strange place, as I have been to so many before!

POSTSCRIPT.

Here the Journal abruptly ends. In all probability the "Montreal" arrived in New York not many hours later. That Miss Low's apprehensions as to the strangeness she was to encounter were not wholly unrealized, we may judge from the fragment of a letter written to her by an old friend, in the most gushing and sentimental style of the day. The change from the comparatively brilliant society life of Macao to the deadly dulness of Brooklyn in 1834 must have been overpowering, and even in the home circle there were changes. The elder sister, for whom the journals were written, was married, the oldest brother was in China, and the next sister (born after a succession of seven boys) was then a child, about nine. Old friends had been left behind in Salem, everything was to be begun again, including the finding of a place in the family circle, so long left vacant, and probably now filled up, as all such gaps are filled in time. There must have been some complaint of loneliness and lack of sympathy to have drawn forth the epistle just mentioned, which sounds as if it might have been written by Amanda Malvina FitzAllan; but it is unsigned, being but a fragment.

"Would that I could open the windows of my soul, dearest H." (the letter begins, it was the fashion then to use initials even in speaking to people), "and enable you to see how fully, how entirely, the spirit understands and sympathizes in all the emotions which dictated your two last precious letters! the sense of loneliness, the incipient discontent of unappropriated affections, longing to rest on some kindred bosom! But, my dear, you would be more than human, could you utterly annihilate such seasons of weakness. If after bright years of youth passed in the hot-bed of adulation, — after living almost exclusively in the softened and tender atmosphere of flattery, admiration, and affluence, where so many studied your happiness, and so many sought but to share it and be blest, — could you return to the still, monotonous course of duty which you now pursue, with only the quiet though inestimable domestic affections living in your bosom, — without experiencing moments like those you have so touchingly described, — of sickening, heartless, uncheered existence? Condemn not too severely the momentary intrusion of such natural emotions, my dear girl, but be comforted, sweetest; moments there are in store, which, if not wholly unspotted, are still bright and glowing, and vivid enough to repay long years of negative existence, here below; and there is, you know, a hope that beyond this terrestrial scene all the most ardent boundings of the heart, if pure, shall be satisfied, — filled to overflowing!"

This "elegant epistle" was dated Sept. 15, 1835, just a year after my mother's return to America, and probably just before her engagement to my father, a younger brother of Hon. George S. Hillard, of Boston, and a man of cultivated tastes and charming manners. They were married on the 3d of November, 1836; and their wedding-cards, which still survive, are quaint and curious. There are two cards, both small and very highly glazed. The smaller of the two bears my father's name in his own handsome handwriting, the larger simply says: "Miss Low, At Home, Thursday evening, November 3, at 9 o'clock," with residence, but says nothing about marriage! The two cards are put up in a small envelope, fastened with a transparent wafer, and that is enclosed in a piece of white paper folded in an oblong shape, and tied up with a piece of narrow white satin ribbon.

Directly after the marriage they went to England to live, where eight children were born to them, of whom three survive. Frequent visits were made to the United States; and, while residing there in 1859, my father died, and my mother preferred to spend the rest of her life among her own people. She passed away in 1877, leaving the fragrance of a most beautiful memory in the hearts of all who knew her.

K. H.

www.ingramcontent.com/pod-product-compliance
Lightning Source LLC
Chambersburg PA
CBHW062035090426
42740CB00016B/2911